KNACK®
MAKE IT EASY

DOG CARE
and TRAINING

KNACK®

DOG CARE
and TRAINING

A Complete Illustrated Guide to Adopting, House-Breaking, and Raising a Healthy Dog

Carina MacDonald
Veterinary Review by Elizabeth Marion Bunting, VMD
Photographs by Stephen Gorman and Eli Burakian

Guilford, Connecticut
An imprint of The Globe Pequot Press

To buy books in quantity for corporate use
or incentives, call **(800) 962–0973**
or e-mail **premiums@GlobePequot.com**.

Editor in Chief: Maureen Graney
Editor: Katie Benoit
Cover Design: Paul Beatrice, Bret Kerr
Text Design: Paul Beatrice
Layout: Kim Burdick
Cover photos by (left to right) ©istockphoto, ©istockphoto,
©istockphoto, Stephen Gorman and Eli Burakian
Back cover photo by ©istockphoto
Interior photos see page 239

Library of Congress Cataloging-in-Publication Data is available on
file.

ISBN 978-1-59921-507-5

The following manufacturers/names appearing in *Knack Dog Care
and Training* are trademarks:
4-H®, AKA American Kennel Club®, Cheerios®, The Humane
Society®, Petfinder™, UKC® United Kennel Club, Yellow Pages™

Printed in China

1 9 8 7 6 5 4 3 2 1

Photographer Acknowledgments

Photographers Stephen Gorman and Eli Burakian would like to thank Robin Young and her dog, Rosie; Charlene Swainamer and her dog, Olivia; Lorelei Westbrook and her dog, Maybe; Kari Nelson and her dog, Yoda; Julia Burakian and her dog, Milton; the Upper Valley Humane Society (Enfield, NH); and Sharon Partridge and the staff at the Lebanon Pet and Aquarium Center (West Lebanon, NH) for their support and help in making this book.

CONTENTS

INTRODUCTION

Are you ready to be a dog owner?

Owning a dog takes money and time: money for food, toys, and other canine accoutrements. You may find yourself browsing pet store shelves for organic venison jerky treats and fashionable doggie coats, hiring a photographer dressed as Santa to pose with Fido for your holiday cards, and contemplating designer dog beds. At the very least, you will have to spring for basic veterinary care and decent dog food. It takes time to train and exercise a dog, along with unglamorous tasks like picking up poop and vacuuming up dog hair.

Most dogs relinquished to shelters are there because owners didn't anticipate that they can be inconvenient, hairy (imagine that), muddy, noisy, and expensive. Dogs are not little people in fur suits. They have animal drives and desires that often conflict with their owners' interests. Dogs dig holes, bark, eat nasty things and throw up, get sick, sometimes want to fight with other dogs, and have to be taught the difference between their rawhide bone and your leather pumps. Dogs are animals, and you have to teach them a tremendous amount about living in a human world.

In return they teach us about living in the moment, loving unconditionally, and going for walkies. Your money and time will be repaid tenfold with love and the joy of welcoming another species into your home. Your dog will be a companion, exercise partner, and protector. The right family dog helps teach children empathy and responsibility. Dog owners and their families tend to be healthier than nondog owners. Owning a dog can expand your horizons, skills, and circle of friends if you decide to get involved with dog sports—and you don't need a purebred dog to play!

Whether you get a bouncy puppy or a sensible adult dog, he is still a long-term commitment.

If you get a puppy when you are fifty, you may be sixty-five and still have the same dog. You may still have the dog you got when your children were in grade school when they are grown, married, and starting families. Depending on the size and breed, a dog can live fifteen years or more.

If you're not scared by now, you're ready!

Choosing the right dog for your lifestyle is the most important first step in your journey. Training and caring for the dog are ongoing, and if you make the right choice to begin with, they won't be chores but rather pleasures. This book aims to help you choose the best dog and provide training and care for life, whether this is your first dog or your tenth.

Choosing a Dog

It's not every day that you get to pick a new family member, so choose wisely. You'll want to consider breed (or type, if picking a mixed breed). Ask yourself plenty of questions: What do you expect from a dog? What are your must-haves (active, quiet, low grooming maintenance) and don't-wants (harder to train, vocal, needs frequent grooming)? Do you really have resources to deal with the considerable work involved in raising a puppy, or would a grown dog be a more practical choice?

Puppies

Oh, so cute. Every puppy is cute. But he is puppy cute only for the first few months after you bring him home, then he turns into a teenager, then an adult dog for many years. Puppies are quite a lot of work and lots of fun. Performing potty training, crate training, and manners training, socializing, dealing with teething, and watching him grow and learn can be very frustrating and incredibly rewarding. How you teach him from the minute he comes through your door will go a long way toward having a stable, well-trained adult dog for life. If it's been years since you've had a puppy, know that a lot has changed in the fields of veterinary medicine, training theory, and nutrition.

Shopping

You don't have to spend a ton, although you certainly can. Which dog toys and chews are safe, and when can a

ix

knotted rope or empty pop bottle be the best toy? You don't have to buy the organic venison treats—Cheerios and hot dog bits are great, too. Collars, leashes, halters, and dog coats—there's a dizzying array to choose from, but it's not hard when comfort and safety are your main criteria. Crates, dog beds, and fences keep your dog secure and comfortable.

Work and Play

Training should be structured play. Whether you're training an eight-week-old puppy or an adult shelter dog, the key is to teach him self-control rather than impose control through correction and punishment. You want him to be well mannered and work willingly rather than obey in order to avoid a correction. Dogs don't want to please us; they want to please themselves. Train to make him realize that doing what you want is rewarding to him, and you've got a confident, obedient dog!

Behavior problems are often caused by a breakdown in communication—you don't understand each other's language. He doesn't understand why you keep insisting that he stop jumping up on guests, and you don't understand why barking at the enticing sight of the squirrel up a tree is more important than coming when called. Sometimes problems are more serious, like aggression or separation anxiety. Usually serious issues are avoidable, both by choosing a dog wisely and raising it correctly.

Whether minor or major, most behavior problems can be addressed or managed.

Exercise

Most dogs were bred for specific jobs. Without a flock of sheep to herd, vermin to control, or an estate to guard, many dogs are chronically unemployed. Both physical exertion and mental exercise are crucial for their well-being. Walks and playtime benefit both dog and owner, and for many dog owners, a walk is incomplete without a dog along.

You don't have to stop with basic walks. It's not difficult to teach a high-energy dog to run with your bicycle or carry a daypack for country hikes. Find classes for agility, rally obedience, or new sports like flyball and dock jumping. Teach your dog to dance with canine freestyle. Try breed-specific sports like lure coursing or terrier racing. Mixed-breed and purebred dogs alike not only can learn for fun but also can compete at the highest level for ribbons in many venues. Even if you never compete, classes are a great way to tap into your dog's—and your own—potential.

Health, Nutrition, and Grooming

Good nutrition helps grow a healthy dog, and the range of diet choices is greater today than ever before. Dog food companies have branched out, and you're no longer limited to bags of dry pellets from the grocery store. Diet and supplements can help dogs with arthritis, dry skin, and plain old "doggie odor."

Food and supplements are not cure-alls, of course. Your dog needs veterinary care. Parasite control and preventative maintenance forestall many chronic problems. Keeping your dog's teeth clean is one of the most important tasks you can perform for his overall health—bad breath isn't normal; it's a medical condition. Knowing how to identify and deal with an emergency is vital.

Fluffy dogs need regular brushing, or you can clip their fur shorter to save grooming time. Even hairless breeds need grooming—teeth and ears cleaned, toenails clipped. You can take your dog to a groomer or save money and bond with your dog by doing this basic maintenance yourself.

Ready, Set, Go

With proper choosing and care, a dog will enhance your life in ways you never imagined. Whether purebred or great mutt, one dog or multiples, couch potato or high-drive athlete, there is no such thing as a zero-maintenance dog. But with the right approach, a dog is never a chore; rather it is a joy to own.

A DOG AS COMPANION

Dogs evolved as human companions and helpmates, so these should be the primary reasons

From the tiny, smooth-coated Chihuahua to the bearlike Newfoundland, dogs evolved from those wolves who learned to scavenge at the edges of human habitation. Dogs were the first animal to be domesticated by humans. Artifacts, fossils, and cave paintings show they were domesticated as long as fifteen thousand years ago. Stone Age burial sites indicate

dogs were highly valued as both working animals and companions. Early wolf-dogs were used for hunting, guarding, and hauling supplies. Wolves who were less aggressive, less fearful of humans, and more trainable were the foundation stock for modern dogs. Over the centuries, selective breeding for working ability, companionship, and appearance has

Companion Dogs

- From guarding to herding, from controlling vermin to hunting and performing police and military duties, dogs have worked for us, but their most constant task has been as companions.

- Dogs have been used as status symbols and prized companions as well as for working purposes for thousands of years.

- Having a dog, especially a large, active one, means outdoor exercise for both of you. A dog can be the best personal trainer you've ever had.

Adaptable Pets

- More than any other animal in history, dogs have served humans. Almost every culture has valued dogs as helpmates.

- Part of dogs' enduring appeal is their ability to adapt and integrate into their human pack, whether as working or companion dogs.

- Newfoundlands historically helped fishermen and were renowned water rescue dogs. Protected by a heavy, water-repellent coat and equipped with webbed feet, the Newfie is at home in the mountains or the ocean.

led to the wide range of today's breeds.

Dogs are still used today for many jobs, from performing police and military work to performing search and rescue to assisting the disabled to herding stock and even such esoteric jobs as keeping geese away from golf courses. At day's end, most working dogs go home to be part of the family.

Dogs are highly social animals, capable of play and empathy and of quickly learning from their human companions. Whether raised in the family from a puppy or acquired later in life, they regard their family as their pack and integrate accordingly. Modern dogs perform a multitude of functions, but even the family dog is more than "just a pet." The smallest dog will bark to warn of possible danger. Big dogs can be gentle playmates for children. Companion dogs keep the elderly engaged.

A dog relegated to the back yard for life or, even worse, to a chain, is an unhappy animal incapable of providing either function or companionship. You want your dog to be a protector, a buddy, and a family member. With training and care your dog will be all that and more.

The Family Dog

- There have been times in history when small companion dogs were thought to be ideal ladies' pets and when any dog with size or working ability was thought to be a man's dog. Times have changed.

- The world of competitive dog sports is populated more by women than men nowadays, and women are usually the caretaker of the family dog.

- The golden retriever is one of the more popular and versatile dogs in the world and an iconic family dog.

Benefits of Owning a Dog

- The company of a dog has been shown to lower blood pressure and stress and to improve heart health.

- Retirees who travel frequently find small dogs easier to travel with. A dog who can fit into an airline crate under the seat can fly in the cabin with its owners.

- Smaller dogs are less expensive to own, costing less to feed, groom, and medicate.

- Almost 40 percent of households own at least one dog.

1

A DOG FOR EXERCISE

Dogs make perfect jogging, hiking, and even boating companions—just ask them along!

For dog owners, a walk isn't fun without a dog along. Having a dog is an invaluable way to get out into the fresh air. If your dog is overweight, you're not getting enough exercise! If an active lifestyle is your thing, then the right dog will be a willing participant and an excellent motivator. A Labrador will be a better jogging companion than an English bulldog, but even the bulldog will benefit from a daily stroll.

There is no better companion for day hikes than a dog. A healthy dog can safely carry up to 20 percent of its weight in a doggie backpack. Let Fido carry the bottled water, water bowl, and trail mix.

Exercise with Your Pet

- With some training and practice, running or walking with your leashed dog can be virtually effortless.

- Be careful, especially in warm weather. Most dogs have a lower tolerance for heat than we do. A dog will valiantly try to keep up even if it's dangerously hot.

- Like people, dogs need to be conditioned for extended exercise. Don't run your dog into exhaustion.

- Avoid jogging with young dogs. Short runs and playtime are great, but overdoing it can damage growing joints.

Hiking

- Use your dog's working ability to carry supplies while hiking. Doggie backpacks are available for every size of dog, and most dogs love to have a purpose.

- Your dog can carry his own fresh water and collapsible drinking bowl. Mountain streams can harbor giardia and other nasties that can cause severe diarrhea.

- It's wise to carry a basic first aid kit when hiking remote trails.

2

Boat dogs have a long tradition of service on the water, and some breeds like schipperkes and Portuguese water dogs were bred to be boating companions. With proper safety considerations, almost any dog can be a boat dog.

Multiple dogs can be walked on split leashes as long as they are trained to do so. Cross-country skiing, bicycling, and even inline skating can be shared with well-trained dogs, and it's a great way to burn off excess energy and have a calmer dog. A tired dog is a well-behaved dog!

ZOOM

Numerous studies have shown measurable physiological benefits to interacting with a dog, such as lower blood pressure and stress hormones. Not only do dog owners tend to get more exercise than nondog owners, but also the presence of a dog in the home makes dog owners live longer and healthier lives.

Boating

- Dogs are versatile animals. From boats to the slopes, dogs can adapt, and some breeds, like Labradors, originally worked hauling nets for fishermen. A dog will accompany you just about anywhere you go, and even poodles can make great boat dogs.

- Most pet and outdoor supply stores carry canine life preservers. Many dogs are not naturally good swimmers, so this is a good safety precaution.

- Bring fresh water and a water bowl when boating.

Beach Dogs

- Most dogs love water, although not every dog can swim. Dogs with very little body fat, like greyhounds, cannot stay afloat. Others, like bulldogs, simply sink when in water.

- In any public space, including wilderness and beaches, carry bags and pick up after your dog. Active dog owners are in the habit of carrying poop-pick-up baggies everywhere. Tuck bags (plastic grocery sacks work fine) into pockets, backpacks, and your vehicle.

- Respect regulations when your dog is at a beach or public park.

3

A DOG FOR THE FAMILY

Many people think a family isn't complete without a dog—here's why

Many people don't consider a household complete without a canine family member. Children raised with dogs learn empathy and responsibility by caring for them. Research suggests that children develop fewer allergies in dog-owning homes. Dog owners tend to be healthier and happier. A dog can fill the void for empty-nesters, keep the single and elderly company, and be an integral part of the family, and you can dress them in cute costumes for family greeting cards.

Consider your lifestyle before deciding whether to get an adult dog or a puppy, which breed to get, or whether a dog is even the right pet for you. Getting a dog for the children is great. But a dog can live fifteen years or more. How old will

Children and Dogs

- A family dog encourages interaction and exercise. Even very small dogs benefit from regular walks.

- Gentle retrievers and retriever mixes are usually excellent with children. Despite their size, they are gentle and willing companions, although they do tend to be boisterous when younger.

- Studies have consistently shown that children raised on farms and in homes with pets are less likely to suffer allergies or asthma and tend to have stronger immune systems.

Training Both Dogs and Kids

- Don't get a dog expecting the children to take full responsibility for his care. Make it a shared responsibility so nobody resents doing all the "dirty work." When all family members are involved, he will become a more valued family member.

- Give children tasks but avoid having small children feed the dog or tease him with food. Bites to children often happen around food.

- Both children and dogs need to be trained how to interact safely and respectfully with each other.

your children be in fifteen years? Chances are the kids will be out of the home, and guess who keeps the dog. A dog is a long-term commitment.

If you travel frequently, consider that for the rest of the dog's life you will have to arrange for her care in your absence. If you are a renter, it will be harder to find rentals, particularly with a large dog. Dogs cost money to feed and care for, so take your budget into consideration.

Before bringing a dog home, have a family conference. Involve everyone in learning about different breeds. Avoid getting a dog just because you like the appearance. Looks count, but it's the dog's personality you will have to live with for a decade or more. Some breeds dig, some bark, some are mellow, and others high energy. Discuss family expectations for the dog. Agree on responsibilities—poop pick-up duty, training, and exercising. Accept the responsibility and be rewarded with security, companionship, and better health that a dog provides any family.

Dog Handling for Kids

- Children can learn a great deal about dogs, sportsmanship, and responsibility by getting involved in 4-H or junior showmanship.

- Children up to the age of eighteen train and handle the dog in the show ring and can compete in many dog sports. Some venues allow children as young as two years old in competition.

- Many junior events allow mixed-breed dogs as well as purebreds.

Picking the Right Breed for your Family

- Whether you have children in the home or not, a dog becomes part of the family.

- Consider more than breed alone when choosing a family dog—every dog is an individual. Although most golden retrievers are gentle and social, not every golden is perfect. Rottweilers and pit bulls might have bad reputations, but they can make fabulous family dogs.

- An impressive pedigree means nothing if your dog is a poor match for your lifestyle.

A DOG TO SHOW

Getting involved with dog shows and dog sports boosts your confidence and social well-being

Dog sports are increasing in popularity. No longer limited to purebred dogs strutting their stuff in the ring with professional handlers, dog sports are varied and egalitarian. Mixed-breed dogs are welcome in many venues. Amateur yet enthusiastic dog owners of all ages are entering the ring, from children in 4-H or junior handling to retirees taking up a new hobby. It is structured play at its best. Owners learn new skills and make friends, and dogs get an outlet for their energy and natural instincts. Don't be intimidated!

Team activities like agility and Frisbee involve dog and handler working together, learning from each other. In freestyle, the owner devises a simple dance routine to mu-

KNACK DOG CARE AND TRAINING

Dog Sports

- People and dogs of all ages, shapes, and abilities play and compete in dog sports.

- Mixed breeds and purebreds alike can compete in many venues, and any kind of dog can train just for fun.

- Your dog doesn't have to be an impeccably trained canine athlete to start learning. Any physical activity can be part of his exercise program.

- Agility weave poles can be hard for a big dog to master!

Stacking

- This Australian shepherd is being "stacked" and baited into position by a young handler. Depending on the venue, food may be allowed in the show ring.

- Stacking is positioning a dog in the show ring to show off his attributes to the judge.

- Many breed enthusiasts show their dogs in conformation and earn working titles, too. Ideally, a dog should both look good and have working ability, especially if it's a breed with a purpose.

sic and teaches the dog to be a dancing partner. Rally-O is a fun, fast-paced obedience routine. A reasonably well-behaved dog can start training at a beginner level for any team sport, and ongoing classes will sharpen obedience skills. Some sports use a dog's natural abilities. Hunting dogs can hunt or enter field trials. Terriers can compete in earthdog, scrambling through tunnels in the ground to find and corner caged rats. Lure coursing for sighthounds lets the dog free to run at high speed after a mechanically operated lure. Dogs with herding abilities can learn to herd geese, sheep, and cattle. Tracking uses a dog's natural scenting abilities. Any dogs who like water can be taught dock jumping, in which they leap from the end of a dock in chase of a thrown toy.

It's easy to find classes for just about any dog sport. Use the Internet to find organizations and trainers. Call local training facilities and ask what they offer. Take classes just for fun but don't be surprised if you get bitten by the competing bug as you progress.

Judging a Dog

- This poodle won a first-place blue ribbon and is being stacked for a win photo with the judge.

- In the conformation ring, a judge looks at the physical attributes, checks for proper dentition, and evaluates the dog's gait.

- The structure and gait of the dog are usually supposed to reflect suitability for the job it was originally bred for.

- Breed standards are supposed to be in place to ensure purebred dogs are physically and mentally sound.

Is Your Dog a Contender?

- If you think your dog is too hyper or wild to learn, think again. In dog enthusiast parlance, this is called "drive," and when that energy is channeled you could have a real contender.

- You don't need to pretty up a dog for sports, but having a well-groomed dog with trimmed toenails makes you both look good.

- Conformation showing is the only time you need a dog who closely matches the breed standard.

A DOG FOR SECURITY

The presence of even a small dog can be a deterrent and provide security

An entryway floor mosaic uncovered in Rome's Pompeii depicts a large chained dog with the warning "CAVE CANEM" (beware of dog) written at its feet. Warning of intruders likely was one of ancient dogs' first uses for early humans. Modern criminals are still deterred by the mere presence of a dog.

There is a difference between a watchdog and a guard dog.

A watch dog is any dog who will bark when he hears someone outside your home. Small, alert dogs often make excellent watchdogs, and the noise they make will keep the majority of would-be burglars away from your home. A guard dog will back up his bark with a bite if necessary.

A dog who bites when he perceives a threat is a potential

Barking

- The mere presence of a barking dog deters most intruders. Many small dogs are alert and vocal, making excellent watchdogs.

- The ideal watchdog barks to alert her owners of people around the house but follows her owner's cue and welcomes all friendly visitors.

- Regardless of size, no dog should be praised for barking and snapping at family and friendly visitors.

Large Dogs

- Large, intimidating dogs are also good deterrents, but any dog who may actually bite in response to visitors to the property must be impeccably trained and managed.

- Don't assume that every dog of a "macho" breed will actually protect his family and territory. Few dogs have the correct temperament and nerves to be truly reliable protectors.

- Never rely on a dog to protect you. Conversely, you should always protect your dog and rely on good judgment and technology to keep your home safe.

liability. Some breeds have a natural tendency to guard their territory, but this tendency must be tempered by proper training and socialization. Many dogs who bite do so out of fear or poor judgment, not discriminating between friendly visitors and intruders. Any breed with natural guarding instincts must be well-socialized and accustomed to interacting with different people to become confident and trustworthy. Keeping a dog isolated and unsocialized will impair rather than enhance his natural guarding abilities by making him unnecessarily suspicious and unpredictable around strangers. Merely choosing a "bad boy" breed does not guarantee a guard dog, but any dog who barks at unusual noise will be an effective watchdog.

Personal and home protection dogs are available for a pretty penny, but do your research extremely carefully if considering this option. Also know that owning such a dog entails extensive owner training. For the majority of dog owners, the family pet dog automatically becomes an integral part of the home security system.

Guard Dog

- Taking a dog walking or jogging can make a single person feel much safer.

- It doesn't require a huge or tough-looking breed to give a sense of security and built-in protection.

- Although it would be unwise to assume that having a dog along gives you a license to take unnecessary risks, most people with bad intent will choose someone without an animal with teeth and a loud bark by her side, given a choice.

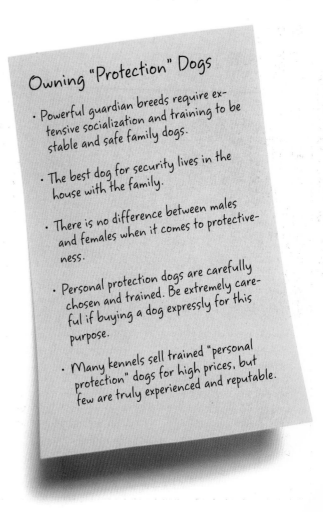

Owning "Protection" Dogs

- Powerful guardian breeds require extensive socialization and training to be stable and safe family dogs.

- The best dog for security lives in the house with the family.

- There is no difference between males and females when it comes to protectiveness.

- Personal protection dogs are carefully chosen and trained. Be extremely careful if buying a dog expressly for this purpose.

- Many kennels sell trained "personal protection" dogs for high prices, but few are truly experienced and reputable.

A DOG AS YOUR HELPER

Dogs have long been recognized for helping people with disabilities

Man's best friend has long been put to work as a leader dog for the blind and an assistance dog for the disabled. Dogs can alert owners to impending seizures and provide auditory help for the deaf and practical assistance for the wheelchair bound. Dog-owning heart attack survivors tend to live longer than their nondog-owning peers. Dogs have been used to help children with ADHD and autism relate better to their

environment. Some dogs even work as psychiatric assistance dogs to increase social and mental functioning for those with mental disorders.

Some people train their own assistance dogs, and such dogs are also professionally trained and available for sale. Although golden and Labrador retrievers are commonly used due to their easygoing temperaments and high trainability,

Assistance Dogs

- It takes extensive work to train an assistance dog; this golden retriever is on the job. Always ask for permission before petting an assistance dog and respect its personal space while it is working.

- Golden retrievers and Labradors are the most

common breeds in many physical support roles, including guide dogs for the blind.

- Support dogs need off-duty time and daily opportunities to be "just dogs." Caregiving is a two-way street.

Helping the Disabled

- Dogs are taking on increasingly complex roles as assistants for the disabled, and their roles have expanded from the traditional guide dog for the blind.

- Most assistance dogs are bred for the purpose, carefully chosen, and trained by volunteers for a year before

going to their forever homes.

- Some people train their personal dogs for assistance work. Doing this is very possible with the right dog and patience. Online communities offer support to those training their own assistance dogs.

many breeds, including mixed breeds, work in partnership with disabled owners.

Because it has been shown that interactions with dogs help promote physical, emotional, and social well-being for their owners, dogs are now used for therapy work in hospitals and group homes. Even short visits can help ease loneliness and anxiety. Programs letting children read aloud to dogs have been implemented in schools and libraries because this practice has been shown to improve reading skills. Several organizations certify dogs (just like yours, perhaps) as therapy dogs,

and their volunteer owners take them to welcoming institutions. Therapy dogs worked onsite during the aftermath of the 9/11 terrorism attack, offering support to survivors and rescue workers along with the rescue and police K-9s.

These formal jobs are amplifications of the roles many dogs serve in their day-to-day lives as "just pets." Although few family dogs perform weekly feats of Lassie-like derring-do, every loyal family dog has the potential to alert her owners to a 3 a.m. fire. Every dog is capable of easing anxieties and promoting well-being.

Therapy Dogs

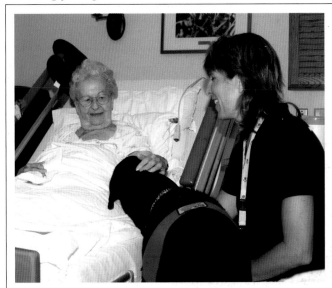

- Volunteering with your dog as a therapy team can be extremely rewarding. Friendly dogs of any size and breed are welcome. Check the resources chapter for the larger organizations offering certification.

- Requirements usually include basic obedience training and friendliness toward people and other dogs. A generally calm demeanor is important, so the dog doesn't spook at wheelchairs and a hospital environment.

- Therapy dogs are welcome in many hospitals, assisted living homes, and schools.

Helping the Elderly

- Caring for an animal can be a lifeline for elderly dog owners, who otherwise may not have much social contact at all.

- Interacting with a dog and using the dog as a catalyst for interaction with others in the course of walking and caring for it carry significant benefits.

- Calm, lower-maintenance dogs usually make the best pets for elderly owners. A large, well-behaved older dog may be more suitable than a small, energetic youngster.

GUNDOGS & SPORTING BREEDS

These breeds are field companions, family dogs, and sporting competitors

Dogs in the sporting group (gundogs in the United Kingdom) include perennially popular breeds like Labrador and golden retrievers and most spaniels, pointers, and setters. Bred to work in woods, field, and stream, these tend to be active, water-loving dogs.

Usually bright and easily trained, sporting dogs need plenty of exercise when young because they are often rambunctious. Although some spaniels are more laidback, most dogs in this group require too much exercise to make ideal apartment dogs. When buying a pup from a breeder, ask if she breeds for field or for show.

"Field-bred" dogs are bred with an emphasis on working

Pointers

- Pointers track the prey by scent, then freeze and point for the hunter.

- The German shorthaired pointer is a versatile hunting dog, proficient not only in pointing but also in tracking and retrieving game. They are medium-sized dogs with boundless energy and enthusiasm.

- As with many sporting breeds, pointers may be bred for show or field, with the field-bred dogs having greater energy and instinct for hunting.

Setters

- Setters find game in the brush by scent, then stop and "set" while the hunter finishes the job.

- Setters are all medium to large dogs with long, flowing coats that require regular brushing.

- Like most dogs in this group, setters are high-energy, gentle, and friendly dogs who thrive on companionship. They tend to be sensitive and do not take well to harsh training.

ability and structure and may be even more high energy. On the whole they are gentle with other dogs and people alike and make excellent family dogs. Retrievers tend to have soft mouths because they were selected for their ability to retrieve downed fowl without mangling them. Most dogs in the sporting group do not make good watchdogs, although they are alert, and some will bark when they hear a strange noise. In general, they are very friendly, social dogs who respond best to gentle training because they can be a bit sensitive.

Sporting dogs tend to excel in any activity that allows them to be physical and learn new skills. Dog agility, dock diving, and canine freestyle are excellent outlets for their skills. Several breeds, most notably golden retrievers, are all-star obedience competitors.

Be aware of the common hereditary problems in your breed and buy puppies from health-tested parents. Sporting dogs tend to be healthy and long-lived, but when any breed becomes extremely popular, breeding quality can be compromised. For a more laidback sporting dog, consider getting an older one from a shelter or breed rescue group.

Sporting Breeds

- Pointers track the prey, then freeze and point for the hunter.

- The versatile spaniel tracks and flushes game for the hunter, then retrieves it.

- Sporting breeds are hunting dogs and are active, highly trainable, and usually excellent, gentle family dogs.

Retrievers

- Labrador retrievers are one of the most popular breeds in the world and consistently hold the AKC top spot in registered breeds.

- Labradors come in black, chocolate, and yellow.

- Retrievers retrieve downed game with a soft mouth.

- Generally speaking, field-bred Labradors (sometimes referred to as "American") are more lightly built.

- Labradors bred for the show ring are called "trial" or "show bred" (or "English") and have heavier bones and thicker coats and are typically less energetic.

THE HOUND GROUP

Bred for hunting by sight or scent, hound dogs are a diverse and energetic group

All hounds were bred to hunt. Some, like greyhounds and whippets, are sighthounds, using keen eyesight and high speed to bring down a kill. Most sighthounds have a very high instinctual prey drive, triggered by anything fast moving, from cats to cars. Although generally gentle and obedient dogs, not all sighthounds can be trusted around smaller animals, and many must be kept on a leash unless inside a fenced area. A popular, breed-specific activity for sighthounds is lure coursing, in which the dogs chase a mechanized "rabbit" at high speed in open fields, similar to greyhound racing. Other hounds were bred to hunt by scent alone. Bloodhounds are renowned for their tracking ability, and many

Beagles

- Beagles are scent hounds, bred to hunt with their noses, in large packs. Scent hounds can be single-minded and determined when on the scent, ignoring everything around them, including their owners.

- Due to their history of living and working in a pack, some hound breeds can be vocal and distressed when left alone.

- Their reputation for being harder to train is a function of their history as independent workers, not a lack of innate intelligence. Hounds can be creative problem solvers.

Dachshunds

- Dachshunds were bred in Germany for hunting badger and other game and are indefatigable hunters and enthusiastic diggers. They are effective watchdogs, with a bigger bark than their short stature suggests.

- They come in three sizes and a variety of acceptable colors. They may be smooth, wire, or long coated.

- Dachshunds are generally healthy and athletic dogs, although they can be prone to spinal problems.

scent hounds can be very single-minded when it comes to following tracks. Dachshunds track prey into the ground, and their low, narrow bodies and powerful front legs make them enthusiastic hunters and diggers.

Most hounds are friendly and cooperative with other dogs, especially those bred to work and live in large packs. They dislike being alone and can be quite vocal. Some hounds are prized for their "voice" or ability to bay melodiously to alert the hunter to a treed or cornered quarry, and training such dogs to be quiet can be challenging. Most hounds have a great deal of stamina and may be good choices for active families.

Because hounds tend to be fairly single-minded and were not bred to work closely with a handler, they can be stubborn dogs to train and would not be a great choice for most competitive dog sports. However, as with any breed, there are exceptions to every rule, and they are usually sweet, gentle family dogs although not stellar watchdogs. As a group, hounds are healthy and sturdy, especially if not allowed to get overweight.

Greyhounds

- Retired racing greyhounds make excellent family pets and are known as "60-mph couch potatoes." There are many retired racer rescue organizations.

- Like most sighthounds, some can be unsafe around cats and small dogs. They are very sweet natured and gentle with people, and many live successfully with cats and other dogs.

- Greyhounds are built for speed. Compared with most dogs, they have a larger heart, better eyesight, lower body fat, and the ability to run at 45 miles per hour.

Whippets

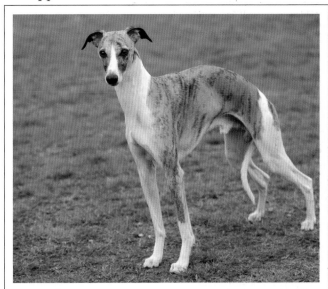

- Whippets are small sighthounds, weighing 25–40 pounds and looking somewhat like miniature greyhounds. They are popular in England and are valued for racing and hunting and as family companions.

- Like most hounds, whippets are known for an independent, sweet nature and are easygoing, well-mannered dogs. Despite their elegant appearance they are sturdy, with few health problems.

THE WORKING GROUP

These dogs are big, strong, and task-oriented and need experienced owners and responsible training

Working dogs are the stalwarts of the breeds. Most often bred as property and flock guardians, they have also been used for pulling carts and sleds and for performing water and high country rescue. Some working dogs are used for military and police work. As guardians, they are independent thinkers and problem solvers and very trainable. Most dogs in this group need an experienced, responsible owner who will socialize and train them fairly. Activity level and temperament vary considerably within this group (and within each breed), so research individual breeds. A knowledgeable breeder will be able to steer you to the right puppy, and adult dogs come with known temperaments.

KNACK DOG CARE AND TRAINING

Huskies

- The Siberian husky has been used primarily as a sled dog and is capable of great endurance and cold tolerance.

- Huskies are extremely intelligent dogs, but their independent and playful temperament and history as a dog-team worker make them care less about pleasing their owners than about pleasing themselves.

- Like other northern breeds, huskies are affectionate and playful, but unlike most dogs in the working group, too friendly to be reliable guard dogs.

Mastiffs

- Large dogs tend to mature slowly and have shorter life spans. Many working breeds are not considered mentally and physically mature until about three years old.

- Mastiffs are all molossers, a term applying to a group of large, heavy-boned dogs. Ancient in origin and used primarily as guardians, many mastiffs retain a strong sense of territory. Devoted to family and suspicious of strangers, they are even-tempered dogs.

- Most working dog breeds are fairly quiet, barking only for good reason.

Some working breeds have become gentled by selective breeding and do not always make great guardians. Great Danes, English mastiffs, malamutes, Newfoundlands, and boxers tend to be more social. Others, like akitas, rottweilers, and other mastiffs, are aloof and discriminating with new people. No dog in any group should be aggressive toward people without good cause, and this is always a disqualification according to breed standards. All should be well-socialized as puppies to prevent a high degree of suspicion toward strangers. This in no way compromises natural protectiveness; rather it encourages the dog to have better judgment and be more confident. Some working dogs have an innate tendency toward dog aggression, particularly dogs of the same sex.

As the term suggests, working dogs can become bored and develop behavior problems if they have no job to do and benefit a great deal from training, productive activity, and plenty of interaction. Although all working dogs can make loving dogs for families with children, only experienced and dedicated owners need apply. In the wrong hands, some can become dangerous, if just for sheer size alone.

Saint Bernards

- Like many large dog breeds with pendulous lips, the Saint Bernard may drool, and a vigorous head shake can send strings of dog drool flying upward to stick to the ceiling.

- Saint Bernards (affectionately known as "Saints") can weigh upward of 150 pounds.

- Big, strong breeds need ongoing training. A single obedience class is not enough. Training should be consistent for at least the first three years of the dog's life, with emphasis placed on socialization and interaction with a wide range of people.

Great Danes

- Great Danes are gentle giants, sensitive and devoted to their owners. It is rare for them to be aggressive, although they should be carefully trained if for no other reason than to control a dog of this size.

- Although their exact history is disputed, it is believed that great Danes originated in Germany and were initially used as hunting dogs.

- Danes come in almost every possible range of colors and markings, although there are precise breed guidelines for correct coloration.

17

THE TERRIER GROUP
Feisty, sturdy, and active, they usually have tons of personality packed into a compact body

Terriers have been bred to hunt and kill vermin for centuries. The word *terrier* comes from the Latin word for "Earth"—terra. Terriers tend to be enthusiastic diggers, smelling grubs underground and diligently working to exterminate them. Most terriers are small, with the exception of the Airedale terrier. Developed primarily in Great Britain, many terriers are named after the region they originated in. Many were bred to go after larger wild animals like badgers, otters, and foxes, and the smaller terriers were mousers and ratters on farms.

As pets, terriers are charming and humorous but have a high need for exercise and ongoing training. They are extremely intelligent and can question authority. Some won't

American Staffordshire Terriers

- The American Staffordshire terrier is an iconic American dog breed. Pete from the *Our Gang* comedies of the 1930s was a Staffie. Although originally bred for dog fighting, many are gentle family dogs and enthusiastic agility and flyball competitors.

- Staffordshire terriers are small to medium sized, and in addition to their dog fighting heritage were used as farm dogs to kill vermin.

- All terriers are very intelligent, love to think for themselves, and are ideal candidates for clicker training.

Jack Russell Terriers

- Jack Russell terriers are indomitable sport dogs, excellent vermin hunters, and enthusiastic companions for active owners. They are definitely a high-maintenance breed, needing extensive training and exercise.

- Avoid "small dog syndrome" by establishing boundar-ies and teaching manners from the start. Many terriers can be willful and bossy, becoming snappy and territorial without training.

- Because of their feisty and sometimes nippy nature, not all terriers are good choices for families with small children.

18

tolerate a lot of rough handling by children and may become nippy. When raised with other animals, they can be safe but may harass and even kill smaller animals, including cats. They are fearless, often won't think twice about challenging much larger dogs, and are often not good "dog park" material. If you have a sense of humor and some patience, you will find terriers fun to train and live with. Like most dogs bred for a purpose, when not given enough exercise and mental stimulation, they can become noisy and destructive.

Terriers can excel at agility, flyball, and any sport requiring them to run and chase things. Earthdog competitions are open to terriers to test their mettle at going down an earthen burrow to "find" a quarry—usually caged rats, which are not harmed.

Terrier coats are wiry and water resistant, needing regular grooming and stripping to maintain the terrier look. Longer-haired terriers can be clipped short in a puppy cute for easier maintenance. Most terriers are hardy, with few congenital health problems, and as a group they are quite long-lived.

Airedale Terriers

- The Airedale terrier is one of the largest terrier breeds, sometimes called the "King of Terriers."

- Airedales are known for their stoicism and athleticism. Like most terriers, they are extremely intelligent but challenging to train because they get bored quickly and like to think for themselves.

- A typical terrier is not a calm lap dog and needs an owner who is willing to spend time training, exercising, and playing with the dog daily.

Schnauzers

- The miniature schnauzer, like other terriers, was developed as a hunting dog, although, unlike most terriers developed in the United Kingdom, schnauzers originated in Germany. Like most terriers, they are effective watchdogs, barking to alert their family of any unusual sound.

- There are three schnauzer types—the standard and giant schnauzer are classified as working dogs.

- Schnauzers are sometimes sold as "hypoallergenic" dogs because of their short, wiry coat, although there is no truly hypoallergenic breed.

THE TOY GROUP

Small in size, portable, and cute, these are ideal big city dogs

Toy dogs excel in their intended purpose as cute house dogs and companions. Bred solely for their appearance and their use as lap dogs, most toy breeds are outgoing and loyal. The reputation that some toy breeds get as yappy dogs or "ankle biters" comes not from their basic temperament but rather from their being spoiled and untrained. Most toy dogs have naturally sweet, playful, undemanding temperaments.

Although not imposing guardians, they can be excellent watchdogs, alert and ready to warn of any strange sounds.

Toy dogs are practical. They can easily be litter trained for apartment living. Although every dog needs outside walks, a toy dog can get a lot of running inside a small apartment, so it's not much work to exercise a hyper little dog. You can travel easily with toy dogs. They cost less to feed, less

Chihuahuas

- The tiny Chihuahua should not exceed 6 pounds and is the smallest recognized breed. The Chihuahua has the familiar short coat or a long, flowing coat.

- Chihuahuas are intelligent and devoted and are prone to being snappy without training. If trained, they can excel in obedience, agility, and several other dog sports.

- Popular toy breeds can have temperament and health problems. Exercise caution when buying a toy breed puppy or consider a grown dog with known temperament and health.

Pugs

- Pugs, with their stout bodies, smushed faces, and endearing personalities, are a popular choice for anyone looking for a loyal companion who doesn't require extensive exercise and training.

- Like most toy dogs, pugs are very intelligent and trainable. Teach your pug basic obedience and tricks and amaze people who aren't used to seeing well-trained little dogs!

- Pugs are prone to eye injuries because of their protruding eyes, breathing difficulties, and heat intolerance.

to buy supplies for, and less to medicate. They are easy to handle and walk, even with less-than-stellar leash manners. Most toy dogs are healthy and very long-lived.

The popularity of toy breeds has resulted in some careless breeding, and there are some inherited problems that can be largely avoided by choosing carefully and not buying any undersized dog advertised as "teacup," which is just a marketing term. Many little dogs are predisposed to poor dental health, so it's imperative that their teeth are properly cared for. Some are prone to have collapsing tracheas and do bet-ter with a harness than a collar. Luxating patellas are more common in little dogs; keeping them at a healthy weight will prevent problems.

Breeds prized for long, luxurious coats, like Yorkies and Pomeranians, require ongoing grooming. Others, like pugs and Chihuahuas, require only basic coat care. Small dogs eat more relative to their weight and may need three meals a day to prevent stomach upset.

Toy Poodles

- The toy poodle has been one of the most popular breeds in the world for over one hundred years.

- Highly intelligent and train-able, the versatile poodle has been used as a circus animal, therapy dog, sport-ing dog, and, of course, an elaborately coiffed show dog.

- Most poodles are natural swimmers because they were originally bred as waterfowl retrievers. Toy poodles have been used in France for finding truffles.

Little Pomeranians

- The little Pomeranian is identifiable by its heavy double coat, foxlike head, and supremely confident demeanor.

- The Pom is a spitz-type dog, bred down in size from northern European sled-pulling breeds. Despite its tiny size, it is a sound and healthy little dog with few common health problems.

- Be careful with table scraps and treats. Tiny amounts of not-so-great food that can be tolerated by a larger dog can make a tiny dog very ill.

21

THE NONSPORTING GROUP

This varied group includes dogs for those who are cat people at heart

In the United Kingdom the nonsporting group is known as "utility" because each breed was bred for a specific purpose but is not covered by the other group descriptions. Some in this group are very ancient breeds, and the true origins are unclear. This is a diverse bunch of dogs, from the small, long-haired Lhasa apso to the distinctive Dalmatian. Because each breed is so different, there are no generalizations to be made about this group. Some, like the standard poodle and bichon frise, are well known. Others, like schipperkes and lowchens, are less common. English bulldogs, originally bred for bull-fighting, have had the fight instinct bred out and are now purely companion dogs. The true history and original pur-

French Bulldogs

- Each dog in this category has a distinct history and original purpose. Even if that purpose is now defunct, the dog may retain the characteristics it was first bred for.

- The French bulldog (also "Frenchie" or "Frog dog")

  was bred down from English bulldogs, but its primary purpose has always been as a prized companion.

- A French bulldog was an unfortunate passenger on the *Titanic* but was insured for an astounding $750—a fortune at the time.

Chows

- The chow chow is thought to be one of the most ancient dog breeds. Originating in China, probably as hunting and guardian dogs, they are aloof, regal, and catlike in temperament.

- Only two dog breeds have black tongues: the chow and the Chinese shar-pei.

- Chows are good guard dogs with natural suspicion of strangers but should never be vicious, although they have a tendency to be aggressive toward other dogs, as do many of the guardian breeds.

pose of the French bulldog are unknown, but it has been a favored pet for over two hundred years. The popular Boston terrier is not a true terrier. Originally developed as a fighting dog in Boston, it quickly became a prized companion dog and has been bred for that purpose for over a century.

For "cat people" considering a dog, the chow and shiba inu are dignified, clean, and aloof, much like cats. Very intelligent yet resistant to training because of their independent nature, these breeds can make excellent pets and watchdogs.

ZOOM

Many rare or regional breeds are not fully recognized by the major kennel clubs but have a true breed standard and long history. This does not make them any less of a dog. Examples are fila de Brasilieros, Pyrenean shepherds, Leonbergers, Sloughis, and many regional hunting and working stock dogs.

English Bulldogs

- The English bulldog was bred for fighting bulls for sport. Early bulldogs were leaner, more athletic, and sturdier than today's bulldogs.

- Bulldog breeders today have come under fire for breeding a dog with such exaggerated features that the dog cannot tolerate much exercise or extreme weather and usually cannot give birth normally due to the puppies' large heads and the dam's narrow pelvis.

- Despite a fighting heritage, bulldogs are sweet and affectionate pets (but they snore).

Dalmatians

- Some dogs in nonsporting could arguably be categorized in another group. The Dalmatian was used to catch vermin in stables and firehouses and to hunt.

- Dalmatians are a true coach dog and the only breed known to have a natural affinity for horses.

- Dalmatian puppies are born white. The black or liver spots appear as they grow, and the underlying skin pigment is also spotted.

THE HERDING GROUP

The ability to move large herds of animals makes these dogs natural athletes

Known in the United Kingdom as the "pastoral group," herding dogs have toughness and the ability to work tirelessly from dawn to dusk. Controlling the movement of animals many times the size of the dog requires both independence and the ability to precisely follow orders when asked. A single dog can move hundreds of animals. Herding dogs tend to have natural stamina, agility, and weatherproof, double coats. Both athletic and highly trainable, most excel at any task before them. Generally, herding dogs are extremely intelligent, and many make good guard and watchdogs. They tend to get along with other dogs and make wonderful family pets if given outlets for their energy.

Border Collies

- The border collie is one of the most intelligent breeds of dog, capable of learning complex instructions and thinking on her feet to control large herds of sheep.

- Proper working border collies do not bark while working because barking would spook the sheep. They work silently and efficiently.

- Plenty of vigorous exercise is mandatory for most herding dogs. Quite often problem behaviors cease if the dogs get enough exercise.

Corgis

- The short-legged corgi, despite a small size, herds cattle hundreds of times its size. Corgis bark vociferously and are very athletic and agile. Corgis do well in dog sports and are easily trained.

- Herding dogs tend to be very alert and may be sensitive to noise. Some, like the corgi, can be quite vocal.

- The Pembroke corgi (above) is smaller and has no tail. The Cardigan corgi is larger, with a longer tail.

As pets, they often need a lot of exercise. Border collies are renowned for being insanely high energy and are not often recommended for an average pet home. Some herding dogs, like collies and corgis, were bred to bark as a way of controlling herds. Collie specialty shows are oddly quiet because the dogs are either trained not to bark or are surgically debarked. Some herding dogs will herd people, including children, using nipping to round up stragglers. This should not be interpreted as aggression, but such a dog needs to be taught that nipping is unacceptable.

Some herding breeds, like German shepherds, bouviers, and varieties of Belgian shepherds, are now used more for police and military work than for herding. Herding dogs tend to be versatile workers and rack up ribbons in the obedience ring and sporting competitions. Although many dogs never see livestock, many organizations and training facilities offer herding for fun or competition, employing cattle, sheep, and even geese for inexperienced dogs or puppies. Go online to find herding organizations and take the test to see if your herder has retained her natural abilities.

German Shepherds

- Some herding breeds are multitaskers, serving as assistance, police, military, and protection dogs. The Belgian sheepdog and the German shepherd (above) are versatile enough to perform several functions.

- German shepherds (or GSDs) are renowned for their courage, trainability, and dignity. They excel in almost any task before them.

- As with any dog who becomes very popular, care must be taken to avoid buying poorly bred dogs with fearful temperaments and heritable conditions like hip or elbow dysplasia.

Australian Shepherds

- The modern Australian shepherd was actually developed in the United States, and its ancestors hailed from northern Europe.

- "Aussies" are a medium-sized dog with a bobbed tail, a heavy coat, and a wide range of coat colors.

- Some herding dogs have very soft temperaments and do best with lots of positive reinforcement training because corrective measures can make them shut down and refuse to learn for fear of punishment.

MATCH BREED TO LIFESTYLE

What do you want a dog for? Find the breed type that will fit your lifestyle

Now that you've narrowed it down to breed and lifestyle, it's time to think about what you want to do with your dog. Undoubtedly the primary function is companion. But even show, sport, and working dogs are also companions first. Dogs are great multitaskers.

If you are looking for a show dog, you will be researching pedigrees and getting to know breeders and show folks. The right hunting breed will depend on the type of hunting you do. If you plan on getting involved in dog sports, trainability and athleticism will be factors. Family dogs for the kids should be happy-go-lucky types. Choose an active, weather-tolerant breed for a hiking companion and a laidback one if

Active Dogs

- Most dogs who are relinquished to shelters are there because the owners did not research the breed traits first. Most herding dogs were developed to work long hours and can run 10 miles a day easily.

- Working border collies are on the job almost every

day. They thrive with owners who will take time to wear them out and train them.

- Many herding breeds make wonderful hiking and agility companions. Most don't do well with hours of inactivity.

Independent Dogs

- Terriers are active dogs who love to be with their owners, enjoy learning, and make very good trick and sport dogs. You have to have a sense of humor with terriers because they like to do things their own way.

- It is possible that some dogs, like terriers, are very

aware of scents and movement underground and will dig to investigate.

- If you are trying to train a terrier, and there is a mouse in the vicinity, you will have to work really hard to get his attention! Many terriers will kill smaller animals if they get the chance.

you enjoy kicking back at home. Getting a particular type of dog because you think it is cute and because celebrities are photographed in tabloids carrying one is fine, but you still have to interact with it.

Are you a renter? Check local laws and homeowner's insurance policies. Some municipalities restrict or ban certain breeds, and insurance companies will not write insurance policies covering them. This may make it difficult to find rentals. If you plan to have children, consider breeds that are typically good with kids and ensure that your dog has plenty of positive interaction with children now.

Some long-coated breeds will require frequent grooming. Some people love floofing a dog; others prefer the ready-to-wear type. Some short-haired dogs shed more than long-haired ones, and long-haired dogs tend to carry dirt and twigs in from outside. Some dogs drool copiously. Large dogs with long tails will knock things over. These are things to consider if you're a fastidious housekeeper.

Relish the decision process—it's not every day you get to choose a new family member!

Energetic Dogs

- Most retrievers are known for being puppy-like and energetic for about the first three years of their lives. Playing fetching games with them satisfies their natural retrieving instincts.

- If weather allows, take water-loving dogs swimming or find dock jumping trials.

- For high-energy breeds, consider doggie day care once or twice a week. The effects of a good day's playing can calm a dog down for days.

High-maintenance Dogs

- Some short-haired dogs shed more than long-haired dogs, although there is less work in grooming them.

- Most hunting dogs get along well with other dogs because they were developed to work cooperatively in packs. Guardian breeds are more independent and more likely to be unfriendly with dogs outside their own "pack."

- There is no such thing as a truly low-maintenance dog, but there are definitely high-maintenance dogs!

FIND A BREEDER

It's not difficult to find a breeder who breeds for both form and function

The Internet makes it easy to look for a purebred puppy. Perhaps too easy. Unfortunately, many people breed indiscriminately and sell puppies, sometimes even with falsified registration paperwork. The Internet is a great way to research breeds and breeders, but be cautious of puppy classifieds sites. A good breeder will rarely use these or sell to pet stores.

Good breeders show and work their dogs. In order to determine good breeding stock and breed the best to the best, the parents should prove themselves exemplary representatives of the breed in both form and function. Good breeders will also do all health testing required to ensure that faulty genetics are not passed on.

Signs of a Good Breeder

- She titles her breeding dogs in conformation and possibly also in working trials.

- She belongs to local and national breed clubs.

- She provides proof of all health clearances specific to the breed. Sire and dam should be at least two years old.

- She quizzes you on your goals for one of her puppies and will probably choose the puppy for you.

- She requires a signed contract with a limited health guarantee.

- She will usually require that pups who are not show worthy be spayed or neutered.

Evaluating Litters

- Usually by the time a litter is six to eight weeks old, a breeder knows which pups are show prospects and which can go to a "pet only" home. "Pet only" does not mean the puppy is lower quality in any way. It means simply that the puppy doesn't meet strict breed standard criteria.

- A good breeder will often have an independent evaluator critique every puppy before placing it with prospective buyers.

- Expect to be quizzed about your suitability as a worthy dog owner.

Typically a breeder will evaluate the puppies and sell pups with show potential to those who will show the pups, with the rest of the litter going to pet and working homes. Puppies will come with both a contract and a guarantee. To find breeders, network. Use the Internet or phone book to find local breed clubs. Ask veterinarians and dog trainers if they know reputable people. Visit dog shows and working trials and talk to participants. Look online for breeders but look for those with websites set up more to brag about their dogs' accomplishments than just to sell puppies.

An older puppy or adult purebred could be a great choice because you can skip most of the teething and potty training work. Breed rescue groups are a great place to start looking for dogs if you are not concerned about pedigree. Sometimes breeders take back young adults who don't fulfill show potential—ask around.

If you are serious about getting a purebred, even as "just a pet," it's worth the effort to buy a puppy who comes from a caring breeder.

Visiting Dog Shows

- The purpose of dog shows is to evaluate the worthiness of potential breeding stock.

- A purebred dog should not be bred unless it meets the breed standard in appearance, temperament, and comportment.

- Visiting dog shows and working trials is a wonderful way to find a good breeder. Don't expect to get a lot of information during the show because people are often preoccupied with their dogs. Get contact information and call later.

Red Flags

- The breeder has no titles of any sort of her dogs. "Champions in the pedigree" means absolutely nothing. Champions often produce puppies who don't conform to the standard or have health and temperament problems.

- Dogs and puppies are in unsanitary, isolated conditions, or you are not able to see any of her dogs.

- The breeder shows little interest in your goals or worthiness as a dog owner.

- The breeder requires no contract and no spay/neuter of pet-quality puppies and will not show you health clearances.

EVALUATE BREEDERS
What to ask and what to expect from a good, reputable breeder

A caring breeder will screen prospective puppy owners because she has a great deal of care invested in the little guys. Reputable breeders don't need to advertise because they either have waiting lists for the puppies or are well known enough that puppy buyers seek them out.

Often, a breeder will pick the puppy who will be best suited to your lifestyle and expectations for the dog. Good breeders observe the puppies carefully as they grow. The puppies are exposed to different people, sounds, and environments early so they are better prepared for the big, wide world when it's time to leave. Between five and seven weeks of age, the basic temperament is observed—some puppies will be bolder and more challenging, others calmer and submissive.

Even in the most carefully planned litters, some puppies

Handling Puppies

- Puppies should be whelped and raised inside the home where they get a lot of handling and interaction.

- Because tiny purebred pups may look a lot alike at birth, they are usually identified with different-colored ribbon around their necks. This way the breeder can monitor their progress and temperaments.

- A good breeder won't let puppies go to their new homes any younger than eight weeks old. In some states it's illegal to sell puppies too young.

Healthy Living Conditions

- Outdoor kennels should be spacious and clean, and the dogs ought to spend time inside as well as out.

- The dogs should appear well-kept, healthy, and confident, with trimmed nails, well-conditioned coats, and bright eyes.

- Even dogs who live primarily outside the house should have a lot of interaction, training, and attention.

- A good breeder is passionate about one, perhaps two, breeds and does not breed "designer" dogs or multiple litters of different breeds.

will not meet show quality—a white spot where there shouldn't be one, incorrect angulation of the shoulder blades, or a poorly set tail may be all it takes to determine that the puppies will not be show quality. These carefully bred puppies make great pets or working or sporting dogs. They are usually sold on a spay/neuter contract and given a limited registration, meaning that if they are bred, their progeny will be ineligible for registration. This practice is to protect the integrity of the breed.

A breeder should be happy to show you her dogs, their living quarters, and proof of health clearances. Ask about health guarantees for both parents and grandparents. These may include clearances for hip and elbow dysplasia, heart defects, hypothyroidism, and genetic eye diseases. Any of these conditions can shorten a dog's life and be extremely expensive to treat. An inexpensive, poorly bred puppy with no health guarantee is no bargain if you are faced with thousands in veterinary bills within a year.

Show Puppies

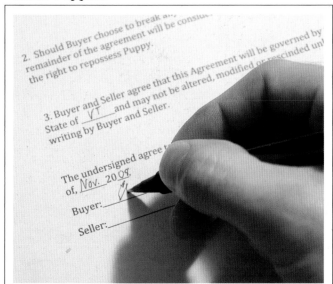

- If you plan to show your puppy, the breeder may wish to co-own the dog and retain some breeding rights. Read and understand all contracts carefully.

- It is not uncommon for the sire to be at a different location or even passed away. Breeding is often done with frozen semen after a careful evaluation of both sire's and dam's strengths and weaknesses.

- Be clear about your goals for the puppy—great family pet or working or show prospect?

Having the Proper Paperwork

- When puppies are born, the breeder registers the litter with the registering organization, which sends her a temporary slip for each puppy. Be suspicious if the breeder does not have the paperwork on hand.

- The new buyer then sends in that paperwork when she buys her puppy and is sent a permanent registration in her name.

- This AKC registration certificate shows the pup's pedigree and registered name, which often includes the breeder's kennel name.

BREEDERS TO AVOID
Don't give your money to careless and dishonest breeders

Puppies are a profitable business for some people. There is nothing wrong with making a profit on dogs unless it's at the expense of their well-being. Unfortunately, it can be difficult to winnow out the good from the bad. There are show breeders who are less than honest in ensuring that genetic defects are eliminated from their lines and small hobby, and "backyard" breeders who put a lot of thought into breeding

their quality bitch to a carefully selected dog.

However, there are plenty of red flags to watch out for. Pet store puppies are never a wise choice. Not only are you invariably supporting puppy mills (no matter what the pet store tells you), but also your chances of getting a physically and temperamentally unsound puppy are very high. Pet store puppies raised in cages are often hard to potty train,

Puppy Brokers and Mills

- Pet stores invariably purchase puppies wholesale from puppy brokers. The price for pet store puppies is often much higher than for pups from a good breeder.

- Often these puppies are farmed like livestock and raised in deplorable condi-

tions in puppy mills. They are cleaned up for sale in pet stores.

- Avoid stores selling puppies. Buying one because you feel sorry for it perpetuates the puppy industry, and these pups often have lifelong health and temperament problems.

Misleading Information

- Slick puppy-selling Web sites often misrepresent their product, and the puppies often come from cages.

- Red flags: breeders charge more for females than males, for "rare" colors, or for "show quality" puppies, especially if they don't have titles on their own dogs.

- Claims like "champion lines" or "imported stock" have nothing to do with quality. Almost every purebred dog—and many a mutt—in the world has at least one champion or import in the pedigree. It means nothing.

and most pet stores charge significantly more than a reputable breeder.

The Internet is awash with puppies-for-sale Web sites. It is easy to make great claims of "family-raised" puppies and impressive pedigrees. Photos of endearing fuzzballs held by children, frolicking amongst flowers and posed on satin pillows, are appealing but can be misleading. Beware of Web sites that are put together primarily to sell puppies. A responsible breeder will showcase her dogs' accomplishments, make health clearances available, and breed infrequently.

Unless you are considering a rare breed, chances are you can find the puppy you want locally and visit the breeder.

What about puppies advertised locally, in the newspaper, on Internet bulletin boards, and at flea markets? You will be taking a chance, and it's highly unlikely you'll get a stellar example of your chosen breed. A carefully bred puppy is your best bet, but buying locally is at least better than buying at a pet store or buying sight unseen online.

Flea Markets

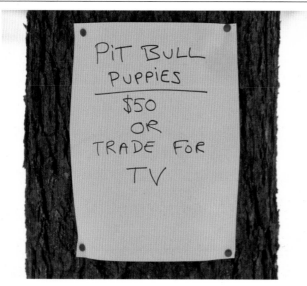

- It's perfectly possible to find puppies, even purebreds, being sold in flea markets, via signs tacked to telephone poles, or in grocery store parking lots. Ask yourself first if the sellers really deserve your money.

- Purebred dogs—some very nice ones—end up in shelters and rescue groups in high numbers. A purebred dog is not intrinsically superior to a mixed-breed dog.

- If you want a purebred dog, your two best choices are a breed rescue group or a responsible breeder.

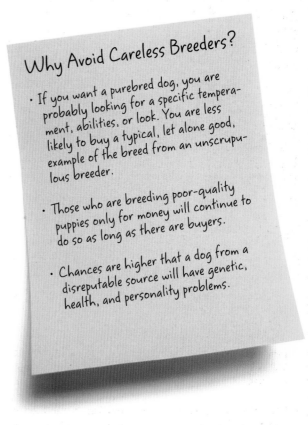

Why Avoid Careless Breeders?

- If you want a purebred dog, you are probably looking for a specific temperament, abilities, or look. You are less likely to buy a typical, let alone good, example of the breed from an unscrupulous breeder.

- Those who are breeding poor-quality puppies only for money will continue to do so as long as there are buyers.

- Chances are higher that a dog from a disreputable source will have genetic, health, and personality problems.

REGISTERING YOUR PUREBRED

There are many registries for your purebred dog, but not all are reputable

To "register" something means to record it. An AKC-registered dog has parents who were recorded as being a particular breed; this signifies nothing about their quality. There are three reputable breed registries in North America—the American Kennel Club (AKC), United Kennel Club (UKC), and Canadian Kennel Club (CKC). There are also for-profit regis-

tries that will register any dog for a fee. Some are set up for the sole purpose of allowing puppy-selling operations "legitimacy" and have similar initials to legitimate registries. There are some reputable single-breed registries that promote breed improvement and working ability, like the American Border Collie Association (ABCA) for working border collies.

Reputable North American Registries

- American Kennel Club (AKC)

- Canadian Kennel Club (CKC—not to be confused with the Continental Kennel Club, which is a for-profit registry for puppy sellers)

- United Kennel Club (UKC), the second-oldest breed registry in the United States; has a limited privilege (LP) program for mixed-breed dogs, who may compete in most sporting events alongside purebreds

- AKC and CKC are purebred registries, with their primary focus being the integrity of breed standards

Use Reputable Registries

- These dogs are competing for best in show, a competition in which the winners from each group are compared to choose the dog who is the best overall example of his breed.

- It is by gathering points at small shows like this that

the big winner dogs make it to Westminster or Crufts.

- Only reputable registries hold shows and trials and keep a database of all the dogs' accomplishments.

34

Bottom line: Don't be unduly impressed by registered dogs. What counts is the care given to the breeding.

The reputable registries offer limited registration (LP) for purebred dogs who do not meet the breed standard but may be otherwise well-bred dogs. For instance, a long-haired rottweiler (long hair is a disqualification according to the standard) may have a limited AKC registration and can compete in all AKC venues except conformation shows, and his offspring cannot be registered. This practice is to maintain the integrity of the breed standard.

Register with Parent Organizations

- To compete in working trials, dog shows, or dog sports, a dog needs to be registered with the parent organization.

- Registration is usually inexpensive, and requirements are dependent on the purpose of the registry.

- Some organizations promote a single working ability, like herding. Usually only certain breeds are eligible for these organizations.

- If you have a collie who has never seen sheep in her life, give herding a shot. You may be surprised to see the instincts kick in.

A dog who is clearly a purebred but has no proof of pedigree may be granted a registration similar to an LP upon approval of photos and a veterinary statement that it is spayed or neutered. This means your pound puppy may be eligible to compete for working titles such as obedience or agility.

Additionally there are sport, hunting, and working registries, most of which accept any dog who wishes to compete. You may want to register your dog with the appropriate organization if you plan on breeding, showing, or competing with your dog.

Reputable European Registries

- The Kennel Club Great Britain

- FCI (Fédération Cynologique Internationale) does not register dogs but rather holds shows and is an umbrella agency for many kennel clubs worldwide, including the AKC. A kennel club will not be recognized by the FCI unless it is in good standing.

- Most European countries have reputable kennel clubs, each with its own system of record keeping and breed standards.

THE MIXED-BREED DOG

Mongrel, crossbred dog, mutt: Mixed breed dogs can be the best

A mixed-breed dog is any dog who is a mix of two or more breeds. There might even be multiple sires for a single litter. The dog may be a recognizable type, like a lab-shepherd mix, or there could be no identifiable breeds in the mix, resulting from a long pedigree of mutt-dom. Designer and hybrid dogs are mixed breeds, as are thousands of dogs in county shelters.

Hybrid vigor is the theory that mixed-breed dogs are healthier and less likely to have congenital problems. There may be some truth to this theory after many generations of natural breeding, as in the case of indigenous dogs in some countries. However, the results of putting different breeds together and asserting that the puppies will have "hybrid vigor" are not the same as those of generations of natural breeding. Mixed-breed dogs carry the traits, including genetic faults, of

Mixed-Breeds

- Some mixed-breed dogs are types, bred for function instead of appearance.

- Lurchers, a cross between a working breed and a sighthound, were originally bred in Europe for poaching game. Although lurchers may look very different from one another, they share the same working characteristics.

- Primitive-type dogs in much of the world have a similar, "generic dog" appearance after centuries of natural breeding. Most are medium sized and brown or yellow with pricked ears and short- to medium-length coats.

Toy Breeds

- Many toy breeds were developed by breeding down for size. Little French bulldogs have English bull-dogs in their lineage, and Pomeranians are miniaturized sledding dogs.

- Small mixed-breed dogs are often quickly adopted from shelters, whereas larger dogs, particularly black ones, are less sought after.

- It used to be thought that a purebred bitch was somehow "ruined" by mating with a dog of another breed.

both parents. It's just as possible that a puppy can manifest both sets of health problems.

Mixed-breed dogs are as competent and intelligent as purebred dogs. They have been search and rescue dogs, therapy dogs, obedience and agility champions, and guide dogs. "All-American" dogs outnumber purebreds as family dogs, possibly because they are usually cheaper to buy and more widely available through shelters.

Purebred dogs were carefully bred by crossbreeding several breeds over generations to achieve a reliable outcome and standard. Breeds such as dobermans and Australian cattle dogs were developed for specific work like guarding or cattle herding. Other breeds, like the pug, were bred for their appearance and value as a companion.

Mixed-Breed versus Cross-Breed

- A mixed-breed dog has two or more breeds, often unknown, in the lineage, whereas a cross-breed dog is a breeding between two purebred dogs.

- Some mixed-breed dogs are influenced by geography. Hound mixes are common in the southern United States, whereas pit bull mixes are not uncommon in large urban areas.

- More popular breeds, like beagles, Labradors, and German shepherds, are often in a mutt's ancestry.

Cross-Breeds

- This dog is probably a husky mix—look at his blue eyes and coat.

- Technically, all purebreds were once mixed breeds. Breeds as we know them today were achieved by crossing and interbreeding different dogs until the desired result was achieved.

- With the rising popularity of dog sports, some breeders are experimenting with different crosses like border collies and Jack Russell terriers for ultimate flyball or agility dogs.

MIXED-BREED STRENGTHS

Weigh the advantages and disadvantages of these dogs—does a pedigree matter?

Whether the lineage is an orderly record of purebred descendants or a motley crew of hit-and-run dogs, even mutts have pedigrees. The primary disadvantage to getting a mixed-breed puppy is not knowing just what she will look like when adult. The purebred dog pedigree offers some guarantee that the dog will be reasonably close to the stan-dard. A mutt's pedigree offers no such clues.

Because of recessive genes, two short-haired, tan parents could produce long-haired, black pups. A small puppy can grow larger than expected. The union of a golden and a German shepherd could result in a happy-go-lucky retrieving dog or the sharper, more work-oriented shepherd tempera-

Mixed Heritage

- Some dogs are such a stir-fry of breeds that you will never really know what makes up their heritage.

- A flowing golden coat could result from a yellow Labrador and Australian shepherd, among others, and not necessarily a sign of a golden retriever.

- Sometimes mixed-breed dogs end up looking like purebreds, even if they have none of that particular breed in their DNA.

Wide Range of Breeds

- There is most likely golden retriever and possibly German shepherd in this dog's heritage.

- The coat, head shape, and soft expression suggest retriever. The coloration could come from several breeds, and mixing more than one can result in some unexpected characteristics that may look like neither parent.

- It doesn't take too many generations of mutts interbreeding randomly to result in a wide range of possible breeds in the mix.

ment. Some people prefer purebred dogs due to the predictability of the outcome. However, it's possible to make educated guesses to predict the adult result of the mutt puppy.

It is usually inexpensive to buy a mixed-breed dog. Shelter and rescue group fees typically include heartworm testing, vaccinations, and "speutering." Check classifieds and find cheap or free puppies and dogs of indeterminate origin. The initial cost of the dog is tiny compared with the lifetime cost of owning a dog, but the high fees for some purebreds deter many people from taking the first step.

High-energy mixed breeds compete at international levels in dog sports. Although a mixed-breed dog should not be bred and is ineligible for AKC events, there are many venues if you want to get out and play.

Every dog is unique, and mixed breeds even more so. You may never know what breeds make up the dog, so you can invent your own designer dog: canardly dog (as in "Can 'ardly tell what breeds he is"). Call him a "Mongolian bat terrier," and most people will take you at your word.

Unique Characteristics

- Mixed-breed dogs are truly unique.

- It is impossible to guess which breeds make up this little dog. The shape of the head suggests Chihuahua or Pomeranian, the ears perhaps terrier. The coat is anyone's guess.

- Mixed-breed dogs can still be prone to genetic conditions like hip and elbow dysplasia. However, overall they tend to be healthier unless all breeds in the mix are those prone to similar congenital problems.

Shelter Dogs

- Mixed-breed and crossbred dogs make up the majority of shelter dogs.

- It is theorized that if people don't pay a lot of money for a dog or get it for free, they see it as less valuable and are more likely to relinquish it to a shelter.

- Up to half of all puppies are euthanized in shelters by two years of age, largely because they were acquired at no or low cost and without much forethought.

BREED CHARACTERISTICS

Use the predominant breed type of the dog as an indicator of his characteristics

Walk through any animal shelter, and you'll notice a prevalence of a certain breed, either purebreds or mixes. Labradors and German shepherds are popular dogs and are represented in many mixed-breed dogs. There may be regional differences—in some areas, hunting and treeing dogs are quite common; in others it may be pit bull mixes or northern breeds.

Individual dogs may have temperaments that are atypical of the breeds that make up their mix, and assumptions shouldn't be made on breed alone. Mixed-breed dogs are neither better nor worse than purebreds, and all dogs may be aloof or affectionate, sickly or sturdy, dog aggressive or socially graceful, be healthy or prone to allergies and con-

Labrador Mix

- "Black dog syndrome" refers to the phenomenon in which large, black dogs like this Labrador mix often languish unadopted in shelters because nobody wants them.

- Young, large retrievers often remain puppy-like for the first several years,

exasperating owners who haven't taken time to work with them. Hence, they are often relinquished to shelters.

- Because Labradors are popular dogs, they often make up part of the genetic makeup of mixed-breed dogs.

Small Dog Ailments

- Small mixed-breed dogs may be healthier than some of their purebred counterparts, but many are still prone to "small dog" ailments. These include poor dental health and luxating patella (slipping kneecap).

- Most mutts are accidental "designer" dogs!

- Unless you plan to show or breed or have an affinity for a particular breed, there is no practical reason not to get a mixed-breed dog. A mixed-breed dog performs virtually the same functions as a purebred.

genital joint problems, and be hyper or be laidback. However, understanding the breeds that make up the dog can give you clues to his likely traits.

A herding or hunting dog mix is more likely than not to be very high energy and possibly quite vocal. Mixes of some of the working or guardian breeds like rottweilers, chows, akitas, and bully breeds may be dog aggressive and stubborn. Terrier-type mixes will usually be intelligent and very feisty. Some breeds are harder to train than others—beagles, pugs, chows, and some of the toy breeds fall into this category.

Aggression

- In some cities people are breeding tough mixes, sometimes for illegal dog fighting. Although these dogs are often very smart and friendly to people, they may have a higher inclination to dog aggression.

- It is normal for some breeds to be aggressive toward other animals. This does not mean there is anything at all wrong with such dogs, but they need to be responsibly managed.

- Never take a bossy or dog-aggressive dog to a dog park.

Less Extreme Temperament

- Many mixed-breed dogs tend to have a less extreme temperament than purebreds, which have been selectively bred for certain traits. Temperament may be "toned down" by mixing breeds.

- However, if a dog is a mix of highly active breeds, such as Jack Russell terrier and border collie, you can end up with a very high-octane dog.

- This may not be the case if purebred parents were not typical of their breed.

CHOOSING MIXED-BREED PUPPIES

Evaluate a mixed-breed puppy by understanding predominant breed and bone size and by temperament testing

Consider what you expect from the dog ownership experience and choose mixed-breed dogs by researching the identifiable breeds. Pay more attention to temperament traits than to appearance, especially with puppies. They're small and adorable for a very short time, but you'll be living with the adult dog for many years.

If both parents are a similar size, it is likely that the puppies will grow roughly that big. If the size of the sire is unknown, it's possible to guesstimate, and the older the puppies, the easier it is to guess adult size. Big feet, wide head, and sturdy bones (compare the puppies in the litter) indicate greater bulk rather than height. At three months old, small-breed

Picking a Puppy

- Ask the litter owner if she has noticed any of the puppies being bolder, shier, noisier, or more social. The more information you have, the better you can predict the adult dog.

- Spend time observing how the puppy interacts—does he follow people, chase thrown toys, calm down or struggle when picked up, or appear inquisitive and social?

- Temperament is hardwired but will be heavily influenced by how the pup is raised.

Determining Adult Features

- This puppy has substantial bone and will be a sturdy, larger dog. She has a broad chest and chunky legs.

- A rough rule of thumb is that the weight at sixteen weeks is about half the final adult weight.

- The long hair on the ears and slight feathering on the back of the legs suggest she will have a medium-long coat as an adult.

- She has slightly open lips, which means she may drool later in life.

dogs will be roughly half their adult weight, and large-breed puppies reach the halfway mark by around four months of age. The larger the dog, the slower it is to physically mature.

Coat type can be hard to predict because coats change texture, length, and color as they mature. A puppy with long hair on its ears by eight weeks of age will probably be a long-haired dog. If both parents are known, their coat type—long, short, undercoated—may be a clue as to the pups' adult coats. In many breeds, white coats—especially on the head and ears—can be a predictor of deafness and skin problems.

Choose neither the feistiest nor the shiest puppy in the litter. Hold a pup gently on its back. The pup who cries and perhaps urinates in fear may be a high-strung and nervous adult. The pup who struggles and bites without calming is going to be one feisty handful and lots of work! The best pick will usually be the pup who struggles briefly before calming.

Visual Appearance

- Longer hair on the ears and legs indicates a longer coat as an adult. Coat texture and even color may change as the pup matures.

- The final adult coat may not be "done" until the pup is over a year old and has gone through one or two shedding seasons.

- White or speckled puppies may gain color as they grow. Some spotted dogs, like Dalmatians, are born white and start developing spots between two and three weeks of age.

Mutt Puppy Potential

- Mixed-breed puppies can compete, even at international levels, in many competitive dog sports.

- They can be shown by children in junior handling.

- They can be registered therapy dogs.

- They can be service and assistance dogs for the disabled.

- They can learn tricks and even be film stars. (Benji was a mutt.)

- Mixed-breed dogs can be excellent watchdogs and guard dogs.

43

"DESIGNER" DOGS

These are a hot item, but in reality they are high-priced mixed-breed dogs

The term *designer breed* is regarded with derision by many, yet such dogs are increasingly popular. All "designer dogs" are mixed-breed dogs. Most are cute, not unlike many of the mixed-breed dogs in shelters. Most are small because there is a demand for small dogs who can be carried and dressed. And most often the price tag for a Yorkiepoo puppy vastly ex-

ceeds that of either a well-bred Yorkie or a well-bred poodle.

If you have your heart set on a particular mix, research the breeds used to create it. Puggles are adorable puppies and no doubt make great little family dogs. Be aware that both pugs and beagles have a reputation for being hard to train, and beagles are notorious barkers. Learn about breed traits in

KNACK DOG CARE AND TRAINING

Cockapoo

- Crossbreeding dogs is not new—poodles and cocker spaniels have been crossbred to create the popular cockapoo for over a century.

- Many sellers mate different breeds to poodles because curly-coated dogs tend to shed less and cause fewer

- allergic reactions in allergy-prone individuals.

- Because poodles range in size from the little minia-ture to the larger standard size, they are mixed with a great variety of dog breeds of all sizes.

Good Breeder Ethics

- Although some designer dog breeders make an effort to breed carefully, many do not.

- Look for breeders who do health testing and generally follow good breeder ethics as outlined in Chapter 3.

- The main difference between a mixed-breed dog in a shelter and one touted as a designer dog (apart from the price tag) is marketing and a catchy, made-up "breed" name.

44

the mix, both good and bad, before writing that check. You are not buying a cute puppy; you are buying a decade or longer of commitment to training and caring for an adult dog.

Beware of marketing terms like *teacup* or *pocket* dogs. Breeding dogs so small that they practically have to be picked up with tweezers magnifies the health problems that many toy dogs are already prone to, including bad dentition, heart and joint problems, and hypoglycemia.

Some purebred dogs started as a mixed-breed experiment. Labradoodles were initially bred in the 1970s in Australia in an effort to develop a hypoallergenic guide dog. That breeding program was abandoned when it didn't produce the expected results, but "doodles" became very popular nonetheless. Some agility and flyball enthusiasts look for "border Jacks," a cross between a Jack Russell terrier and a border collie, for the ultimate fast sport dog. There is nothing wrong with spending a lot of money on a mixed-breed dog. Just go into it with your eyes open.

Labradoodles

- Labradoodles were created in Australia by breeding standard poodles to Labradors in an effort to create a hypoallergenic guide dog for the blind.

- The breeding program was abandoned because the dogs were not hypoallergenic. There is no such thing as a truly hypoallergenic dog, although some breeds tend to cause fewer allergic reactions.

- Labradoodles became a popular commodity, and now many types of "doodle" mixes are sold worldwide. They tend to be intelligent, sweet, and active.

Designer Dog Traits

- A mating of two toy breeds prone to luxating patellas (slipping kneecap), bad teeth, and heart defects are as likely to produce these problems in their offspring as dogs of the same breed.

- However, some traits can be improved by crossbreeding— a pug's injury-prone eyes and very short snout are modified by breeding it with a beagle, so the offspring may have fewer eye and breathing problems.

- Designer dogs can be sport and competition dogs, therapy dogs, and obedience dogs and can fulfill all purposes like normal dogs.

REGISTERING A MIXED BREED

Here's why you might want to register a mixed-breed dog

When most people think of dog registration, they think first of the AKC. But there are many legitimate ways to register a dog and many reasons to do so. As the unofficial United Kennel Club slogan states, "Our Dogs Do Stuff." In order to "do stuff," you often have to register somewhere.

The AKC is a purebred registry and as such does not currently allow mixed-breed dogs. However, any mixed-breed dog can qualify for AKC's "Canine Good Citizen" certificate program, usually run through training facilities. The AKC is the second-oldest registry in the United States, with the focus on performance. Mixed-breed dogs are eligible to compete in obedience, agility, dock diving, weight pulling, some hunting programs, and even protection.

There are several national and international flyball and agil-

UKC and AKC

- The United Kennel Club (UKC) accepts some mixed-breed dogs in hunting programs. Generally they have to be hunting dog or retriever mixes.

- The AKC offers a "Canine Good Citizen" (CGC) certification for all dogs, including mixed breeds. Training and testing are done at many training facilities. Call around or check the AKC website for details.

- Some landlords and municipalities waive bans or restrictions on dogs who have earned a CGC certificate.

Registry Requirements

- With few exceptions, mixed-breed dogs can compete to the highest levels in the popular sport of agility, and many have achieved international titles competing alongside purebreds.

- Depending on the type of registry, some require that your dog is spayed or neutered. There is often a minimum age for competing. This requirement is for the well-being of the dog.

- To join some organizations, like therapy dog registries, your dog may first have to pass a temperament and basic obedience skills test.

ity registries for the hyper canine. Don't assume that dogs must be impeccably trained and that owners must be athletic to be involved. A visit to any class or event will disabuse you of that notion! The focus is always on having fun with your dog first. Regional clubs offer competition for weight pulling and herding, often open to mixed-breed dogs. Canine freestyle, in which dog and handler perform a dance routine together to music, has spawned international competition. 4-H and the major registries offer junior handling programs so the whole family can be involved. To find any of these activities, use the Internet and call local training schools to see what they offer.

Dogs of any breed can be registered as therapy dogs, visiting hospitals, schools, and group homes to lift spirits. Mixed-breed dogs can be registered search and rescue dogs. There are programs to help children learn to read by reading aloud to dogs, and any friendly, well-behaved dog is welcome.

So register and do stuff!

AMBOR and MBDCA

- Two North American registries accept mixed-breed dogs only. They are the American Mixed Breed Obedience Registration (AMBOR) and Mixed Breed Dog Clubs of America (MBDCA).

- The Cross Breed and Mongrel Club in the United Kingdom caters to British mixed-breed dogs.

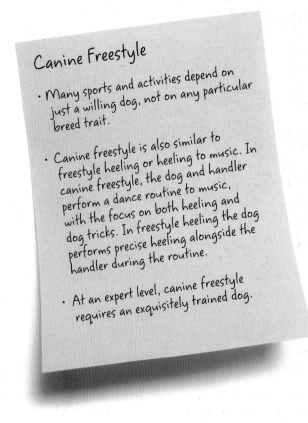

Canine Freestyle

- Many sports and activities depend on just a willing dog, not on any particular breed trait.

- Canine freestyle is also similar to freestyle heeling or heeling to music. In canine freestyle, the dog and handler perform a dance routine to music, with the focus on both heeling and dog tricks. In freestyle heeling the dog performs precise heeling alongside the handler during the routine.

- At an expert level, canine freestyle requires an exquisitely trained dog.

MIXED BREEDS

FINDING AN ADOPTEE

Shelters, rescue groups, and classified ads are all great sources for your next dog

Dogs in shelters aren't there because there is something wrong with them. Overwhelmingly, they are relinquished because of a change in owner circumstance. The family moves and cannot take the dog; the owner doesn't have time to train and exercise the dog; there's a new baby in the home, and the dog loses its appeal. Most dogs in shelters are relatively young, and many have received little obedience training. Having grown out of the cute puppy stage, the untrained dog becomes a bother. This means that there are thousands of perfectly good young dogs, past the teething and potty training stage, who need some guidance to become a great pet.

Rescue Organizations

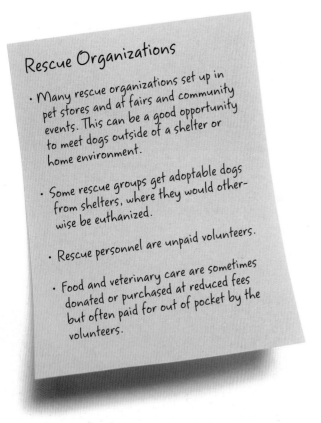

- Many rescue organizations set up in pet stores and at fairs and community events. This can be a good opportunity to meet dogs outside of a shelter or home environment.

- Some rescue groups get adoptable dogs from shelters, where they would otherwise be euthanized.

- Rescue personnel are unpaid volunteers.

- Food and veterinary care are sometimes donated or purchased at reduced fees but often paid for out of pocket by the volunteers.

Shelters and Foster Homes

- Some shelters have personnel who will help you evaluate a prospective dog, and some run training classes.

- Dogs who have spent time in foster homes have often lived with other dogs, cats, and children. A foster volunteer who has cared for such a dog can tell you a great deal about its temperament.

- Choose wisely when adopting a dog from the classifieds. If possible, ask to talk to the vet and neighbors for insight and opinions before making a commitment.

48

Shelter dogs have usually been checked for parasites and heartworm. They've been vaccinated. The adoption fee generally includes spaying or neutering. You can find purebreds and puppies at the shelter. You get bang for your buck with a shelter dog and save a life. Dogs in rescue groups and foster homes often come from shelters. Deemed adoptable by rescue volunteers, they are placed in foster homes and advertised for adoption. The greatest benefit to getting a dog who has been living in a foster home is that the dog's temperament has been evaluated. The foster home can tell you what the dog's strengths and weaknesses are.

Many people advertise unwanted dogs for free or a nominal fee. If you go to someone's home to meet a dog, vow to give yourself a twenty-four-hour waiting period before making a decision. It's too easy to feel obligated to take a cheap, friendly dog home with you, but impulse decisions are often regretted later. No matter where the dog comes from, you owe it to yourself, the dog, and the previous owner to make the right choice. Some shelters will help you evaluate and even train a prospective pet.

Know Dog History

- Most dogs, like this hound mix, will adapt and bond quickly to their new families. The more information you get and the more evaluation you do beforehand, the better the chance of a successful adoption.

- Find out as much as you can about the known history of the dog.

- Be aware that some people who relinquish their dog may be less than truthful about the dog's behavior and history.

Where to Find Dogs

- Municipal shelters are taxpayer-supported, and most euthanize animals regularly to make room for more.

- Private shelters usually are supported by donations and grants. Some may be no-kill; many accept only adoptable animals.

- All-breed rescue groups are not-for-profit groups that usually operate on a shoestring or at a loss.

- Pure-breed rescue groups are similar to all-breed rescue groups but focus on a particular breed.

- Individuals often resort to classified ads as a last resort before relinquishing a dog to a shelter.

PURE-BREED RESCUES

Some rescue groups specialize in adopting out purebred, even registered dogs of all ages

Up to 25 percent of dogs in a shelter may be purebred. The puppy whom someone paid $1,000 for last year can easily end up at the pound. Purebred rescue groups routinely check shelters for purebred dogs and sometimes are contacted when a shelter receives suitable dogs. Dogs are also relinquished to rescue groups by owners. Sometimes breed-ing operations are seized by authorities, and a rescue group steps in to take dogs. Breeders may let a rescue group know when they have a dog who cannot be shown or bred because it doesn't meet the breed standard. This flaw could be as minor as the wrong eye shape or misplaced markings.

Few rescue groups operate out of kennels. Dogs are fostered

Breed Rescue Groups

- Many who work, show, or breed are also involved in rescue.

- This nice looking golden could be a show breeder "reject" for some imperfection as simple as an incorrect bite.

- A well-bred purebred like

this will probably come speutered and with a limited registration.

- Volunteers who work with breed rescue groups are often very knowledgeable about their breed. Use this knowledge to your advantage and ask lots of questions!

Breed-Specific Bans and Restrictions

- American pit bull terriers are not recognized by AKC (although the similar Staffordshire terrier is) but are a recognized UKC breed.

- A proper pit bull temperament means that she is loving, loyal, and affectionate with people. There is a breed tendency to be

aggressive toward animals, but many co-exist perfectly with other pets. Aggression toward people and animals are two different mechanisms in a dog's psyche.

- Some municipalities have breed-specific bans and restrictions.

by volunteers in their homes. Many who foster already own dogs of that breed and are knowledgeable about their health and temperament. In fact, many are such advocates for their breed that you may find yourself quizzed about your expectations and circumstances in an effort to ensure that you will be a suitable owner. People who have kept foster dogs in their homes become attached to them, get to know them, and want to be sure the dogs are going to the best possible homes. Dogs adopted from rescue groups may cost slightly more than those adopted from shelters.

Rescue Groups around the Globe

- Rescue volunteers often transport dogs from states where too many of that breed are found to states where there may be more of a desire for that breed.

- This is often how breed rescue groups in northern states end up with southern hunting dogs, for example.

- Some areas have been so successful in reducing unwanted dogs that small and medium breeds may be imported from other countries like Mexico and Puerto Rico.

- There is a list of purebred rescue groups on the AKC Web site.

Trial Periods

- You may have to wait to find a perfect rescue dog for you, especially if your preferred breed is uncommon or in high demand.

- Some breed rescue groups will have mixed-breed dogs available and very occasionally puppies.

- Breed rescue groups will require a signed contract and sometimes a home visit to ensure a suitable match.

EVALUATING A RESCUE DOG

Learn some of the basic characteristics before signing the agreement

Whereas dogs in foster homes are easy to assess, dogs in shelters are often stressed by the environment. You need to observe a dog both in and out of the caged run. Most shelters have quiet areas so prospective owners can interact with dogs.

Ask shelter personnel what they know about a dog you're interested in. They may have volunteers who interact with the dogs; ask if you can talk to them. If the dog was owner-surrendered, the owner may have left information on the dog, although many gloss over the dog's faults to make it more adoptable.

Bring a dog-savvy friend with you for a second opinion, and

Introducing Dogs to the Home

- If you already have a dog at home, arrange for a meeting between your dog and the potential adoptee.

- Most shelters have a "meeting area" where potential adoptees can meet both human and canine family members.

- Watch the body language of both dogs. The puppies above are young enough that it's unlikely there will be an altercation, but dogs of the same sex can sometimes challenge each other as they mature.

Judging on an Individual Basis

- Don't make assumptions about any dog based on the predominant breed. Judge each individually.

- Pit bull mixes can be extremely animal-friendly; rottweiler mixes can be goofy and easygoing; a pug mix may be a potential obedience champion.

- A relaxed dog will happily roll on his back without tucking his tail or looking anxious. A very submissive dog will tuck her tail and refuse to meet your eyes. Overly submissive dogs may need help integrating into your family.

if this dog will be a family dog, bring the family. Don't go to the shelter planning to bring a dog home that day. You are just going to look. Walk through the shelter and observe the dogs. Those who ignore you or act threateningly may not be the best choice for a family pet. If you see a dog who appeals, crouch down and make eye contact. Is the dog wagging her tail, meeting your gaze, and acting relaxed? Is she shy or eager? Rule out dogs who act defensively and aggressively with eye contact.

When you take the dog out, see how she acts when you put a leash on her. Dogs who aren't used to being handled by a leash may be unsure. This tells you she could need a lot of training. Ask for a "sit" and a "down" and see whether she comes when called. Observe how she responds to other dogs when walking through the shelter, and if you have children with you watch her body language with them. If she wants to chase or jump up or seems nervous, she is not the best choice for kids.

Training the Dog

- Bring some small treats with you.

- See if the dog will obey basic commands like "sit," "down," and "come" in exchange for a treat.

- Avoid forcing a dog or grabbing the collar. Doing this can make some dogs become nervous and even growl or snap because they have no reason to trust you yet. Be gentle and encouraging.

- Decide beforehand how much work you are prepared to put into a new dog. Are you willing to train an adult dog from scratch?

Introducing Family to the Dog

- A confident dog will accept being handled by everyone in the family with a happy, relaxed expression.

- If you have children, bring them to meet potential dogs.

- When adopting an adult dog, it's a good idea to have a dog-savvy friend along for a second opinion. You can't take them all home, but it's heartbreaking to have to return a dog because it didn't work out.

- Put more importance on temperament than appearance.

BRINGING YOUR DOG HOME

Integrate the new dog into your household with the minimum of stress for everyone

It can take one to three months for a dog to become fully acclimated to a new family. Bring her home when you have some free days to spend. While you get to know each other, keep her close to you in the house so you can be alert to bad habits. Let her trail a leash so you can give gentle corrections or redirect her. Use baby gates or a crate to confine her when alone.

Establish a routine and rules right away. Dogs are more secure when they know that their environment and humans are predictable. Teach her that she gets food and treats only for polite behavior. Have everyone in the house follow the rules. Avoid spoiling her because she's "already had a rough life."

Dog, Meet Cat

- Teach your dog that the resident cat is your property, same as a shoe or table leg, and must not be chewed on.

- Feed your cat before the dog, because the cat should rank higher in your pack structure. (The cat certainly believes this.)

- Make sure the cat has a safe place to eat and use her litter box—many dogs think litter boxes contain gourmet treats. It's easier to restrict access than to train your dog to leave it alone.

Dog, Meet Boundaries

- Let your new dog earn his right to get onto furniture, if at all.

- Avoid letting him get away with anything because he's "had a rough life." This isn't fair. Dogs are secure with having rules and knowing clearly where they stand. It's not "mean" to set boundaries; it's kind.

- Even as benevolent dictator, you can cuddle and baby talk your new dog! You can set boundaries and love him up at the same time.

Be prepared for some potty accidents. Even trained dogs can make mistakes due to stress or a new diet, and recently neutered males may still mark. Treat her like a new puppy—take her out to potty after eating and upon waking and praise for pottying appropriately.

A resident cat will be appalled by a new dog, but dogs and cats can get along fine. Make sure your cat has safe egress if the dog gives chase. Introductions with the dog on leash are wise. Praise and reward the dog for calm or neutral behavior toward the cat. Don't hold the cat in your arms and "show" it to the dog—the cat will be terrified with no escape route, and the dog will think you are bringing her a toy.

Dogs are best introduced to each other on neutral territory, in the absence of food or toys that can cause jealous spats. If you and another person can take them for a leashed walk together, this will be an excellent bonding experience for both.

Dog, Meet Yard

- Evaluate your fencing and yard security and accompany your new dog outside at first. Some dogs are proficient escape artists. It's better to go out with her than to leave her out by herself.

- The stress and confusion of a new home can make the best-behaved dog forget potty training. Be patient and give her plenty of time to eliminate outside.

- The longer the leash, the better.

Dog, Meet Food

- Give her space to eat and don't crowd her. To a dog, home is where the food is!

- Rather than feed a new dog a big meal, feed small meals to begin with. New food, new water, and stress can add up to gastrointestinal issues, which aren't fun for anyone on a new dog's first day.

- Find out what the current diet is and mix in the new diet slowly to avoid digestive upset.

- If you are using a crate, feed her there so she associates her crate with positive things.

COST OF RESCUE
The fee for a rescue dog seems high, but it's usually a great deal

Dogs cost money. A free dog is no bargain if you later find out it needs to be treated for heartworms. Free dogs often need grooming, vaccinations, and speutering. Older dogs may need dental work or other medical attention for minor ailments.

Most rescue groups rely on discounted veterinary fees, donated food and medication, and volunteers' own time and money to ensure that their dogs are healthy and ready to go. Typically,

adoption fees cover little more than costs. The cost for speutering, vaccinating, and making sure a dog is disease free at retail veterinary prices can be much higher than the adoption fee.

Additionally, many rescue dogs are unsocialized and untrained when they enter a foster home. The foster "parent" may have spent weeks or months working with the dog to make it a canine good citizen for the benefit of the dog and

Why Dogs Become Unwanted

- Dogs are rarely taken to shelters due to behavioral problems.

- Overwhelmingly, people abandon a dog because they are moving or their landlord does not allow pets.

- Abandoned dogs were never highly valued in the first place. Few have had basic training.

- Most were received for free from friends or the classifieds.

- Most are relinquished between five months (when they grow out of the cute puppy stage) and three years of age.

Understand the Contract

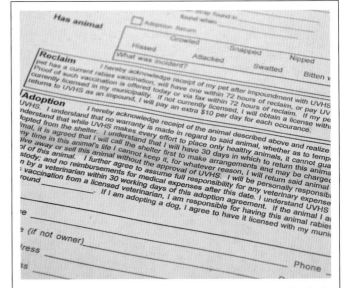

- The contract from a rescue group or shelter usually includes a no-questions-asked return policy, so you may return the dog if he doesn't work out.

- Read and understand the contract. Most contracts are boiler-plate contracts, but some are very detailed. Remember that you are signing a legal document.

- Be cautious about paying an adoption fee to anyone who doesn't require a contract.

the future owner. Check the cost of having a dog professionally trained!

A good rescue group will make sure the dog is placed in a suitable home both by being honest about the dog's limitations and by evaluating the potential adopters. The group will take back any dog if it doesn't work out in that home, for any reason, saving new owners the difficult task of relinquishing the dog.

Keep Records

- Volunteers often transport dogs from a low-demand area to a higher-demand area. Private citizens and even truckers will drive dogs.

- Many dogs come from shelters or rescue groups microchipped. Record your information right away with the microchip organization and put a tag on your dog's collar as a backup.

- Ask for any vet records with your new dog, so that you at least know her immediate health and vaccination history. Give a copy of these to your vet.

What to Expect with Your New Dog

- She'll be up to date on vaccines and tested for heartworms.

- She will be free of fleas and other parasites. You may want to have a fecal test run by your own vet to double check for intestinal bugs.

- You will get a copy of her vet and shot records.

- She will be spayed (or neutered).

- You will be advised of any behavior or training issues that need work.

- If known, her behavior around children and other animals will be disclosed.

SPECIAL-NEEDS DOGS

Some rescues specialize in these dogs, which can make perfect pets

A special-needs dog could be deaf, blind, or missing a leg. A special-needs dog may be a senior citizen or one with epilepsy easily controlled by daily medication. Sometimes veterinarians take dogs whom the owners cannot afford to treat and turn them over to a rescue group. A dog's owner passes away, and her family takes her faithful old hound to the shelter. Badly injured dogs are taken from dog fighting rings, and

puppy mill breeding dogs are seized by authorities.

Some rescue groups specialize in rehabilitating and rehoming these dogs. Most dogs are astonishingly resilient. They adapt well to being sightless or deaf. They run and play on three legs, and they still trust people after being removed from abusive situations. They can teach us a lot about survival and good cheer. A dog doesn't know he's elderly or disabled.

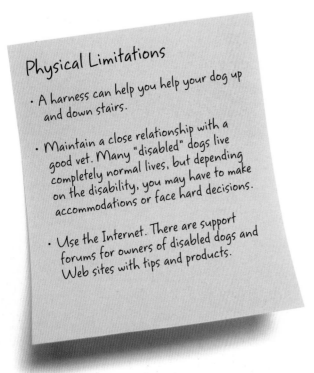

Physical Limitations

- A harness can help you help your dog up and down stairs.

- Maintain a close relationship with a good vet. Many "disabled" dogs live completely normal lives, but depending on the disability, you may have to make accommodations or face hard decisions.

- Use the Internet. There are support forums for owners of disabled dogs and Web sites with tips and products.

Deaf and Blind Dogs

- Deaf and blind dogs are often less vocal because they have less auditory or visual stimuli to respond to.

- Senior dogs can be a delight to live with and can be particularly suitable as pets for the elderly or anyone who doesn't want to spend

a lot of time training and exercising.

- There are several organizations and books for those dealing with a special-needs dog. Check the resources chapter.

Most special-needs dogs are used to a lot of handling and are tolerant, patient animals. Senior dogs generally come pretrained and mellow, perfect for those who want a couch potato buddy. Older people may prefer the company of an calm senior dog to that of a rambunctious young dog who needs more attention.

If you enjoy a project, learning to communicate with a deaf or blind dog is like learning another language. Deaf dogs are very adept at learning sign language. The loss of eyesight to a dog is less important than it would be to a human because sight is a less important sense for dogs. After they are familiar with the layout in their environment, they adapt extremely well.

Although increased medical costs may be a consideration, remember that many serious and expensive conditions happen early in a dog's life, and with older dogs what you see is what you get.

Disabled Dogs

- Dogs with disabilities don't see themselves as disabled and don't feel sorry for themselves. Reminiscent of the Marine slogan, they adapt, improvise, and overcome.

- Three-legged—or "tripod" — dogs can run, walk, jump, and play fetch just about as well as a dog with all four legs.

- As always, it's very important to keep any dog from getting overweight. It can mean the difference between mobility and true disability.

Behavioral Limitations

- These limitations can be harder to manage. They include noise phobias, fear of certain types of people, severe separation anxiety, and dog aggression.

- Some limitations can be cured, others only managed. Your vet or a veterinary behaviorist may be able to help with medications in conjunction with behavioral management. Also consult a good trainer.

- Again, use the Internet to look for forums and tips. For advice, stick to vet school or other reputable Web sites instead of those also selling products.

ESSENTIAL PUPPY SUPPLIES

Time to go shopping for puppy supplies—what you need before she comes home

A trip to a pet emporium can make your head spin with possibilities, but you'll need essentials, such as a crate. The wisest buy is a wire crate with an adjustable divider so you can give your dog more room as she grows. She'll need bedding for the crate, but don't buy a lavish bed because you risk a teething puppy shredding it. A baby gate can be handy, too.

Get separate water and food bowls instead of the ones sold in pairs because food can easily foul the water in side-by-side bowls. Stainless steel and ceramic are a better choice than plastic, which can be chewed up and may also cause a skin reaction.

To acclimate your pup to her crate, consider a hard rub-

Collars

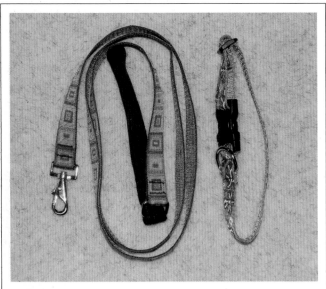

- Buy only a buckle collar for a puppy, never a chain or choke collar.

- Get an inexpensive, comfortable adjustable collar. You won't be using it for very long because she will grow out of it within a couple of months.

- A lightweight leash is better than a big, heavy one. Make sure it feels comfortable in your hand. It won't hurt to buy a 20- to 30-foot cotton training line now, too.

Grooming Tools

- Grooming tools—at least a soft brush and a pair of nail clippers—are important because you can get her used to being groomed right from the start.

- If she is very small, human fingernail clippers will work fine for her nails.

- Short-haired dogs shed— sometimes worse than long-haired dogs.

- If you buy shampoo, get a very mild one and make sure it's OK for puppies.

60

ber toy that you can stuff with food or treats. Puppies need to chew. The best commercial chewies are nylon or rubber bones. These are a better choice than rawhides, which can be chewed apart and swallowed, causing possible choking or impaction. Until you know your pup's chewing style—dainty or power chewer—avoid toys that can be decimated and swallowed.

She will need an adjustable collar that can grow with her. If she has very short fur, avoid the cheap nylon collars, which have hard edges, and choose cotton webbing or leather. You will need a lightweight 6-foot leash, and again cotton or leather is a more hands-friendly choice.

Because you want her to get used to being handled and groomed right away, buy a dog brush and some good nail clippers. If you plan on brushing her teeth, get a doggie toothbrush and toothpaste, too.

Decide what she will eat and buy food and treats. Finally, stock up on paper towels and pet stain clean-up supplies.

Toys

- Take a list when you go shopping. It's easy to get overwhelmed when you're in the store.

- Don't go overboard on toys and chewies and make sure the ones you get are safe, especially for power-chewer puppies.

- A pet store is the best place to buy clean-up supplies. You'll find a wide range of odor- and stain-control products.

Food and Water

- Weighted water bowls are a good idea because many puppies like to play with the water and tip over bowls. Hanging a water bucket hung from the side of a crate (inside or out) or putting a large clean rock into the bowl will prevent this as well.

- Often puppies will be sent home with a bag of whatever they've been eating so far, but stock up anyway.

- Choose treats wisely. You'll be going through a lot for training, so pick something with nutritional value.

PUPPY VET CARE

Establish a relationship with a good vet and get your puppy on a wellness schedule

Your puppy will need to go to the vet for vaccinations and a check-up. If you got the pup from a breeder, your contract may mandate a vet visit shortly after you get the puppy. If you don't have a regular vet, ask knowledgeable people such as your breeder, dog trainers, and dog enthusiasts for a recommendation. Not all vets are created equal, and because

your vet should be a lifelong team member in ensuring that your puppy grows up healthy, don't choose just the most convenient vet's office.

Puppies need vaccinations, and protocols are changing. Most vet schools now caution against combination vaccines because of poor results and possible allergic reactions, and

Core Vaccines

- All dogs should get core vaccines. These are for canine parvovirus (CPV), canine distemper virus (CDV), canine adenovirus (CAV), and rabies.

- Noncore vaccines are given depending on the geographic and lifestyle risk. These vaccines may be for canine leptospira, bordetella, parainfluenza, and Lyme disease.

- Most noncore and optional vaccines like those for leptospira or giardia and Lyme disease are not 100 percent effective and may carry heightened risk of complications.

- Heartworm screening is recommended for pups over seven months before starting preventive meds. For younger pups, preventive medication should be started at eight weeks.

Vet Visits

- Busy vet offices can expose a vulnerable puppy to illness. Keep him in a crate or in your arms and avoid contact with other dogs.

- Distract him with a small treat when he gets a shot and praise him for being brave.

- Make a list of questions to ask the vet. If possible, have all family members who will be caring for the puppy at the vet's office so everyone gets the same information.

the vaccinations suggested may depend on your geographic area. All puppies need distemper, adenovirus, and parvovirus vaccines. You should also discuss if your puppy needs leptospira or kennel cough vaccines. Your vet can help you decide the risks. Three sets of vaccines should be given at six to eight, nine to twelve, and no later than sixteen weeks. A rabies vaccination is legally required in most of the United States; ask your vet.

Unless your puppy has fleas, don't worry about it. Most flea treatments are not recommended for young puppies. Ask your vet for treatment options when the puppy is older or ask if treatment is even necessary.

A vet and her staff should take the time to answer questions about your puppy's health. It is OK to ask about fees and payment policies. You might want to inquire about veterinary insurance for your puppy. On your first vet visit, bring whatever veterinary records you may have from the breeder or shelter. Bring a fresh fecal sample so the vet can check for parasites. Also bring treats for your puppy. It's much easier for everyone, including the dog, if he enjoys vet visits.

What to Discuss and Bring

- If possible, bring in small fecal and urine samples so your vet can check for parasites and abnormal bacteria levels.

- Be prepared to fill out some paperwork, just as with a first visit to any doctor. You might be asked about your puppy's diet and behavior.

- Discuss flea control and a vaccination schedule. Ask about spaying or neutering your puppy if you plan to do so.

- Most vets will put a microchip in your pup (see page 90), and it's easy to do this at the same time as vaccinations.

Puppy's First Exam: What to Expect

- The vet will examine your puppy's mouth, ears, and eyes. She will assess the skin and coat and check for parasites or mange.

- She'll check his heart and lungs, feel his abdomen for lumps or abnormalities, and make sure there's no incipient umbilical hernia at his bellybutton.

- She will check your puppy's genitals for discharge and for normal development for his age.

- She may manipulate his legs, feeling for any looseness or popping indicating abnormal joints.

CHEWING

Your puppy inevitably will chew stuff up, so make sure it's the right stuff

Puppies chew. It's one of the ways they explore their world. Some puppies are less bitey, some are destructo puppies. From four to seven months, your puppy will be teething, so expect chewing to escalate as he tries to relieve teething pain and chews to help loosen baby teeth. While he is teething, you may notice that he has bad breath. This is normal.

His ears may be crooked or asymmetrical during teething. This is also normal.

It's up to you to direct his mouthiness to less-valuable items than books, shoes, and furniture. A crate or containment system can be invaluable when you can't watch him.

Protect valuable or dangerous items. Buy electric cord pro-

Toys

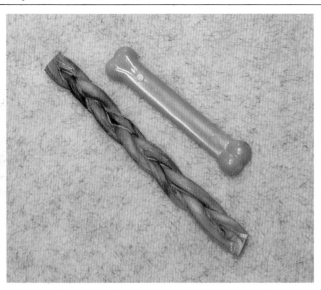

- Keep only one or two types of chewies available. This will help your puppy discriminate between "his" chewies and forbidden objects.

- A toy that can be stuffed with food plus yogurt or water and frozen makes a time-consuming chew, and you can even feed him his meals in one.

- Control, contain, and substitute! Keep moving forbidden objects out of a puppy's reach. Contain him in a crate when you can't monitor his activity. Substitute his chewies for forbidden items.

Forbidden Items

- Don't grab things out of his mouth (unless he's got something really dangerous).

- It's better to exchange the forbidden item with an approved chewie. Start using your "drop it" command right away and praise him when he takes the correct item.

- Tug-of-war is a great game, but don't play it with little puppies who don't know the rules yet.

tectors, which will prevent your puppy from electrocuting himself and burning the house down. Use bitter spray, available at pet stores, to spray table legs. Keep shoes and books out of the way. Give him plenty of exercise and training play to keep his mind off his sore gums. Watch him carefully and redirect him with a gentle correction and an appropriate chew toy when necessary.

Ice cubes with little treats or hot dog pieces added will soothe his gums. Get safe chew toys like nylon bones and rubber rings. Bully sticks are a safer and more digestible choice than rawhides. If you're OK with raw bones, beef soup bones make great chewies.

Teach him from day one that it is never appropriate to put teeth on human skin. When he play-bites, shriek loudly and immediately freeze and ignore him. Correcting him might seem like a game. Make sure everyone in the house follows this rule because even play-biting can be dangerous when he gets bigger.

Dental Problems

- He's teething, and his gums hurt. Putting a treat into an ice cube makes a crunchy, soothing chew. Low-sodium broth can be used instead of water.

- Check his mouth periodically. An adult tooth may come in without dislodging a baby tooth. If the baby tooth doesn't fall out within a few days, check with your vet.

- Baby teeth may be stuck in toys, spit out, or swallowed. Swallowing baby teeth will not harm your puppy.

Bitter Spray Deterrent

- Bitter spray deterrents can be used on items you can't move out of the way, like table legs.

- Pick your battles. It's virtually impossible to expect a puppy to ignore trash, cat food, and cat litter boxes. It's a win-win solution to simply make them inaccessible.

- If your puppy is in another room and being very quiet, he is doing one of two things: sleeping or chewing something up. Best go check!

65

POTTY TRAINING PUPPY

Establishing a routine and learning to recognize "gotta go" will make this phase easier

There are three main components to potty training. First, recognize when your pup needs to go and take him out to do it on schedule. Every time he is praised for pottying outside, the right behavior is reinforced. Second, time both corrections and rewards appropriately. It is counterproductive to punish him after the fact. A "Good puppy!" and even

a treat right as he potties outside let him know he's on the right track. Finally, set him up for success by using a crate and being vigilant. Puppies have the attention span of gnats and will pee without thinking, but they don't like to soil their sleeping quarters.

Puppies aren't capable of much bladder control, and this is

Keep an Eye Out

- Be vigilant at first to recognize signs that he needs to go. The fewer opportunities he has to go inside, the quicker he'll learn.

- If he goes inside, remove all traces of the smell with commercial odor neutralizer or a mixture of vinegar

and water. Otherwise he may use that spot again.

- Most puppies can't hold it through the night until about three months, so until then expect some wee-hours potty trips outside.

Find a Designated Area

- If you put him out the back door, and he potties there, you are training him to go right by the back door. Take him to a designated area.

- If you take him out on a leash, he'll get used to that, which is handy for walks or traveling.

- Don't play with him until after he goes. If after ten minutes he hasn't pottied, bring him in, crate him, and try in another fifteen minutes.

even truer for toy breeds. They gain full control between five and seven months old. They need to pee after waking up and shortly after drinking. They poop about thirty minutes after eating. A puppy will signal that he has "gotta go" by circling or sniffing the ground. Be alert and take him outside to the same place each time.

Don't overcorrect him if you find him in mid-potty on the rug. He might think that pottying gets him punished and will start hiding to go and unwilling to potty outside in your presence. Saying a neutral "whoops" and whisking him outside to finish are more effective. Never correct him after the fact because he won't understand and will think you are a very unpredictable creature. Every time he goes in the designated outside spot, give praise like crazy.

Use the crate to your advantage and confine him when you are away. Young puppies won't be able to hold it all day, so expect some crate messes at first. That's normal. He should grow out of this soon if you are consistent with the other training.

Reward with Treats

- If you think a small treat reward afterward will help, go for it. This really works with some puppies.

- Have a "potty word" and use it every time he goes outside to reinforce the behavior.

- Using a word association lets you practically have him go on command if you time it correctly.

- If you take him for a walk, don't forget poop pick-up bags. Exercising and running often make a pup go.

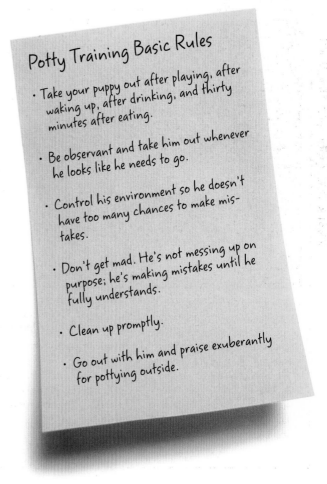

Potty Training Basic Rules

- Take your puppy out after playing, after waking up, after drinking, and thirty minutes after eating.

- Be observant and take him out whenever he looks like he needs to go.

- Control his environment so he doesn't have too many chances to make mistakes.

- Don't get mad. He's not messing up on purpose; he's making mistakes until he fully understands.

- Clean up promptly.

- Go out with him and praise exuberantly for pottying outside.

SOCIALIZING YOUR PUPPY
A well-socialized puppy grows up to be a cheerful and confident dog

Many dogs who are isolated in puppyhood remain fearful and suspicious their entire lives. The developmental period between one and five months is extremely important for puppies. Providing them with a stimulating, varied environment virtually ensures confident, cheerful dogs.

You want your puppy to grow up thinking that all people are friendly. Don't worry that he will be any less of a watch-dog as he grows up. A well-adjusted dog knows the difference between friend and foe.

Invite people to your home to visit the puppy. Make sure that all interactions are pleasant and fun. Don't allow anyone to roughhouse, tease, or play chase games, especially children. Ask your visitors to gently enforce any obedience rules you have established, like not jumping up and not play-

KNACK DOG CARE AND TRAINING

Meeting People

- Carry treats in your pocket, so if the puppy is nervous about some people (men in hats, people of different ethnicities, children) you can hand them a treat to give him.

- It's fine if people you meet ignore him. You want him to accept strangers in a calm, neutral way rather than assume that every person he meets ought to make him the center of attention.

- He doesn't have to greet everyone he meets. Not all breeds are social butterflies.

Short Walks around the Neighborhood

- Taking him on short walks gets him used to the distractions of different vehicles, weather, noises, and smells.

- Puppies who rarely leave the property may bark excessively and be apprehensive about the world outside. Being outside of the house reassures a puppy that it's not a threatening place.

- Don't put him into a situation where he will get scared by a dog or person. Puppies can retain vestiges of fear for life.

biting. Let friends run a brush through your puppy's coat and handle his feet gently. Doing this will get the puppy used to being groomed and going to the vet. Don't force anything at this point. Make it pleasant and use treats.

Build physical confidence by letting the puppy explore smells and different types of footing, climbing over logs and being in and around water. Take him to pet stores and walk him around the neighborhood. Occasionally drive him places. Many dogs develop stress and carsickness because the only place they go anywhere by car is the vet. This stress is easily avoided if the puppy associates car trips with fun and the reward of being with you.

Talk to your vet about when your puppy will be protected by immunizations before taking him to places like pet stores and public parks. A puppy is not completely protected until about two weeks past the final set of vaccines at sixteen weeks. By then he's ready for puppy kindergarten and training classes, which will provide structured socialization and learning.

Country Settings

- Country settings, even parks, provide a rich, natural environment for a curious pup.

- Getting a puppy to a farm to meet different species and smell different smells will help boost his confidence about other animals in general.

- Let him off leash or use a long line to let him be independent.

- Avoid comforting a scared puppy. Doing this can reinforce anxiety. Be cheerful and distract him instead.

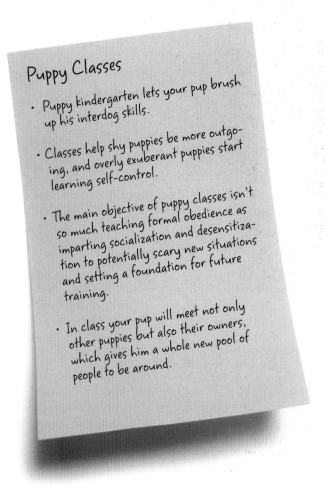

Puppy Classes

- Puppy kindergarten lets your pup brush up his interdog skills.

- Classes help shy puppies be more outgoing, and overly exuberant puppies start learning self-control.

- The main objective of puppy classes isn't so much teaching formal obedience as imparting socialization and desensitization to potentially scary new situations and setting a foundation for future training.

- In class your pup will meet not only other puppies but also their owners, which gives him a whole new pool of people to be around.

CRATE TRAINING

Teach your puppy to love her crate right from the start with simple techniques

Crate training is a great tool. Although puppies don't learn anything by being shut in a crate except how to stay quietly in a crate, it's the safest place for a puppy when left alone in the house. Dogs may be den animals like wolves, but wolves spend a lot of their time hunting and traveling and rarely den alone, unlike a crated dog.

Make the crate a rewarding place and don't overuse it. A puppy who spends too much time crated may start thinking it's OK to potty in the crate. She is not learning to interact with her family or behave when she's in there. Spending all day in the crate and then part of the evening and overnight in the crate is excessive. Use it for necessity, not convenience.

KNACK DOG CARE AND TRAINING

Crate-Training

- If a pup is properly crate trained, she will come to regard the crate as her own special place and will choose to go there to nap or relax.

- Crate-trained dogs don't get as stressed when crated at the vet or groomers or when traveling. If you plan

- on showing or doing sporting events with your pup, she will be spending some time in her crate.

- Make the crate comfortable with a bed or blanket, some water, and something to chew.

Use Food

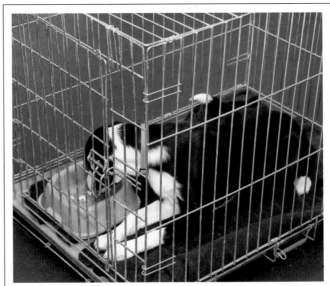

- Food is one of your most powerful tools for training. Feed your pup in her crate.

- Always sound excited and happy when your pup goes to her crate. Use a consistent phrase such as "crate up!"

- After she realizes that the food won't get put down until she's all the way inside, she'll race in. This is setting a very strong foundation.

- Set your criteria and require that all four feet plus her head be inside before putting down food.

Feed your puppy in her crate with the door open. Food is a powerful motivator, and doing this creates a strong positive association. Play crate games. Throw treats and toys into the crate for her to eat or chase. Make the crate fun.

Don't put her into the crate as punishment or in anger. Being isolated in a crate can be a bewildering experience for a puppies. They don't understand "time out" and ponder the evil of their ways like children do.

Dogs learn quickly through association, so prevent her from associating her crate with being left alone. Crate her when she's ready to crash when you're around the house. When leaving, give a safe, long-lasting chewie to occupy her time. Hollow rubber toys that can be stuffed with food or treats and frozen are an excellent choice. She should have some water if being left for several hours. Buy a flat-sided water bucket that can be hung from the side. Make the crate a comfortable, rewarding place, and she'll adjust quickly.

Positive Associations

- Dogs learn by association, so make all her crate associations positive.

- Play is a strong motivator for puppies, so incorporate her crate into games like fetch and chase.

- Build drive by putting a favorite toy or treat into the crate. Make sure she knows it's there and restrain her by the collar while asking her if she really, really wants to go "crate up." She'll shoot in there like a rocket when you release her.

Crate Dividers

- Many crates are available with dividers, so the space can be increased as the puppy grows.

- Ignore whining and let her out only when she's quiet, even momentarily. It can be hard to ignore whining at first, but if you're consistent, she'll understand that fussing won't make you open the door.

- While she's quiet, quietly drop a treat into the crate and walk away.

- If your pup is very vocal, draping a blanket over the crate may help calm her down.

TAKE TIME OFF
Have at least a free weekend to help your puppy get settled in

A puppy is a lot of work. Bring him home when you have some days off, at least a weekend. It's a confusing time for a puppy. Until now his whole life has been limited to the company of Mama and littermates. Depending on his temperament, he might adjust very quickly, or he may whine and cry for a while. Be patient with the little guy; he has a lot to take in.

A baby gate will help keep him confined to one area so he doesn't get himself into trouble. The more time he spends with his new family, the quicker he will learn the routines, so right from the start be with him as much as possible. Avoid overwhelming him with all your friends and neighbors until he's settled in.

Do not correct him now; redirect instead. Accidents happen, and he has yet to learn your rules. Take him out on

Puppy's First Day

- Understand that the little guy is going to be quite bewildered because his entire world just turned upside-down.

- Feed him a small meal as soon as is practical in his sleeping area or crate. Nothing says "I'm home" to a puppy like food.

- Let him explore safely at his own pace and try to get him outside to potty.

- After all this, he will be ready to crash. As he starts to fade, put him to bed with a little treat and cover his crate.

X-Pen Location

- Put his x-pen in a busy area of the home, so he doesn't feel ostracized.

- When you're able to watch him, let him be out. Use the crate and x-pen for times when you can't watch him or for nap time.

- Determine which toys and chewies he responds to and let him have only those instead of toys scattered throughout the house. A limited choice makes it easier for him to understand what's allowed and what's not.

schedule and give lots of praise. If he starts chewing something forbidden, hand him an appropriate chewie and praise him for taking it. Start right now using his name and basic commands like "come," rewarding every time he responds. Establish words to associate with actions and be consistent. When he goes outside, say "outside!" In the house use "crate up," "come," "wanna eat"—start growing his vocabulary. He is a little learning sponge. The more consistent and positive you are, the faster he will learn.

If you are using a crate, put it where the most household activity is. You may even want two crates or an x-pen in the living room and a crate in the bedroom. Dogs are social animals, and he has never been alone before. Don't let it be a scary experience. Give him this time to start learning and adjust without stress.

Creating a Comfortable Space

- Make his space comfortable and enriching. Put food down for mealtimes only but let him have ready access to water.

- To make it easier for him to go through the night without needing to pee, it's OK to restrict water overnight.

- Puppy pads in the x-pen will minimize clean-up.

- Make sure he can't climb out of his pen. Some models have extra panels that can be used as a roof to prevent escape.

Night-time Preparation

- A covered crate in the bedroom at night will keep your pup feeling like part of the pack.

- Expect some whining and fussing for the first few nights. Ear plugs do help! It's important to be able to ignore him.

- Be prepared to get up in the wee hours and let him out to potty.

- Don't play with him when you go out. Potty trips at 2 a.m. are strictly business.

73

BABIES NEED QUIET TIME

A puppy needs a lot of sleep, so make sure he gets his quiet time

Puppies take sleeping very seriously. Even the most hyper puppy runs out of gas, and learning to calm down is an important skill. When she nods off, put her into the crate. It's fine to leave the door open—you are giving her the idea that her crate is a refuge. It's OK even to pet her gently as she drowses. Remember that puppies learn through association. Reinforce calm behavior whenever you get the chance.

If you are not going to let her onto the furniture as an adult, don't let her onto it now, even in someone's lap. It's no fair changing the rules later! Similarly, don't let the puppy sleep in your bed. Even if you plan on letting her sleep on the furniture when she gets older—and be very sure this is what you want because it's extremely hard to untrain—let her earn the right to be on furniture.

Sleeping Time

- Covering a crate or turning off lights for sleeping time will help your puppy be calm and stay asleep.

- Avoid the temptation to bring a new puppy into bed with you at night. She can share your bed later. It is healthy for a pup to learn to spend some time alone. Constant contact can set some pups up for separation anxiety later in life.

- If you leave her, turn on the radio or TV.

Keep the Crate Warm

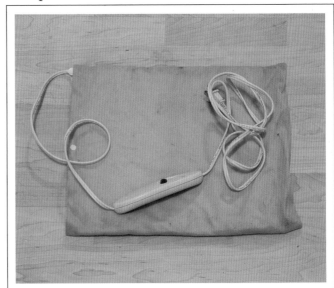

- A hot water bottle wrapped in a towel might help, especially for the first few nights. Your puppy is used to spending his sleeping time nestled in a warm pile with his littermates.

- Some puppies, especially short-haired toy breeds, are sensitive to cold. They can be chilly and unhappy if you keep your house cool at night.

- Be aware that some pups might chew on a hot water bottle, although this is more likely when they start teething.

Your puppy should spend the night in whichever room she will sleep when she's grown. For most people, this is the bedroom. Prepare yourself for several weeks of interrupted sleep! A puppy younger than about twelve weeks old simply cannot make it through the night without needing to potty, even with a right-before-bed potty trip outside. Try wearing ear plugs and setting your loud alarm for the night's midway point to take her out on a schedule.

Chances are she will whine at night initially. She's not used to sleeping alone. Taking her out to potty before bed and letting her burn energy in the evening will help. If your bedroom is cool, it could be chilly for a puppy, especially a short-haired toy breed. Wrapping a soft blanket or flannel sweatshirt around a hot water bottle will keep her warm and sleepy.

Puppy Massage

- Puppies spend more time sleeping than playing.

- Try using touch to relax a puppy. Massage the upper jaw, just below the ear opening, with small circular movements. This is a calming touch.

- When your puppy is winding down and getting sleepy, handle his feet, teeth, and ears. Doing this while he is very relaxed helps get him used to being handled without wiggling.

Avoid Overstimulating

- Your puppy's breed may dictate how much energy he has and how much he sleeps. Active breeds like terriers and herding dogs may be more excitable and energetic. Giant and toy dogs are usually more laidback.

- Just like children, puppies can get overexcited and cranky if they are overstimulated or too tired.

- Don't let him get too overwhelmed and hyper playing with children or visitors. Calm him before putting him down for a nap.

SET BOUNDARIES RIGHT AWAY

Start training the minute he walks in your door

Puppies are smart. Your puppy will learn whatever you teach him. If his progress stumbles, as it will, don't blame him. Step back and assess what he is learning from you and how you can communicate more clearly. It is so easy to miscommunicate.

When you tell a puppy "sit," you probably think of a sitting position. But the way it's usually taught is that the puppy lowers his rear from a standing position, which is why "sit" is meaningless to him when he's lying down. For him, sitting is an action, not a position. If you repeat the word "sit" several times and then praise him for finally complying, you are teaching him to sit . . . eventually. Even though that is not your intention, he's doing precisely what you have trained him to do!

Have Puppy Earn Treats

- Not only is a puppy learning manners from you right away, but also he is learning to learn. Teach him early that paying attention to you brings good things to his life.

- Have him earn every treat and meal by sitting and "taking nice" instead of grabbing.

- Self-control is not a normal canine trait, but it's a mandatory skill for a dog who will live with a human family. Teaching a pup to sit for food is an essential first step.

Training Boundaries

- Most puppies are natural followers and want to be with you. As soon as a puppy realizes that coming when called means good things for him, he'll happily comply.

- Even if he tests you during adolescence, you are laying a very important foundation now.

- All training cements the dog-owner bond. Untrained dogs are poorly bonded with their families. This poor bond inevitably manifests in behavior problems.

Don't let your puppy do anything now that you don't want him to do as an adult. It's not fair to change the rules. Pulling on your pants leg might be cute when he weighs 8 pounds, but it won't be cute when he's 80 pounds.

Be consistent. Use the same words for everything and watch his vocabulary grow. After he connects a word with an action it can become a command later: "Let's go outside" to "Go outside." Use his name and call him to you only for praise, never for punishment. When he's little, don't punish him. Re-direct unwanted behavior and reward good behavior. It takes patience to train a puppy, but he'll get it.

Expect him to sit nicely for food and treats without lunging or being bitey. There is no reason to give treats to a puppy just because he looks cute. Expect a lot from him and be rewarded with a confident, can-do dog. Dogs enjoy working and having structure. Dogs love their leaders.

Be the Leader

- If your pup doesn't come right away, turn and start running away. Nine times out of ten, he will follow.

- If he doesn't follow you, calmly go and get him.

- It's great to play chasing games as long as your puppy gets to chase you and not the other way around.

- In all interactions, you are the leader, your puppy the follower. Whether on leash or off, your puppy follows you.

Use a Leash

- Letting a puppy drag a lightweight leash gets him used to the leash. A gentle tug can remind him that he is doing something naughty like chasing the cat or jumping onto furniture.

- Don't ever drag your pup. When he first feels pressure, he will automatically pull back in response. Use treats and encouragement to get him used to it.

- Use a drag leash only when you're there to supervise. A drag leash can get caught or wrapped around a pup's legs.

77

INTRODUCTION TO OTHER PETS

Introduce the new puppy to resident pets with the minimum of stress and hassle

How your puppy gets along with other pets in the house depends on three things: the temperament of your other pets, the temperament of your puppy, and how well you control the situation. Don't expect that when you put the puppy with other pets they'll automatically "work it out."

Make sure your cat has a safe place to go on her own terms.

Bring the puppy into the room on a leash. Some puppies are fairly neutral about cats, some apprehensive, and others intensely curious. Calmly praise your puppy for anything other than lunging. Use a toy or treats to refocus him. If he gets too wild about the kitty, simply lead him out of the room and try again later. Repeat this exercise until the puppy remains

KNACK DOG CARE AND TRAINING

Dog Meets Puppy

- Unless your current dog has a long history of welcoming other dogs, the first introduction should be with one crated or separated by a gate.

- Your new pup may not recover from a bad initial scare by your resident dog.

- It's normal for an adult dog to growl at a puppy. Separate them immediately if you see bared teeth or a stiff body.

- Later introductions can be on loose leashes, with treats in pocket to distract and reward for polite behavior.

Puppy Meets Cat

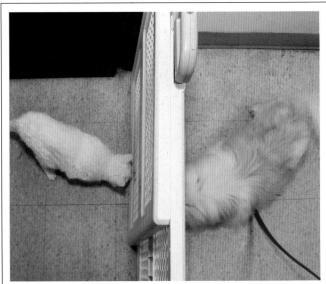

- Most puppies are curious about cats and want to chase and play. Reward calm behavior and redirect if he gets overly rambunctious.

- Much will depend on how dog savvy your cat is. A dog-savvy cat will hold her ground, and if she swats, she will do so without claws.

- Be very careful if your cat uses her claws because she can easily injure your puppy. Eyes in particular are vulnerable, and many cats aim for the head.

somewhat calm in the cat's presence. This could take days or weeks. It's OK; you have plenty of time! Let the calm puppy sniff the cat. Avoid letting the cat get cornered because she can swipe and scratch the pup's face. Use baby gates and the crate to give your cat time to stroll around her territory and the puppy time to get used to her.

Hopefully you already know how your current dog is with other dogs and puppies. Most adult dogs are naturally tolerant of puppies, but some can be overly aggressive in their corrections. It's normal for an adult to correct a puppy for various infractions, sometimes with snarling and great drama. However, a wise adult dog can be the best teacher of manners. Introduce puppy and dog on loose leashes and praise both for polite behavior. Bring them into the yard and let them walk close to each other. Make introductions away from food and valued toys so no dog feels he has to defend property.

Interaction with Dog and Puppy

- It's a positive indication of acceptance when your adult dog is willing to play with the new puppy.

- A puppy may reinvigorate an older dog or pester him. Make sure your dog has time to relax and special time with you without the puppy around.

- Feed and pet your resident dog before the puppy so he doesn't feel like his pack status is threatened. If you give the puppy food or a treat, give something to your other dog, too.

Separate Dog and Puppy

- Let your current dog boss the puppy around as long as he is not too aggressive. This is normal pack order behavior.

- Never leave an adult dog and a puppy alone together, no matter how well they seem to get along in your presence.

- Feed them separately.

- Spend time with each, making sure your pup bonds with you as well as the resident dog.

FEEDING YOUR PUPPY
Don't overwhelm his digestive system with new food and many treats

Dog people are opinionated about what they feed, but here's the truth: There is no one, ideal canine diet. Most people agree that cheap supermarket kibble is never the best choice. The fact is that dogs can do very well on decent kibble, on raw diets, on home cooked diets, or even on a combination of these. The most important things for puppies are eating the correct ratio of protein and minerals and not getting fat. Eat-

ing an incorrect diet and being overweight are strong predictors for joint problems. If you got your puppy from a good breeder, follow her feeding recommendations.

Eight-week-old puppies typically eat three times a day, although some experts recommend that four meals are best for toy breed puppies. Between three and four months old, they can be weaned down to twice-daily feedings. Free

Puppy Diets

- Whatever you feed, particularly if you are feeding a raw or home-cooked diet, do extensive research to avoid feeding an unbalanced diet.

- Puppies require a higher calcium intake than adult dogs. Feeding inadequate amounts of calcium or excess phosphorus (found

in muscle meat) can cause bone abnormalites.

- Some people feed kibble until the pup is grown, then switch diets, whereas others raise multiple litters on "unkibble" food.

- Your breeder is a good source of nutritional info.

Special Foods for Development

- Consider large-breed kibble formulas or good all-life stages formulas to grow big puppies slower.

- Avoid high-protein and grain-free kibbles.

- The percentage of protein in dry dog food should be 22 percent or higher. High

calcium and high energy diets can cause excessive growth spurts, encourage too much weight gain, and harm joints.

- Use the recommended feeding guide as a rough estimate. Your pup may need more or less to grow at a proper weight.

feeding is not ideal. It encourages many dogs to overeat and some to guard "their" food. By leaving kibble out all the time, you also lose a powerful training tool—a meal!

How much to feed is an art, not a science. Dogs have individual metabolisms, just like people. Start with the recommended amount but be prepared to adjust it if the pup is looking a little too chubby or too ribby. Your vet can help determine whether your pup is at a correct weight. A little on the lean side is best, and growing puppies go through leggy stages and growth spurts. You may be adjusting food amounts frequently, especially in fast-growing, large-breed pups.

Treats and "extras" like people food should be kept to a minimum. If training takes up a lot of treats, lower meal amounts to compensate. Avoid too many highly processed, cheap treats. String cheese, low-fat hot dog bits, Cheerios, and carrot pieces are all great alternatives.

One caveat: When you work with a raw food diet, you must maintain strict hygiene rules and be wary of diet imbalance in puppies.

Raw Feedings

- Raw feeding is becoming increasingly popular. However, it is easy to do incorrectly with puppies. Calcium levels (critical for proper joint development) should be carefully monitored and bacterial contamination could cause serious illmess.

- If possible, find a mentor who has successfully raised puppies to healthy adults on a raw diet.

- Be cautious about online nutrition advice because there's a lot of bad advice as well as good advice. Consider the source carefully.

Limit Treats

- Treats should be very small and healthful. Break commercial treats into smaller pieces.

- Small pieces of chopped, crunchy vegetables, cooked meat, and unsweetened oat cereal or popcorn make easy, cheap treats.

- Remember to make your puppy "work" for every treat!

- Sometimes teething puppies will refuse a meal because their mouth hurts. Refusing treats or two or more meals warrants a call to the vet.

81

COMMONSENSE PRECAUTIONS
A puppy is a baby and has some vulnerabilities; keep him safe

As sturdy as puppies may seem, they are curious, don't have common sense, and eat inappropriate things, and their immune systems are not very strong. You have to keep them safe and keep your possessions unchewed.

Get down on your hands and knees and crawl around your house. Pretend you're a puppy. What do you see? Furniture legs, shoes, kids' toys, electrical cords, potted plants, the TV remote, open cabinet doors, and the Holy Grail—a bathroom trash can. The other Holy Grail would be the cat litter box. Move what you can and secure cabinet doors. Use bitter no-bite spray for furniture legs. Puppies like to chew cords, so block off rooms with messes of electrical cords or buy cord protectors. Be vigilant. Puppies need to be watched closely; keep your home picked up. A puppy will swallow anything

Protect Puppy

- Puppies are like babies and will put anything into their mouths. Swallowed items, from stones to poisonous foods and plants, can kill a puppy or mandate difficult surgery to remove. Be absolutely vigilant about what the puppy has access to.

- Puppies explore. Keep your yard secure and don't leave a puppy out there alone.

- Use baby gates to keep a puppy from stairs until he can handle them.

- Dog toys should be sturdy and too large for him to swallow.

Puppy Safety

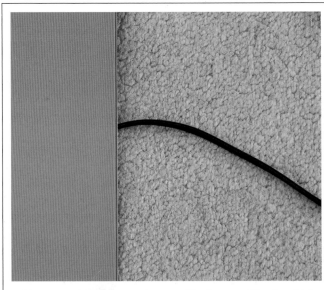

- Many puppies are prone to chew on electrical cords, garden hoses, and anything else that has a bit of flexibility and give.

- Carpet fibers, wool, and thread can be very dangerous if swallowed. Watch your puppy with towels and rags.

- *Pica* is a condition in which the pup will obsessively eat (not merely chew, which is normal) nonfood objects. Medical causes should be ruled out, and in an extreme case he may need to wear a lightweight basket muzzle.

from carpet fibers to cooked bones, and if it doesn't kill him, it can cost a lot of money to surgically remove.

Check your back yard for edible toys, thorns, and spaces under the fence. A puppy shouldn't be unattended outside, but it doesn't hurt to puppy-proof the yard. Antifreeze and some garden chemicals are deadly to dogs. Make absolutely certain they are out of the way. Dump standing water anywhere you find it because it can be contaminated by harmful algae or bacteria.

Some puppies like to eat feces. It's a disgusting habit but usually not harmful, and they usually grow out of it. Pick up in the back yard every time he goes, so he doesn't get the chance and make sure he can't get to the cat litter box. The poop probably won't hurt him, but ingesting cat litter might.

For most puppies, the mouthy phase lasts only until they're done teething. Be patient!

Spot Danger Areas

- Looking at your home from a puppy's-eye view will help you spot danger areas.

- Check your yard for mushrooms and harmful plants like common deadly nightshade and morning glories. Check the resources chapter for a full list.

- There are dangers outside your home as well. Limit his exposure to parks and strange dogs until he's completed his vaccinations.

Put a Cap on Smells

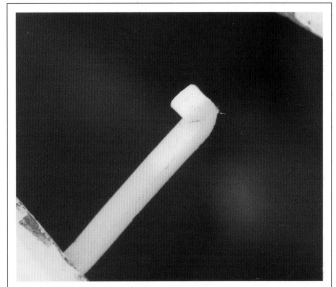

- Puppies have a keen sense of smell, and tasting what they smell is a normal way for them to explore their world.

- Keep medications, vitamins, cleaning supplies, and anything potentially poisonous completely out of your puppy's reach. Puppies have no common sense at all about what they put into their mouths!

- The smell of trash under the sink can be an incentive for a puppy to force his way into a cupboard. Child-safe locks are an inexpensive insurance.

DOG COATS AREN'T SILLY

Some dogs are not equipped to handle inclement weather; keep yours warm and fashionable

Some dogs, like greyhounds, evolved in the desert. With short, sleek fur and little body fat they are well suited to hot weather but don't tolerate cold well. Northern breeds like huskies have kept their natural, wolflike traits. Heavy double coats keep them warm in winter but uncomfortably hot in summer. Some very modified breeds like English bulldogs

don't tolerate any temperature extremes well, getting chilled easily and being susceptible to heat stroke. Toy breeds can get miserably cold very quickly.

Dog coats and sweaters aren't just fashionable; they're functional. Dog coats with reflective stripes are great for walking or jogging in the dark. Dressing a greyhound or Chihuahua

Coat Designs

- Some dogs resist wearing a coat, especially complex ones with hoods and multiple straps. Try a loosely fitting sweater or simple lightweight coat to get her used to the idea.

- Check the design, especially if you have a male dog who lifts his leg to pee. Some

coats that extend down the dog's belly can be easily soiled.

- If the weather is extremely hot or cold, postpone long walks and exercise your dog inside for the day.

Reflective Stripes

- Dark-colored dogs become practically invisible to drivers at night. Reflective stripes on a dog coat are an important safety feature when walking your dog in the dark or when it's raining or foggy.

- Reflective tape is available at hardware stores if you

want to decorate your dog's existing coat.

- For walking on snow or ice, dog boots are tolerated well and prevent irritation from snow and deicing chemicals.

for cold weather is simply the kind thing to do. Dogs walked on city streets in winter might be wearing boots to protect paws from salt and de-icing chemicals. Naturally you want your dog to look attractive when dressed. Even hunting dogs are often outfitted in camo or hunting orange coats to keep them warm and dry—a dog won't work efficiently if it is too cold.

Dogs can be dressed for hot weather, too, if they absolutely must be in the heat. Unlike humans, dogs don't sweat, and breeds with thick coats and short snouts overheat easily.

Show and sport dogs often trial outside in the summer and may wear cooling coats to keep them from getting too hot while waiting their turn in the ring. Cooling coats may be reflective silver mesh to deflect the sun's rays; nylon capes, when soaked in water, keep the dog's skin cool.

Of course, it's best to keep your dog from temperature extremes when possible. But when duty calls, or when a longer wintry walk can be taken because everyone is warmly dressed, a doggie coat might be just the thing.

Bright-colored Safety Vest

- A brightly colored safety vest with or without reflective stripes is also a good idea if you bike with your dog, day or night.

- Hunting dog coats are sold in bright safety orange or yellow to increase hunting dogs' visibility in the field.

- Look for a waterproof coat with a removable fleece lining for versatility.

- Hunting supply and outdoors stores usually carry well-made, very durable foul-weather dog gear.

Cooling Coats

- Cooling coats may be reflective mesh that deflects the sun's rays or gel-filled coats that, when soaked in water, remain cool against the dog's coat.

- They are a boon for dogs who spend the day at sporting events, by water, or at dog shows, cooling them down between work or play.

- For your hard-working sport dog, also consider a gel-filled crate bed, which when wetted down gives him a cool place to rest.

COLLARS

Collars serve many functions, but there are times when your dog should be collar free

Collars are used to restrain, to identify, to decorate, to protect, and to attach things to. Saint Bernards historically carried small kegs of brandy on their collars when they were on rescue missions to find people stranded in snowstorms. Rottweilers had their owners' money tied to their collars to keep it safe. (Today one can buy collars that have more practical features, such as a pocket for tucking keys or poop pick-up bags into.) Guardian dogs used to wear metal spiked collars to protect their throats.

The best collar for the dog is comfortable and looks good. Cheap nylon collars, with their sharp edges, may irritate thin-coated dogs by rubbing the skin. If you notice your dog

Collar Types

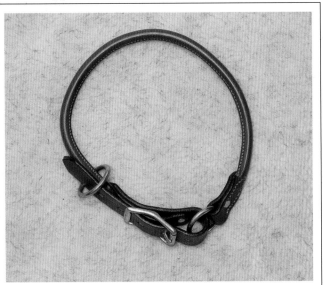

- Many dog show people use a collar only when necessary and let dogs run "naked" otherwise. This protects the coat from breakage.

- A rolled leather collar is gentler on long fur.

- Stainless steel or brass buckles tend to hold up longer than plastic snap buckles.

Signs of Wear

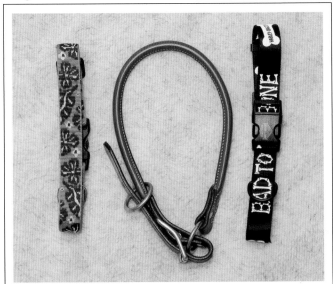

- A collar can send a message about your dog. A cute, flowery collar on a bad boy breed has a different implication than a spiked or studded collar.

- Leather collars can get cracked or worn with age, leading them to break at stress points, such as where the D-ring is attached.

- Signs of wear mean you should replace the collar, or else you risk it breaking if your dog pulls or lunges.

scratching her neck, remove the collar and check for skin irritation or rubbed fur. For most dogs, cotton or leather collars are both comfortable and attractive. Some dogs, like pugs, because of their body and head shape can easily back out of a collar and instead should wear harnesses. Fluffy dogs may look best in rolled leather collars that don't mess their long fur.

A collar should be loose enough to be comfortable without slipping over the dog's head. For a medium-sized dog, you should be able to slip two fingers under the collar.

Collar Fit

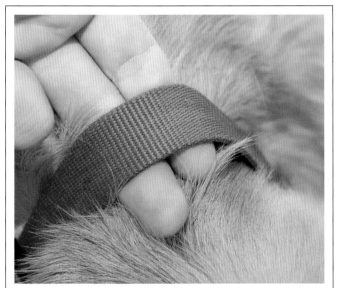

- The collar should be loose enough that you can slip two fingers between the neck and collar on a medium- to large-sized dog yet not so slack that it can slip over the dog's head or get caught.

- If your dog is still growing, or if her weight is changing,

check the collar regularly to ensure that it's still comfortable and fits properly.

- If your dog pulls a lot on a leash, a leather collar can stretch, so also check that it hasn't become too slack.

Harnesses

- Harnesses are necessary for dogs whose necks are the same widths as their heads. They're also recommended for dogs who are prone to breathing problems or for toy breeds who are susceptible to collapsing trachea.

- Most harnesses offer less leash control than a

regular collar, although this isn't usually as much of a problem with small, easily controllable dogs.

- If your dog wears a harness all of the time, make sure it's soft and loose enough to allow unrestricted movement.

DOG GEAR

LEASHES

Here's what to look for among the many leashes on the market

Your leash is an invaluable tool for controlling your dog. A lightweight 4- or 6-foot leash clipped to a dog's collar is useful in the house because it allows for quick control if he is about to hike his leg on the couch. For dogs who need constant supervision, the leash can be attached to your waist so the dog is with you all the time. The more time a dog spends with his owner, the faster he'll learn good behavior.

Six-foot leashes are standard in training classes. They allow the dog enough room to maneuver and the handler the right length to control the dog. Chain leashes are not as effective. The dog gets used to the weight dragging on his collar and is less amenable to corrections and more likely to pull. Nylon leashes can cut into your hands. Cotton and leather are better choices.

Long Lines

- If using a long line for rural walks, consider clipping it to a harness instead of a collar. It's less likely to get tangled between the dog's legs this way.

- Dogs tend to pull less on a long line, although you have less control.

- Retractable leashes are handy but not great for training. The constant slight tension and the variable distance at which the dog gets corrected or tugged don't send him clear signals.

Leash Material

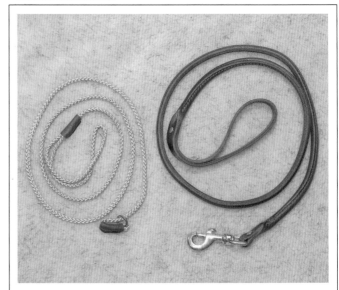

- Choose a leash that feels comfortable in your hands.

- Leather leashes get more pliable and more "character" with age. Braided leather leashes are very strong and soft.

- True dog geeks have multiple leashes in different materials and styles and can't walk past a leash booth at a dog show without stopping.

- Try a splitter leash for walking two (or more) dogs simultaneously without tangling.

Retractable leashes are great for walks, but don't use one for teaching a dog leash manners. The constant tension teaches a dog that a little pulling is acceptable. A better choice for training dogs and for teaching distance work is a long line. Usually 20–40 feet long, such a leash requires handler dexterity to keep it from tangling around a dog's legs or trees, but it allows for loose-leash romping and effective control. Most dogs pull on shorter leashes because their natural speed is much faster than ours. They're less restrained on a longer leash.

Dogs still have to learn to walk at our speed, especially in cities or crowds. Some 4- or 6-foot leashes have loops near the dog's collar. Grabbing a loop is easier when you need the dog to stay close than bunching up the leash in one hand.

Six-Foot Leash

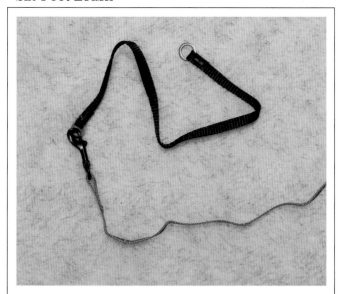

- For city walks, a comfortable 6-foot leash is versatile enough to keep the dog close yet give him space to sniff and potty.

- Some dogs think it's fun to bite the leash. Spraying it with bitter-tasting spray will deter this behavior.

- Some leashes are furry or thickly braided felt. Sold as "tug leashes" for agility and flyball dogs, they are meant to be tugged on as reward for a successful run.

Features

- The most common leash clip features a little bar that you clip onto the collar with your thumb.

- The locking jaws type of clip is much more secure than the traditional type, which can pop open under pressure or inadvertently get stuck in a partially open position.

- Some clips swivel, which results in less leash tangling.

- A far greater range of leash choices is available online than in pet stores.

ID TAGS & MICROCHIPS

No collar is complete without an ID tag; microchipping gives you peace of mind

Dogs get lost all the time. Without ID, their chances of being returned are lower. A dog without any form of owner identification is seen as a stray or abandoned dog. If the dog has ID, it's assumed that someone is looking for her.

Collar ID is important, but collars and tags can come off. Many dog owners use microchips as well as collar ID. Im-

planted between the dog's shoulder blades with a needle, a microchip is the size of a grain of rice. Owner information is registered with the microchip registry, and the dog can be scanned by shelters and vets. There are several registries and some scanner incompatibility, meaning not all chips can be read by every scanner, so it's best to choose one of the larger

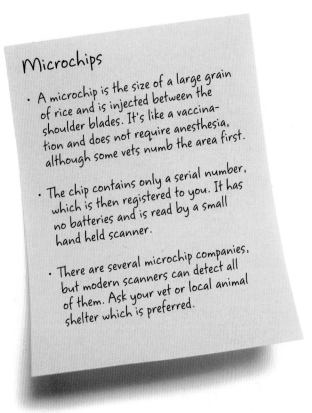

Microchips

- A microchip is the size of a large grain of rice and is injected between the shoulder blades. It's like a vaccination and does not require anesthesia, although some vets numb the area first.

- The chip contains only a serial number, which is then registered to you. It has no batteries and is read by a small hand held scanner.

- There are several microchip companies, but modern scanners can detect all of them. Ask your vet or local animal shelter which is preferred.

Tags

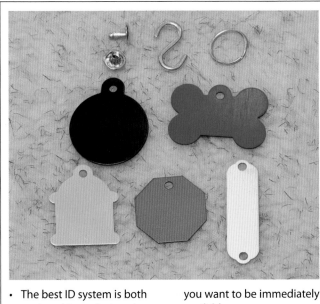

- The best ID system is both a microchip and a tag attached to the collar. Make sure you keep the contact information current.

- If you have a cell phone number, put that on the tag instead of your home land-line number. If you're out looking for a lost dog,

you want to be immediately available.

- Some owners put their vet's number or the number of an easily reached friend or family member on the tag as well.

registries. Because the injection is mildly painful, consider having the chip implanted during another surgical procedure like speutering. Often shelter and rescue dogs come with a microchip included, and for a small fee the new owners register their own information.

Tags are the first line of defense. They are less likely to be pulled off when attached by a sturdy S-hook than by the round wire clip. If you dislike the jingling sound that tags make, you can buy plastic dog tag covers that quieten them.

Another option is buying a collar with the dog's information engraved on a metal plate riveted to the leather. These are also more secure as long as the collar stays in place.

With the growing popularity of microchips, tattooing is less common now, but there are still companies that do it. Dogs are sedated and tattooed with a serial number on the inner ear or thigh, and this number is visible proof that the dog is an owned animal. Check with local vets to find one who participates in a tattooing program.

Collars

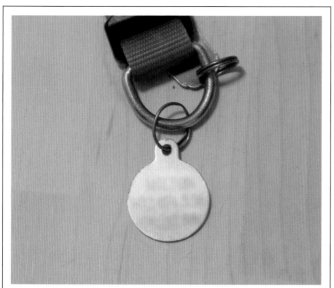

- Collars can be ordered with riveted ID tags, which are more secure, although they may be missed by someone who has found your dog.

- If you dislike the jingling of metal tags, get plastic ones or buy a plastic silencer, which holds the tags together.

- Medical information or a statement that a reward is offered for safe return of the dog can be put onto the back side of a tag.

- An S-hook is a sturdier attachment than the ring type.

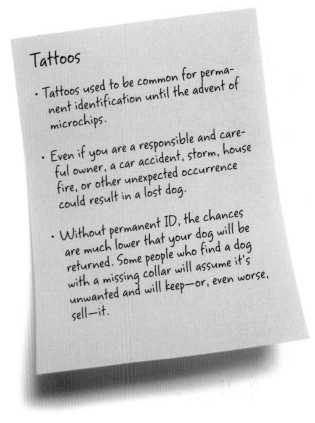

Tattoos

- Tattoos used to be common for permanent identification until the advent of microchips.

- Even if you are a responsible and careful owner, a car accident, storm, house fire, or other unexpected occurrence could result in a lost dog.

- Without permanent ID, the chances are much lower that your dog will be returned. Some people who find a dog with a missing collar will assume it's unwanted and will keep—or, even worse, sell—it.

DOGGIE BACKPACKS

Whether you're hiking trails or taking city walks, let your dog carry the essentials

Dogs love jobs. Several breeds were used to pull carts and sleds or to carry packs. Today doggie backpacks for recreation are widely available. When a dog associates his own backpack with walkies, he'll really look forward to the job. Plus he can carry his own poop bags. Most doggie backpacks are like saddle bags, with straps wrapping around the dog's forechest and ribcage. They range from lightweight "city packs" to complex constructions with multiple compartments and features. Because there's no "average" shape for a dog, you might have to try several types to find a comfortable one. When buying online, take all of your dog's measurements and contact the company to find the best fit.

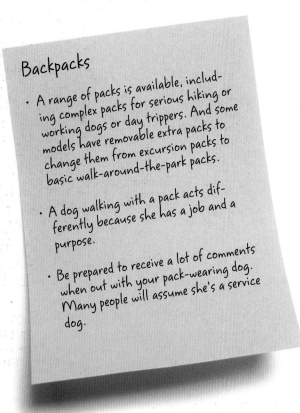

Backpacks

- A range of packs is available, including complex packs for serious hiking or working dogs or day trippers. And some models have removable extra packs to change them from excursion packs to basic walk-around-the-park packs.

- A dog walking with a pack acts differently because she has a job and a purpose.

- Be prepared to receive a lot of comments when out with your pack-wearing dog. Many people will assume she's a service dog.

Backpack Fit

- Make sure your dog has unrestricted range of motion with the backpack both empty and weighted.

- There are many styles to choose from. Look for quick-release clasps and soft fabric or padded straps.

- If you plan on doing some serious hiking, look for weather-resistant packs with rainproof zippers and closures to keep your gear dry.

- Some packs have grab handles on top so you can assist your dog over rough terrain.

A healthy dog can carry up to 20 percent of his weight in a properly distributed backpack. If you have a long-bodied breed prone to back problems or a dog with joint issues, check first with your vet. A young dog shouldn't carry much weight because the weight can stress growing joints. However, even an empty pack will get him used to the idea. You'll want to start with minimal weight and shorter walks. Think of how heavy a 30-pound pack will feel to you at the end of a 5-mile hike! Watch your dog for signs of discomfort or fatigue and remember that the extra work could make him thirstier. The point is to efficiently exercise your dog, not to exhaust him.

High-energy dogs will get more of a workout when walking with a backpack. Working breeds especially will love wearing a pack because they'll feel a sense of accomplishment and duty. Even tiny dogs enjoy them and look darned cute wearing one. Avoid cargo that might poke him and keep the weight evenly distributed. Water or pop bottles work well to start with.

Adjustable Packs

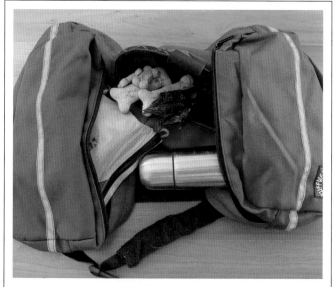

- For hotter days, try putting ice packs into the saddlebags to keep your dog cooler.

- Wrap hard or sharp objects in a towel. Your dog can't tell you if something is uncomfortably poking her.

- To add weight for exercise, try dry beans.

- Carry water and collapsible water bowls, your keys, rain gear, sun block, and even dog treats. Keep the weight equal on both sides of the pack.

Different Packs for Different Dogs

- Backpacks are available for any size of dog. Although most pet stores carry them, your best bet for a really wide range of styles and sizes is online.

- Be careful with long-haired dogs when tightening the straps to avoid pinching or tangling the fur.

- Don't put objects with sharp corners or edges into the pack without wrapping them first; otherwise your dog may be unnecessarily poked or chafed.

93

CAR SAFETY
Keep your dog safe in the car and protect your upholstery as well

When you are driving, loose dogs are unguided missiles in an accident or sudden stop. They should be contained or harnessed for the same reason you make sure that everyone else is safely buckled in. Dogs should never ride on the driver's lap. Not only is this practice unsafe for both, but also it could be against the law in your state. Loose dogs in pickup beds are extremely unsafe, if not illegal. And although dogs might enjoy hanging their head out of the window of a moving car, they're vulnerable to injuring their eyes or falling out.

If space allows, the safest place for a dog to ride is in a crate that's secured so it won't tip or go flying in an accident. A crate can be secured in a back seat with a seatbelt or strapped to the floor of a van. If there isn't room for a crate, get a seatbelt harness for your dog and buckle him into the back seat. He'll

Dog Safety

- Use treats and praise when getting your dog used to a seatbelt. Dogs who are hyper in the car often calm down when in a seatbelt harness.

- Seat belt harnesses for large dogs usually clip into the existing seat belt fastener.

- When driving a two-seater vehicle, like a truck, you have no choice but to have your dog in the passenger seat. If there is a rear seat, this is a better choice. Like children, dogs can get hurt if the air bag deploys.

Mesh Dividers

- A mesh divider in an SUV or station wagon contains your dog in the rear of the vehicle. Some models are sturdy enough to withstand some impact in an accident.

- No matter where your dog rides, teaching her to wait for permission before jumping out is a good safety strategy.

- Until you're sure she won't bolt out of the vehicle, attach a leash to her before she gets out.

be able to lie down, turn around, and be comfortable. A third option is a mesh barrier that keeps the dog confined to a rear area of the vehicle.

Unless your dog is crated, you'll probably want to keep your car interior protected from fur, muddy paws, and the occasional pile of dog puke. Stain-resistant washable seat covers are an absolute must, especially for larger dogs.

Not all dogs ride easily in cars. If the only place they ever go is the vet, riding can be really stressful. Take your dog to fun places, too, even for just quick drives around the block.

Teach her to wait for permission before she leaps in and out of a vehicle, using a leash and rewards and the same command words each time. With good car manners and sensible restraint, your dog will be an easy traveling companion.

Car Seat Covers

- A car seat cover or even an old quilt protects your car upholstery.

- Vinyl and leather seats can be difficult for dogs to maintain footing on. Unless securely belted in, they can slide—and if you have an open window and take a corner quickly, they can slide right out the window.

- It might be OK to let your dog hang her head out the window on a trip to the corner store, but close the windows at higher speeds.

Car Extras

- Put a small treat or chew toy into the traveling crate to get her used to it.

- Never, ever leave a dog in a hot car, even when just running into a store for a minute. A closed car can get dangerously hot in minutes.

- A tub of wipes is handy for dog accidents, paw prints, and nose smudges on the window glass.

CRATES

A crate doesn't have to be merely functional—it can also be decorative

There are three main styles of dog crates—and then there are custom dog crates that double as bedside tables and functional decor. A crate doesn't have to be an unattractive box taking up space. Wire crates allow for maximum air flow and destructo dogs can't chew them up. Some are collapsible, folding into a fairly compact suitcase-style shape, which makes them easy to store and handy for traveling and dog shows. They come with a washable plastic bottom tray. Companies make very attractive fabric crate covers, or if you're handy you can make your own to match the decor. Wire crates aren't approved for airline use, so if you want the crate to double for air travel, get a plastic airline crate.

Crates

- Your dog may not need to be shut in a crate. However, if you have the space and she likes it, leave it with the door open or even removed. A lot of dogs choose to nap and spend their downtime in their crate.

- A crate should be large enough for your dog to stretch out comfortably.

- Pet supply stores have flat-sided water buckets designed to be hung on the side of the crate.

Proper Location

- Crates can be functional and used as end tables.

- For multiple dogs, crates can be stacked. Make sure they are secure by setting them up against a wall and putting smaller crates on top of larger ones.

- The best place for a crate is where the family activity is, but if the only time your dog is crated is when nobody is home anyway, a little-used room works fine.

Plastic airline crates are a bit bulkier, and although they can sometimes be broken down for easy storage, doing so is a bit more cumbersome because they need to be unbolted. They're often available in several colors. Check the construction—some have interior ridges that can be chewed by a bored dog.

Fabric crates come in a multitude of colors and designs, and all collapse for storage. They are not as secure as wire or plastic crates and not the best choice for dogs who may try to escape or are left unattended for longer periods of time.

You can check independent pet stores, online sellers, or custom woodworkers for high-end habitats made of anything from bamboo to exotic hardwoods if you want a haute decor dog crate.

Of course, your dog needs a crate blanket. This can be anything from a cheap faux fur rug or old quilt to a sheepskin bed. Make sure your dog isn't one who shreds her bed when left in the crate before spending a lot of money.

Fashionable Crates

- Make a fabric crate cover to match or complement existing upholstery, complete with matching crate beds and pillows.

- Real sheepskins as crate beds look great and are washable, and dogs really love them. Look online for "seconds," which can be quite inexpensive.

- Cardboard boxes (make sure there are no staples) are a low-cost solution for destructo dogs who shred bedding.

Custom Crates

- Look online or locally for artisans who can make a custom crate if you can afford something really fancy.

- Don't place a crate right next to a heating or air-conditioning vent unless you're sure your dog won't get overheated or chilled.

- Don't use ammonia or bleach-based cleaners in the crate. A mix of water and vinegar does a fine job without irritating the skin or causing unpleasant fumes.

DOG BEDS

Your dog's bed is more than an alternative to your couch—it's his own place

Unless your dog gets to sleep on the furniture, he needs his own bed. Not only is a bed his own comfy place, but also you can train him to go to it if he gets too bouncy with guests or if he's chewing a messy bone. Choose a bed with quality filling and a removable, washable cover. You often get what you pay for—poor-quality beds get lumpy, and the covers

can become so misshapen after one washing that they won't ever fit right.

Until you are sure your dog won't destroy his bed, stick to inexpensive bedding and let him earn his fancy sleeping quarters. Puppies and young dogs often chew up their bedding, especially in crates. Bathroom rugs or old towels and

Couch and Bed Covers

- Every dog loves couches, and if yours isn't allowed onto the furniture, get him his own.

- Look online for custom covered beds to match your decor. Dog beds come in a huge array of decadent and fanciful styles.

- Decide if you want a bed with a washable cover or one that needs to be cleaned like any other piece of furniture. No matter how well groomed the dog, the sleeping area can get grubby and full of dog hair.

Raised Beds

- Raised dog beds support a dog's spine and joints. They keep a dog from a cold floor and are easily cleaned.

- Raised beds can fit inside wire crates and can be a good alternative to fabric beds for dogs who shred bedding. Be aware that

- chewies and toys can fall between the edge of the bed and the crate, out of the frustrated dog's reach.

- For dogs who spend time outside, beds like this are weatherproof.

quilts work well for chewers. If your pup tends to chew and swallow, don't use fabric: if swallowed, it can cause intestinal blockages. Cardboard boxes (check for staples) are perfect for these puppies. They're free; ingesting them isn't likely to cause blockages; and your pup will still have something other than a hard surface to lie on.

Arthritic or older dogs, baby puppies, and very tiny dogs will love a heated dog bed. Beds specifically for arthritic dogs come in many other types, from slightly elevated sling-type beds to ones filled with body-conforming buckwheat hulls.

Hot dogs appreciate cooling beds. These are usually soaked in water, which plumps the bed up into a cushion of cool, moist gel.

Train a dog to go to "bed" or "place" with treats and chewies. Reinforce his staying there with rewards. Gradually increase the time he must stay there and always have a release word so he knows when he is free to go. "Place" can be a great command during mealtimes or when you want him out from underfoot.

Inexpensive Covers

- If your dog is used to sleeping on the couch, an old quilt can save your upholstery.

- Make your own inexpensive dog bed using fabric remnants, second-hand quilts or blankets, and inexpensive batting.

- Children's mattresses or old futons make economical beds for giant dogs, and the waterproof covering on a toddler's mattress is a bonus if the dog is elderly and incontinent at times.

- Toy dogs may like circular cat beds.

Orthopedic Beds

- You may notice that an old dog who previously slept happily on a hard surface will start looking for somewhere soft to lie down.

- Many orthopedic beds are heated, cooled, and made of memory foam to provide maximum comfort for a sore dog.

- The filler is the most important component of any bed. Inexpensive batting will become lumpy and flattened. Look for foam or cedar chip filling.

INVISIBLE FENCING

This barrier is becoming more common, but it's not for all dogs

Invisible fencing is a boon to dog owners in subdivisions where regular fencing isn't allowed. It's cheaper than most other fencing, and most homeowners can install it in a day. With a wireless system, you simply plug in the transmitter to set up a circular boundary. For a more traditional invisible fence, an underground wire is laid around the perimeter of the yard; either way, the dog wears an electronic collar that

first warns and then zaps him when he gets too close to the buried wire. Dogs are usually fully trained to the system in about three weeks, using flags in the ground to give him a visual cue, followed by a leash correction when he gets too close, and finally a zap when he reaches the perimeter.

For many dogs, invisible fences are fine used under owner supervision. Most dogs quickly learn the boundary and over

Invisible Fence Collar

Set-up

- The invisible fence collar should be worn whenever the dog is outside but taken off when the dog is inside because the prongs can irritate his skin with constant contact.

- Long-haired dogs need to have the contact area shaved or to wear longer

- prongs, available as an option with most collars.

- The shock is similar to the zap from static electricity. Most dogs heed it. Those with high pain tolerance and drive may ignore it.

- Although you may save money by installing an invisible fence yourself, you won't have the advantage of the fence professional's training and guidance. If doing it yourself, follow all training instructions methodically.

- Use leash corrections at the perimeter and praise and reward your dog for turning away from the boundary.

- Set the collar to the lowest setting and increase the intensity only if your dog ignores the zap.

time don't even need the collar on to correct them. However, it works well for only some dogs, and dogs shouldn't be left unattended with just an invisible fence keeping them contained.

Dogs with high pain tolerance and a strong prey drive will brave the zap to go after a squirrel or, even worse, a person or other dog. Many hunting and working dogs are pain tolerant and prey driven. After the dog is out of the boundary, it faces another zap to get back into the yard, and if there isn't a real motivation for him to return, he'll remain loose.

An invisible fence won't stop other animals from entering the dog's territory—a situation that could be unpleasant, depending on the animals involved. Nor will it deter someone who wants to steal a dog. Passers-by and delivery people might see a furiously barking dog in an unfenced yard and have no faith that there's anything stopping the dog coming after them. If an invisible fence is your only option, be aware of its limitations and supervise the dog.

Installation

- Leave an invisible fence sign at the front of your property so passers-by understand that your dog is contained. The sight of a barking dog with no apparent fence can be unnerving!

- Some companies will not install a fence if the resident dog has a history of ag-gression, and some rescue groups and shelters won't adopt out dogs to homes where invisible fencing is the only containment.

- Two dogs can use the same area, but each should be trained separately and wear the collar.

Installation within the Perimeter

- Invisible fencing can also be installed within the perimeter to keep your dog away from flower beds, vegetable gardens, or swimming pools.

- Perimeters can also be set up inside the home by running the wire under carpeting.

- If both you and your neighbor use invisible fencing, collaborate so that both dogs can be secure and safe.

- You may have to advise your homeowner's insurance company of the type of fencing you have for your dog.

101

THE FENCED YARD

Learn how to make your back yard secure and safe for your dog

Much though they love us, our dogs enjoy exploring and following their noses. For many obvious reasons, dogs shouldn't be allowed to roam freely. Part of the contract of living in a busy human world is the dog stays on his owner's property most of the time. By far the safest way to keep your dog secure in the yard is with a wood or chain link fence. Most zoning laws allow these types of fences up to 6 feet high, which is more than enough to prevent all but the bounciest and most determined dog from scaling.

Tall wooden fences allow privacy and security. Children can't stick their fingers in or throw things to tease your dog, and the dog isn't constantly stimulated and frustrated by seeing the world going by beyond the fence. Chain link fences are cheaper and every bit as secure, although some visually

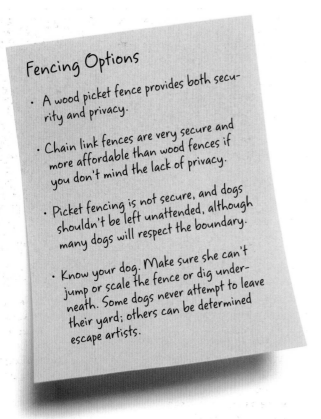

Fencing Options

- A wood picket fence provides both security and privacy.

- Chain link fences are very secure and more affordable than wood fences if you don't mind the lack of privacy.

- Picket fencing is not secure, and dogs shouldn't be left unattended, although many dogs will respect the boundary.

- Know your dog. Make sure she can't jump or scale the fence or dig underneath. Some dogs never attempt to leave their yard; others can be determined escape artists.

Repair Fences

- Some dogs enjoy watching the world go by on the other side of the fence; others get frustrated and bark or act tough.

- If your dog regularly spends time alone in the yard, make a habit of patrolling the perimeter to check for loose fencing or areas where she may be digging out.

- A wood fence in good repair is generally the most secure fencing to contain a dog.

stimulated dogs may bark more when out there. Some dogs like to dig under the fence. A shallow trench filled with concrete along the base deters digging. No matter what type of fence you have, the gate should be securely latched or, better yet, locked from the inside.

If your dog spends much unattended time out in the yard, a draft-free doghouse is a good idea. In summer many dogs love plastic wading pools to cool off in.

Check your yard for anything poisonous, like cocoa bark mulch or plants that could harm your dog. Make sure garden chemicals are well out of his way. Eliminate standing water wherever possible, and if you have a pool be sure either that it is fenced or that he knows how to get out of it if he falls in. Be aware of what your dog does outside and keep him, and your neighbors, safe.

Watch Dog Behavior

- Many dogs have little interest in leaving the property and can be contained safely with a picket fence. Be aware that this fence can make a dog more vulnerable to dognappers, though.

- Any more than two dogs is a dog pack, and pack mentality can make a group of dogs act differently than one or two dogs. It can increase the drive to roam.

- Make sure your dogs aren't barking and terrorizing passers-by.

Securing the Area

- A secure latch is essential if your dog spends time alone in the yard.

- A gate that cannot be accessed from outside is safer, although you may have to make arrangements with utility companies if they need access to meters.

- A sign alerting people that there is a dog in the yard both deters people with bad intent and warns everyone that there's a dog on the other side of the gate.

103

OUTDOOR KENNELS

Outdoor-only dogs need extra care given to their housing and security

Perhaps your dog spends a lot of time outside, or you have an outside-only dog. Dogs really shouldn't live in isolation because they are such social animals, and hopefully if your dog is an outside-only dog she has at least another dog to keep her company. Some dogs spend the workday outside and come in when the family is home. Leaving a dog in a

fenced yard might not be an option, and a secure kennel run can be designed for comfort and security.

Spacious free-standing chain link kennels are the easiest choice. To prevent dogs digging out, many are installed on concrete pads or have a chain link subfloor. The flooring can be pea gravel, outdoor kennel flooring, wood shavings, or

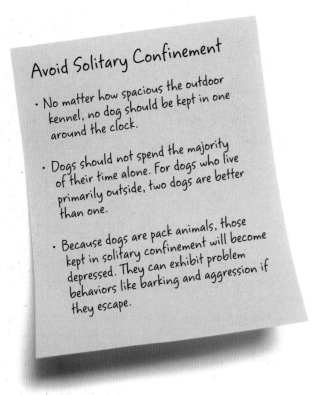

Avoid Solitary Confinement

- No matter how spacious the outdoor kennel, no dog should be kept in one around the clock.

- Dogs should not spend the majority of their time alone. For dogs who live primarily outside, two dogs are better than one.

- Because dogs are pack animals, those kept in solitary confinement will become depressed. They can exhibit problem behaviors like barking and aggression if they escape.

Prep for Cold Weather

- In cold weather especially, doghouses should be raised off the ground, protected from drafts, and completely weatherproof.

- The rounded "igloo" style of doghouses is inexpensive and does an excellent job

of conserving body heat in cold weather.

- Don't leave a dog outside in very cold weather. Dogs are stoic, but few breeds should endure subfreezing temperatures for very long.

straw. Absorbent material needs to be replaced regularly because it will absorb urine.

Shelter from the elements is essential. Heavy, reflective tarps provide shade. A doghouse should be elevated so it stays dry and should have a flap covering the door for wind resistance. A doghouse just big enough for a dog to sleep in conserves more body warmth. In cold or wet weather, never use fabric to line the doghouse because the dog will track in moisture, and if the moisture gets cold enough, it will freeze hard. Clean straw is a better choice.

Dogs need something to occupy their time, even if they have a canine buddy. Provide long-lasting chew bones and toys. Make sure the dogs have fresh water at all times.

Few dogs can tolerate extremely cold or hot temperatures. They'll be miserable and can suffer frostbite or heat stroke. Big "tough" dogs like pit bulls are very susceptible to frostbite. Please make sure your dog is protected, even if that means she has to be brought inside or you have to buy a heated doghouse.

Provide Toys

- Provide wading pools, toys, and chewies for a dog who spends the day outdoors.

- All dogs should be on heartworm preventative and outdoor dogs especially so. Stagnant water encourages mosquitoes to breed. Eliminate or change standing water regularly. Ask at a pond or garden store about pet-safe mosquito repellent that when added to water prevents breeding.

- Clean pet waste regularly; otherwise flies can become abundant.

Clean Up

- Pea gravel makes easily cleaned, nonabsorbent kennel flooring. Hosing it down every week or two washes urine into the ground and eliminates odor.

- Put down a 3- or 4-inch base of gravel.

- If you want to keep a gravel-covered potty area separate from the rest of the outdoor run, use a 2-by-4 or rubber (not metal because you risk injury to your dog's feet) lawn edging to contain gravel.

DOGGIE DOORS

These entryways give your well-trained dog convenient access to the back yard

Let dog in. Let dog out. Let dog in. Let dog out. Doggie doors have pros and cons, but it's certainly convenient to be able to let him go in and out as he pleases, and you don't have to worry about him crossing his legs needing to potty when you're gone for hours. Make an educated decision.

Unless you have the collar-mounted remote control type, it is possible for your home to be broken into through the doggie door. Although some burglars will be deterred by the sign of a dog in the home, not all will. If there is wildlife around you, they may come in, too, attracted by food smells or warmth. Most dog doors are designed to be lockable if you want them secured.

Introducing a Dog Door

- Dog doors are easily installed in wooden doors. Installing a dog door in a metal door requires a bit more work.

- Be proactive with your neighbors by asking them if the dog barks in your absence before waiting for complaints. A dog who may never bark when his family is home can become vocal when left alone.

- Most dogs quickly understand how to use a dog door, especially when coaxed with treats or a meal.

Training a Dog

- There are pet doors for any kind of door, including glass doors and even windows.

- Access to a doggie door won't help to potty train a dog because if he doesn't have access to one, he won't understand about holding it until he can go out. Make sure your dog is potty trained before relying on a dog door.

- Toddlers in a home with a dog door need to be monitored because they may be tempted to copy the dog by crawling through.

If the dog comes in the door and has full run of the house, you could find muddy pawprints everywhere or twigs and gross things on your couch. You can prevent this by allowing access to only one room from outside.

Even if you have a secure yard, the dog can spend a lot of time out there alone. He could bark all day or escape. He could be teased or stolen. In short, he will be spending a lot of unmonitored time outside. You have to decide if you're comfortable with this.

A dog door can be great for elderly dogs who have a hard time holding it while you're at work. Installing a dog door is a cheaper option than hiring a petsitter and less stressful for a dog, who will be distressed that he's pottying in the house, and for you, who has to clean up.

If you're the handy type, dog doors are available at home stores, but hiring a professional who provides a guarantee may be worth it.

Advantages and Disadvantages to a Dog Door

- Dog doors offer a great deal of convenience and flexibility, but it's worth investing in one operated by a remote on the dog's collar.

- Stray cats and wildlife may be enticed into the house by warmth and food smells.

- Even inner cities have their share of raccoons, possums, and even foxes.

- An electronically operated door reduces your chances of burglary through the door from slim to none.

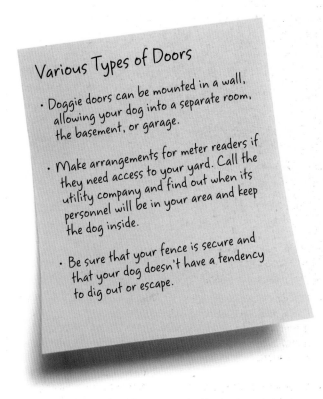

Various Types of Doors

- Doggie doors can be mounted in a wall, allowing your dog into a separate room, the basement, or garage.

- Make arrangements for meter readers if they need access to your yard. Call the utility company and find out when its personnel will be in your area and keep the dog inside.

- Be sure that your fence is secure and that your dog doesn't have a tendency to dig out or escape.

DOG MEETS DOG

Dogs rely almost exclusively on body language to communicate with each other

Dogs communicate with each other mostly via body language and often very subtly. Dogs who have been raised with other dogs "speak dog" better than those who have grown up primarily with their human families. Dogs are social, pack animals, and packs work more efficiently when there is a recognized and respected hierarchy. Dogs gener-

ally work to avoid conflict, and their interactions are more complex than the frequently used terms *dominance* and *submission* suggest.

A passive dog will often assume a lower position than the more assertive dog. She will lower her head and tail and possibly roll onto her back. She will turn her head away and

Social Grooming

- This golden retriever is happy to accept ear-grooming from the Sealyham terrier. Her face and body position are relaxed.

- Social grooming is a natural pack behavior, reinforcing both pack status and bond among animals. Most animal species, including

humans, engage in mutual grooming.

- Although a subordinate dog is more likely to groom a dominant dog, this isn't always the case. Pack rank behavior is complex and nuanced, with many layers of give-and-take.

Play Fighting

- These dogs are play-fighting. Much canine play involves mock-fighting and chasing. Dogs who know each other well can look and sound quite vicious while playing.

- With dogs who haven't fully worked out their relation-

ship, playing can quickly turn into squabbling.

- The dog in the submissive position above is unsure whether she should submit or retaliate to gain the upper hand, and this interaction could go either way.

avoid eye contact and allow herself to be sniffed. After she is certain she's not in danger, she will relax her stance and possibly invite play by running in circles or play-bowing. If she is afraid, she will remain prone; she may urinate, shake, lick her lips, and keep her tail between her legs. Some fearful dogs will try to avoid interaction completely. Hackles raised, tail down, and ears back, they will bark fiercely, bluffing the other dog.

Assertive dogs stand tall, with tail up and ears forward. They make eye contact. They may place their heads or legs over the shoulders of the other dog and even hump the other dog in a dominance move. After she decides the other dog is not a threat, she will relax. Serious fights often erupt when each assertive dog decides the other is a challenge.

Most dogs fall somewhere in the middle. They greet each other without overt displays of either dominance or submission and agree to get along. Many dogs feel emboldened and perhaps a bit stressed if they're being held on a tight leash by an anxious owner and act overly brave or defensive.

Playful Stances

- This is a classic play bow. A dog who assumes this position is saying only one thing: "Please play with me!"

- A dog in this position with a toy in her mouth is usually inviting the other dog to take the toy. Lying down or standing over the toy is a challenge to keep away.

- Look for a playful stance, side-by-side body positioning, upright ears, and relaxed expressions. These indicate friendliness and nonchallenging greeting behavior.

Dogs on a Leash

- When letting two dogs meet on leash, stay relaxed. Keep the leashes loose and observe their body language.

- Tightening up the leash, even momentarily, both transmits tension and makes the dog feel safe because you're backing him up. Keep a loose leash unless you need to pull the dogs part quickly.

- Dogs who stand face to face with eye contact, upright ears, and raised, even wagging, tails are challenging each other. Quickly distract them and move apart to avoid a fight.

WHAT IS HE SAYING?

Understand what your dog is telling you with his ears, tail, and stance

We expect dogs to learn our language, so it's only fair that we learn theirs, too. Training is easier when we understand how our dog perceives the process. More importantly, thousands of dog bites can be avoided if more people understand when a dog is stressed or warning that he may bite.

It takes a little time and experience to learn to read a dog.

Like people, dogs have different personalities and reactions. Also, the dog's body language has to be understood in context. Bared teeth could be an aggressive threat or a harmless, submissive "smile." Raised hackles might mean "I'm going to whip your butt" or "I'm really afraid." A dog who approaches you with ears down, wagging his tail at half mast and curving

Friendly Dogs

- A friendly dog has relaxed, soft eyes and mouth, often "smiling." Sometimes a dog will bare his teeth in a sub-missive smile—look at the rest of his body language. His ears will be up, and he will invite contact.

- A wagging tail can mean ei-ther friendly or threatening behavior. If the whole rump is wagging, you can be sure he's happy to see you.

- Friendly dogs often pant, whine, or bark with excite-ment.

Puppies and Submissive Dogs

- Puppies and submissive dogs roll on to their backs, offering proof that they are not a threat. Dominant dogs don't force another dog into this behavior; it is always voluntary.

- Most puppies will natu-rally roll over at any sign of dominance from an adult

dog. Most dog interaction aims to avoid conflict, and this puppy is being very appropriate.

- Don't force a dog onto its back for discipline; this is not natural dog behavior and can get you bitten.

his body sideways as he approaches you with bared teeth is probably friendly. A dog who walks toward you stiffly and straight on, with a tail carried high and ears forward is warning you to leave. Now. Dogs raise their hackles to look bigger, either to warn scary people away or to appear more intimidating to a threat. Generally speaking the lower the tail, the less confident the dog, but either situation could result in a bite if the dog feels threatened.

A dog who urinates when greeting people is doing it involuntarily out of excitement or nervousness. Getting angry with her will make her just more stressed and even more likely to pee. A dog who ignores an angry command to come and starts sniffing the ground and avoiding eye contact may not be stubborn; he could well be nervous. Unless he's a beagle following a scent, in which case he probably doesn't even hear you!

If your dog, regardless of size, is showing threatening behavior, guarding food and toys and growling, get professional help right away.

Confrontational Dogs

- Dogs who stand face to face with eye contact, upright ears and raised, even wagging, tails are challenging each other. Quickly distract them and move them a safe distance apart to avoid a fight.

- A dog confronting a human with this position isn't kidding, especially if his teeth are bared. Stay quiet and don't run.

- Avoid eye contact, look downward, keep your arms still, and remain motionless. Often this behavior will defuse the situation.

Nervous Dogs

- Dogs who are nervous will have lowered tail and ears, will avoid eye contact, and often will turn their bodies away from the perceived threat.

- A dog who sees every stranger as a threat and barks threateningly is often misperceived as "protective."

A dog who acts like this toward friendly or neutral strangers both on and off her property usually lacks confidence and is afraid rather than protective. This behavior warrants work with a trainer to correct.

- Avoid corrections and never punish a dog who is fearful.

APPROACHING A DOG

Learn how to safely approach a strange dog by modifying your body language

Dogs are amazingly patient with us. Many dogs are expected to allow complete strangers to pet them, without proper introduction. Luckily, most friendly dogs don't mind this. However, some dogs are naturally aloof. Others are shy or nervous about new people and feel very threatened by strangers doing what in dog language would be rude or challenging behavior. Some dogs are going to warn you with threats, growls, and barks to stay away.

Making direct eye contact is a challenge in dog language. So are making direct approaches (notice that friendly dogs usually don't approach each other face to face) and putting the body over another dog's head or shoulders. Yet, when

What Not to Do

- Never sneak up on a dog, especially one who is eating or is sleeping, as this may lead to being bitten or startling the animal.

- Never approach a wild or unfamiliar dog, especially one who is off leash or by himself, even if it's behind a fence.

- Do not approach a dog from above, with direct eye contact, and do not approach him quickly or abruptly, as this might startle the animal or make him growl or bite.

Ask Permission

- Before you approach someone else's dog, always ask the dog's owner for permission.

- Once you obtain permission, approach the dog slowly and quietly, often avoiding eye contact or with your eyes down.

- Slowly bring your hand towards the dog from the side.

- Allow the animal to sniff your hand first to get a good gauge on your smell. Then pet the dog's side or back.

people meet strange dogs, they often approach them head on, stare at their faces, loom over them, and put their hands on their heads. These actions all are very threatening in dog language!

A dog who is naturally aloof may just tolerate petting or move away from a pushy stranger. A nervous dog might urinate, growl, or even snap. He is letting you know with all his might that he's stressed. There's no rule that every dog must be man's best friend right away, but if you want him to relax, here's how.

Keep your body sideways to him and avoid eye contact. Keep your hands low with no sudden movements. Keep your voice calm and quiet. Try bending down and touching the ground—this is a nonthreatening signal and will transfer the dog's attention from you to the ground. It might sound silly, but it can work well. When he approaches, keep looking away and scratch him under the chin instead of the top of his head.

If a dog threatens with bared teeth and raised hackles, avoid eye contact and back slowly away. It's not worth the risk.

Strange Dogs

- Do not approach a wild or unfamiliar dog, especially one who is off leash. Do not allow your child to approach the dog, either, and take extra steps to go out of the animal's way.

- If you encounter a strange dog, stand tall, with your eyes averted and hands at your side, and back away slowly.

- Never try to outrun a dog. If you stand still or back away slowly, a dog will most likely only give you a sniff and then move on.

Calming Signals

- Dogs will pick up on your physical behavior, so here are a few tips for projecting a calm demeanor.

- To calm a dog, avoid eye contact, which some animals perceive as being a threat or a challenge.

- When possible, do not approach the dog head-on; rather, take a sideways stance, with your hands low and close to your body.

- Stay closer to the ground and the dog's eye level to appear friendly and calm.

113

DOGS & CHILDREN

The primary victims of dog bites are children; teach them to be dog savvy

There are many reasons why dogs bite children, and most bites can be avoided. Children need to be taught how to behave with dogs. Ask your school or Humane Society about dog bite prevention classes. Dogs should be well socialized to children from an early age. Finally, monitoring both and not leaving them together unattended are critical.

Many dogs have a natural prey drive. Some working and herding breeds (herding is modified prey drive behavior) may be triggered by children's high voices and quick movements. A single dog might be fine, but several dogs together can engage in pack hunting behavior. Other dogs have been given too much lenience in their homes and feel entitled to snap

KNACK DOG CARE AND TRAINING

Proper Petting

- Many children want to pet a strange dog on top of the head, which makes some dogs uncomfortable. Show your child that the best way is to pet below the head, on the chin, chest, or flank.

- The family dog should accept gentle petting and

handling without discomfort or protest.

- A good daily exercise for everyone in the family is to stroke the dog from head to foot. Doing this gets him used to being handled by everyone in his "pack."

Gentle Approaches

- Puppies and children are naturally attracted to each other, but some children are unintentionally rough and need to be taught to gentle down.

- Teach children to give treats to dogs properly without teasing. Dogs of any age can learn to be gentle with

children, but it's easiest with a puppy so he can grow with the family.

- Watch for any signs of resource guarding (Chapter 13) because children can get bitten when a dog is guarding "his" possessions.

at children who get too close to "their" food or toys. Dogs who have been chained or fenced, perhaps being teased by kids, can become so frustrated that they'll bite when they can. Some dogs, unused to children, get stressed and may snap when a child is at eye level.

Don't let your children play tug or chasing games with a dog. Teach them not to tease any animal. A child can be taught empathy and care for the family dog by helping with daily care. Children must ask permission to pet others' dogs and be taught never to approach a strange dog. Children should be taught how to pet a dog (below the face, fingers curled closed to avoid nipping). Don't let a young child walk a dog alone. When out with the family dog, use two leashes so the child can hold one and an adult the other.

Getting general obedience training, having structure in the home, and making sure your dog is used to kids are the best defense. Dogs and kids can be magical together, but never forget that your dog is an animal with instinctual drives.

Age-appropriate Responsibilities

- Many kids love walking dogs, but a responsible adult should be on hand.

- Don't give a child the responsibility of controlling a dog in public. Should something unexpected happen, a bite can happen very quickly.

- Ask yourself if a child is strong enough to hold the dog back in a pet store or in the street if another dog rushes toward her dog. If not, she can walk him only with adult help.

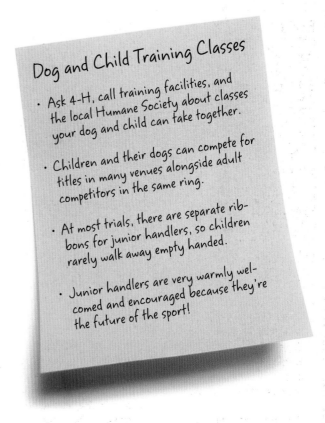

Dog and Child Training Classes

- Ask 4-H, call training facilities, and the local Humane Society about classes your dog and child can take together.

- Children and their dogs can compete for titles in many venues alongside adult competitors in the same ring.

- At most trials, there are separate ribbons for junior handlers, so children rarely walk away empty handed.

- Junior handlers are very warmly welcomed and encouraged because they're the future of the sport!

STRESS & AGGRESSION

Warning signs of stress leading to aggression or unwanted behavior often go unheeded

Millions of dogs—the vast majority—never act aggressively toward humans. Considering that humans kill and neglect millions more dogs than dogs kill or neglect people, their restraint should be admired. But dogs do act out— sometimes with restraint and a warning nip, and sometimes with tragic consequences. Dogs rarely "snap" suddenly. They've usually exhibited warning behaviors for a while before finally biting.

Strong-minded dogs, often the working or terrier breeds, can become overly dominant if not trained. Many a dog has been ruined by spoiling and not enforcing basic rules. The dog feels entitled to the couch and to its possessions and food, entitled even to "protect" one family member from

Aggressive Behavior Signs

- This Pomeranian is indicating she may bite if approached. Small untrained dogs who are often spoiled and carried can become defensive or territorial, leading to unpleasant, aggressive behavior.

- Bared teeth and a direct stare are a threat.

- Whether a dog is 6 pounds or 60 pounds, unwarranted aggression toward humans is never acceptable.

- Large dogs can do more damage, but small dogs have sent many people to the hospital and even been responsible for deaths.

Prey Drive

- Prey drive can be positively channelled with play, such as ball chasing, or with work, such as herding.

- Prey drive is the instinctive canine drive to chase and hunt. It has been modified and tempered by centuries of selective breeding, but most dogs still retain it.

- Children often trigger prey drive and subsequent bites when running and playing. The primitive part of the dog's mind takes over, and an undersocialized, dominant, or poorly trained dog can inflict great harm.

another. This is all bossy resource guarding and very disrespectful. Dogs don't get to choose what they protect in your house because you own all of it! These dogs stiffen and growl when approached by a family member while eating. They may growl and resist being ordered off furniture or act aggressively possessive of a family member.

Other dogs are defensively aggressive. Usually these are dogs with softer temperaments and what some dog trainers call "weak nerves." These can be very sweet pets but have a natural tendency to be apprehensive about life. Two things can mess these dogs up. Not socializing them makes for fearful, mistrustful dogs who bark wildly at strangers, try to bite the vet, and are unpredictable with everyone. They are not "mean" or wrong; they are stressed out. And if too many harsh corrections make a dog feel that her environment and the people in it are unpredictable and dangerous, she can react with defensive aggression when pushed.

Stressed-out, dominant, and aggressive dogs are fixable. It usually takes a combination of behavior modification (on the part of the owners) and consistent, fair training for the dogs.

Behavior Modification

- Whether a dog is dominant or defensive, she will be happier and more secure with consistent training and structure. She can relax knowing that she doesn't have to defend or maintain her position.

- Behavior modification on the owner's part means being consistent, firm, and fair and not spoiling the dog.

- Aggressive behavior must be dealt with, no matter what the size or breed. Contact a positive behaviorist or trainer for help.

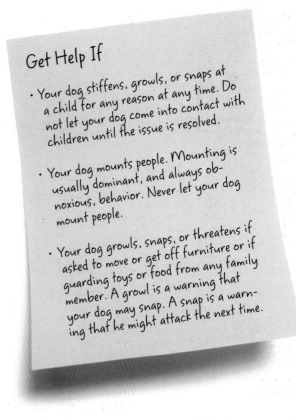

Get Help If

- Your dog stiffens, growls, or snaps at a child for any reason at any time. Do not let your dog come into contact with children until the issue is resolved.

- Your dog mounts people. Mounting is usually dominant, and always obnoxious, behavior. Never let your dog mount people.

- Your dog growls, snaps, or threatens if asked to move or get off furniture or if guarding toys or food from any family member. A growl is a warning that your dog may snap. A snap is a warning that he might attack the next time.

SPEAKING DOG

BODY LANGUAGE & TRAINING
Build a better training bond with your dog with nonverbal signals

You might think you are using words to train your dog, and because he's smart, he'll learn them. However, he's learning more from your posture and tone of voice than your words.

Let's pretend your dog's name is "Rover." Pick a two-syllable word that sounds similar, like "Bacon," and call him from another part of the house using an encouraging tone of voice. He'll come running. Now call him using his name, in a low, neutral tone. Chances are he won't come, or he'll come very hesitantly. He's not responding to the word; he's responding to your happy tone. An upbeat, relaxed, and authoritative tone of voice always works best.

Call your dog with welcoming body posture. Open your arms a little, stand tall and relaxed, and if you want him to speed up, back away from him or crouch down.

Proper Shoulder Position

- Most dogs follow our shoulder position. Call your dog and start turning as if to walk away. He will often speed up to get to you faster.

- If you have a dog who is absolutely refusing to come, turn and run in the opposite direction. Despite his bullheadedness, chances are he won't want you out of his sight.

- If you have to go get your dog, just calmly get him leashed and don't correct him. He won't understand.

Keep Calm

- Project an aura of calm, friendly confidence when working with your dog.

- Getting excited or frustrated inhibits or confuses him by sending mixed signals. Dogs are better at reading our body language than hearing our words; a sensitive dog will quickly pick up on negative emotions.

- Engaging with your dog while walking keeps his focus on you.

- Try walking backward with your dog on leash for a change. Your different body position and gait will get his attention!

If your dog is somewhat submissive, telling her to sit while you bend over her will make her nervous, and although she might comply, it won't be with enthusiasm. Looming over a dog is threatening. Because you want to both project authority and be encouraging, stand up straight and relaxed when you give commands. If you don't think dogs take body position literally—the higher position being one of authority— lie face down on the floor and see what happens when you ask your dog to sit!

Your dog follows you. When you learn heeling, you will learn to always take off with your left foot, closest to the dog. This immediately cues the dog to start heeling. When you tell the dog "stay" and leave him, you'll leave with your right foot first, and he will know that means to stay put.

Matching words with body language makes it much easier for your dog.

Maintain Confidence

- This little dog is unsure or questioning (look at the laid-back ears) but willing to follow her leader.

- The dog's owner is confidently striding forward, acknowledging and encouraging the dog and expecting her to follow.

- Depending on the situation and the dog, talking a lot can be either distracting or motivating. Agility handlers sometimes practice running an entire course without saying a word, forcing both dog and handler to focus on body language.

Keep Dog in Check

- A dog running ahead of his handler isn't necessarily being "dominant." Sometimes the dog is just exuberant, full of joie de vivre, and usually a faster runner!

- A dog's natural gait is usually faster than ours. It can be difficult for them to adjust to our slower pace.

- If your dog is ahead of you, periodically call his name and heap on the praise for any attention, even if he just slows and looks back at you.

119

COLLARS, HARNESSES, & LEASHES
How to choose and use the most important tools in your training toolbox

Training collars are tools in your training toolbox. Puppies should always be trained using a regular collar, and specialized training collars should be used later only if necessary. A well-trained dog with no major issues may never need a training collar.

The choke collar is often used to "strangle" a pulling dog in-stead of the fast pop and release it's intended for. The choke collar may cause neck and throat damage if overused. A prong (or "pinch") collar looks barbaric to some, with its inward-facing metal prongs. However, a properly fitted prong collar can be gentler than a choke collar, offering power steering for large leash-pullers.

Training Collars

- The majority of dogs will never need a training collar if effective, positive training is implemented from the start.

- Training collars should not be used to correct lunging or aggressive behavior toward other dogs. Because your dog will associate the

discomfort with the sight of other dogs, it will usually make him even more reactive instead of better behaved.

- Many trainers believe in positive reinforcement only and do not allow chain or prong collars.

Head Halters

- Head halters work by turning the dog's head toward the handler when he pulls, breaking focus on what the dog was pulling toward and putting focus back on the handler.

- A head halter is self-correcting, so the handler shouldn't pull or jerk on it.

In fact, a dog could be injured by a sharp backward jerk on the head halter.

- Never leave any training collar or halter on the dog unless you are actually walking or working with him.

Nylon limited-slip collars and martingale collars are similar to chokes, except they don't tighten all the way. Head halters have become popular and are effective for leash-pullers and those dogs who lunge at other dogs. Toy dogs and pugs often use harnesses instead of collars. There are also harnesses that discourage jumping and pulling.

A 6-foot leash is standard for training classes. During class you may need to secure your dog to free your hands, and most training facilities have hooks for this. Buy a carabiner from a hardware store and attach it to the leash for a hook-up.

Cotton long lines let the dog have more freedom yet still remind him that you are in control even when you're 20 feet away. A learning dog who might think that he doesn't have to sit or lie down when commanded from a distance may think twice after a quick leash tug. Sometimes young dogs realize they can run faster than you and decide not to come when called. A long line is a great way to remind them that distance from you doesn't mean they can blow you off.

Leashes

- In training, the dog walks on the left. Holding the leash in your right hand leaves the hand next to your dog free to give signals, pet, or give treats.

- Never pull constantly on the leash. If this actually worked, it would be easy to teach a dog not to pull!

- The heavier the leash, the more your dog feels it. For transitioning to off-leash control, use a very light-weight leash.

Harnesses

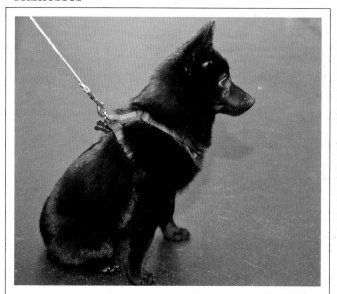

- A harness doesn't give as much control for teaching a dog not to pull unless it's especially designed for that.

- A no-pull harness works by tightening across a dog's chest and restricting front leg movement when he puts tension on the leash.

- As with a head halter, there is no training involved with a no-pull harness. The dog simply finds it uncomfortable to pull while wearing one and stops pulling.

ELECTRONIC & BARK COLLARS
These can be excellent tools, but you must have expert advice on using them

Electronic collars are controversial because many think they are cruel. However, the zap isn't necessarily any stronger than the zap from the commonly used invisible fence collar. Electronic collars can be set to give a warning beep only or anything from a mild tickle to a noticeable shock. The electronic collars works like an electronic leash tug to get a dog's

attention and to direct him from a distance. It's often used for hunting and field dogs because they must learn to obey while out in the field under considerable distraction.

Electronic collars should be used only under the tutelage of someone very experienced with them. One doesn't just put the collar on the dog and start zapping. Timing is crucial in

KNACK DOG CARE AND TRAINING

Electronic Collars

- Timing the correction properly is crucial. Mistimed corrections are not fair to the dog.

- Detractors say that electronic collars are cruel and punitive and that a more humane option is to use positive training methods

- to encourage a dog to willingly comply.

- Proponents say that a few strong corrections are more effective and kinder than months of nagging or simply not being able to deal with a behavior that threatens the safety of the dog and those around him.

Shock Ranges

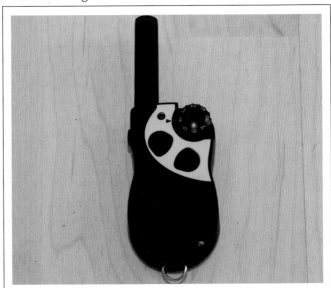

- A high-quality modern electronic collar can have over one hundred settings, from a warning beep to a definite shock.

- At the low settings, most training electronic collars deliver a milder buzz than a common invisible fence collar.

- Most collars have a range of 100–300 yards, but some models work at up to 1 mile.

- Some collars give just a vibration, not a shock. These are sometimes used for training deaf dogs.

proper electronic collar use, and misuse can create serious, potentially irreversible problems. Properly used, an electronic collar can be highly effective and should be used with rewards and motivation. It teaches the dog that the correction comes not as a consequence of the handler but rather as a consequence of his own behavior, which will make the dog think and work independently. It's important to find a reputable and considerate trainer if you consider this tool.

Bark collars come in several designs. The most common design spritzes the dog's face with citronella spray when trig-gered by barking. Others give a zap. Some trigger after about thirty seconds of barking to let the dog know it's fine to bark at strange noises and newcomers but not fine to bark for thirty minutes nonstop.

Not every dog is a candidate for an electronic collar for invisible fencing, barking, or training. Some dogs will be too distressed by the correction, and like any training tool, electronic collars are easy to misuse.

Obeying Commands

- Hunting dogs are trained to obey commands from great distances, often for their own safety. Electronic collars have been used for decades to teach dogs to stay on the trail instead of veering off after deer and to reliably come when called.

- Training is first done without the collar. It's used only to correct incompliance after the dog is familiar with the commands.

- Many hunters successfully train their dogs without electronic collars.

Get Expert Instruction

- There are very few instances when an electronic collar is warranted for training. If used incorrectly or used on a sensitive dog, an electronic collar will confuse the dog and make some behaviors worse.

- Use an electronic collar only with expert instruction, at the lowest possible setting, and in conjunction with rewards for desired behavior.

- Work only with a trainer who has a lot of experience and uses modern electronic collars.

TRAINING TREATS

The taste, consistency, and even color of your training treats can make a big difference

Food is a powerful motivator for dogs, which is why food works so well for training. To dispel a common myth: Using treats for training will not make a dog "work only for treats." Given correctly, treats are used as markers for good behavior, not as bribes and only rarely as lures when teaching a brand new skill. They work to form a positive association in the dog's mind, let him know when he's done just the right thing, and to keep his attention on the job. After he has learned the skill, the treats are used intermittently and can be phased out. Some trainers don't believe in treats, and that's fine. They are merely a tool in the toolbox and like any other tool can be abused!

Size

- Training treats should be very small and soft.

- Don't be constrained by the available size of commercial treats. Many can be pinched in half.

- Use little crumbs for rewards and a whole treat for extra special performance.

- There is no rule that treats all have to be the same. Use tiny treats and reserve cooked chicken chunks for his "jackpot" reward.

Meats

- Hot dogs can be cut into little pieces or held hidden in one hand for the dog to nibble at for reward.

- Low-fat cheese, liverwurst, and lunch meats all make excellent training treats.

- Very nutritious liver treats are made by cooking liver in the oven at low heat, liberally sprinkled with garlic powder. Cut the treats into small cubes and store in the freezer.

- Don't overdo liver treats. Too many at once can cause diarrhea.

Good training treats should be very small. You are not feeding the dog; you are giving him tiny little rewards. They should be soft, so he doesn't inhale one and then get distracted coughing it up when he's supposed to be doing a perfect heeling pattern. They shouldn't be crumbly, so they don't sprinkle all over the ground and distract him, or worse yet, other dogs in a training class. Finally, if you're doing training like agility, where treats are often thrown, they should be a different color than the ground so he can get them fast.

Some obedience trainers tuck treats into their mouths and spit them at the dog to keep their hands free and the dog focused. This explains the rapt attention that competition obedience dogs often have on their handlers' faces. Choose special treats that your dog really loves and use them only for training. You can find many training treats on the market or use your own. Hot dogs cut into tiny pieces work well, as do cheese and lunch meats.

Light-colored Treats

- Most indoor training facilities use black matting, so light-colored treats are easy to see when thrown or accidentally dropped.

- In class, ask permission before giving someone else's dog a treat. Some dogs are intolerant of certain ingredients; some owners are particular about what they feed.

- To reward tiny dogs while heeling, smear some peanut butter or soft cheese onto the end of a dowel and let them have a quick taste as reward. That is much easier than constantly bending down!

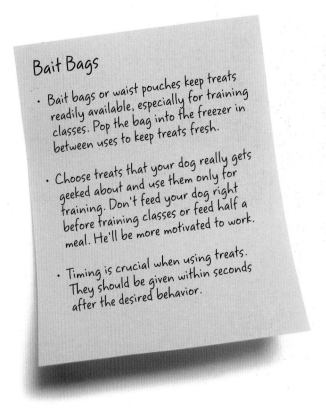

Bait Bags

- Bait bags or waist pouches keep treats readily available, especially for training classes. Pop the bag into the freezer in between uses to keep treats fresh.

- Choose treats that your dog really gets geeked about and use them only for training. Don't feed your dog right before training classes or feed half a meal. He'll be more motivated to work.

- Timing is crucial when using treats. They should be given within seconds after the desired behavior.

CLICKERS
A little training tool can make your dog think, choose, and behave

Developed initially to train large marine mammals, clicker training has become a useful dog training tool. The operant conditioning theory is that an animal will learn to repeat an action if the action has a positive consequence, usually food. A clicker is a small plastic box with a metal strip that when pressed with your finger makes a sharp click. Unlike your voice, the distinctive click is a clear signal to a dog that she's performed the desired action when immediately followed by a small treat reward.

Very specific behaviors, like tail wags are easily taught with a clicker. Because the click occurs at the moment the dog performs the behavior, it bridges the gap between the behavior and the treat. Think of the clicker as a camera, with the click taking an imaginary photo of the behavior.

Preparing a Dog

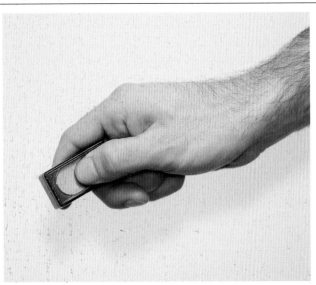

- A clicker has to be "primed." This means making the dog aware that the click she hears will be immediately followed by a food reward.

- Have a handful of very small, soft treats in one hand and the clicker in the other and your dog in front of you.

- Click and immediately treat without saying anything. Repeat this. It usually takes three to ten repetitions before your dog is looking expectant, waiting for the click sound. Your clicker is now primed.

Shape Behaviors

- Shape a behavior, even a simple one. This is fun. Equip yourself with clicker, treats, and your dog and wait quietly.

- Eventually she will move— a paw motion, a head turn, an ear twitch. Immediately click-treat. Wait for her to make the same move and again click-treat.

- Within one short session, she'll start offering this behavior in order to get the click-treat. After she does, put a command to it. You have just shaped a behavior.

126

Clicker training makes a dog work to figure out what she has to do in order to get the click-treat, and because it makes her think, she learns fast and retains what she's learned. Clicker training involves only guidance, not corrections. Incorrect actions are simply ignored. As a result, the dog works hard to figure out how to get *you* to perform and give her a treat.

Increase Your Criteria

- Increase your criteria. Using the head turn example, say you want her to turn her head all the way back instead of making a quick half-turn.

- Now ignore her quick half-turns. There are no corrections in clicker training—simply don't acknowledge unwanted behavior.

- She will try harder to get that click-treat and at some point will turn her head farther. Quickly reward that, and from this point forward you will reward only complete head turns.

General Training

- A clicker can be used to conduct general training, to teach tricks, or just to shape very specific behaviors.

- Even "hard to teach" dogs can grasp concepts quickly through clicker training.

- Teach a beginner dog away from distractions at first. Increase distractions as she gets more proficient.

- Don't do any treat-training right after a meal unless yours is a real chowhound. A dog who is a little hungry will work harder.

TRAINING TOYS

Using your dog's favorite toy just for training sessions can be a great motivator

Trainers talk of dogs having "play drive," which means just any dog who likes to chase, tug, and "kill" toys. It's another great way to motivate and reward a dog during training. Some dogs get more geeked about toys than food, which can make for some high-energy training sessions. Because most training should be structured play, it's wonderful if you

have a play-driven dog. Terriers are often extremely focused on toys due to their development as vermin-killing dogs.

As with treats, it works best if you have a special favorite toy that your dog adores just for training sessions. Again, you are creating a positive association—obeying is a fun game.

The type of toy depends on what you're teaching and what

Training Toys

- Have a special toy or two reserved only for training.

- Many dogs are highly motivated by toys made of real instead of faux fur. Many online training supply stores sell sturdy tugs made from sheepskin or rabbit fur.

- If using a ball for training or fetch, make sure it's too large for a dog to swallow. Large dogs can choke on thrown tennis balls. A baseball is a better size for big dogs.

Playing Tug

- Playing tug is very satisfying for many dogs. An unconfident dog may be hesitant to "challenge" his person over a tug, even in play. These dogs will quickly drop the toy or have a half-hearted grip.

- Encourage a shy dog to take the toy and tug. Don't

pull too hard and give him plenty of praise when he drops it on command.

- Try snaking the toy along the floor, as you would if playing with a cat. Doing this helps trigger a dog's prey drive.

your dog likes. It could be as low-tech as a length of heavy knotted rope or empty plastic water bottle, or it could be an expensive rabbit fur woven tug. If choosing toys for group training classes, avoid squeaker toys, which can completely unravel the other dogs. Toys in class can keep your dog focused on you and having fun while you wait for other dogs to take their turns. Take a toy along on walks and play-train in the park for distraction training. Stop your training sessions before he starts to lose interest. Short sessions work better and keep his motivation high.

It's OK for you to play tug-of-war with your dog as long as you set the rules. Use it to teach your dog the "drop" command—his reward is that he gets to play again after he releases. Work on sits, downs, and stays and reward him with a brief tug session each time. No matter what you're using play-training for, it strengthens your bond with the dog and builds motivation.

Frisbees

- Frisbees come in a plethora of styles and materials, including floating Frisbees for water retrieval.

- If your dog doesn't take to a Frisbee right away, use it as a food bowl for a few days to create a positive association.

- Start by rolling it along the ground and doing short tosses with it. Work up gradually to the spectacular airborne leaps unless he's a natural disc dog.

- Don't encourage a young dog to jump too high. Wait until his joints are done growing.

Proofing for Distraction

- Carry a toy with you on walks for impromptu training play.

- This is called "proofing for distraction." Many dogs will obey beautifully at home, but it's out in the real world where much of the training really counts.

- Every time you increase the difficulty level, you may need to take a step back in training. Don't expect your dog to handle a sixty-second down stay in a busy park right away.

CLASSES

Group training classes are fun, inexpensive, and a great way to learn new techniques

There are some misconceptions about dog training classes. Beginner and novice classes are not just for novice dog owners. They're for beginner and novice dogs, often brought to class by experienced dog owners. The dogs learn to pay attention to their owners in the face of distractions and interact politely with other dogs and people. Another misconception is that basic obedience classes are for puppies and young dogs. Most are held for beginner dogs of any age because old dogs can learn new tricks. Finally, many people think their dog is too wild for classes. Many classes are tailored exactly for the unruly dog—how will he learn to behave in public if he's never in public?

Class Benefits

- The difference between an unruly dog on the first night of class and a controlled canine at the end of the course can be quite dramatic!

- Unless a dog has serious aggression issues, group classes work very well to teach restraint and calm around other dogs.

- Most training facilities will do some private lessons to evaluate and work with a dog before it enters group classes. If you're unsure how your dog will do, call and ask first.

Structured Classes

- Even serious obedience classes should be structured play. Effective trainers encourage the use of treats, toys, and games for control and attention.

- Puppy and beginner classes are usually more lax. At higher levels, especially competition-level classes, dogs are expected to be controlled and to ignore other dogs during class or competition.

- A more experienced dog is expected to keep his focus on his owner and the job in class. He can play with his owner but not other dogs.

130

Obedience training isn't just an eight-week class, and you're done. It's a process, and it's even OK to repeat classes. You and your dog will learn from the different participants, and it will strengthen your dog's social graces. Most good dog training facilities teach not only basic skills but also dog sports and advanced obedience, so you can continue to higher learning.

The AKC offers the "Canine Good Citizen" certification to any dog, regardless of breed. The CGC certification proves that your dog has the basic skills to be a mannerly dog in areas from walking with a loose leash to being friendly with other dogs and people. Many training facilities offer CGC classes, followed by the test.

There are several right ways to train dogs and some wrong ways, and every trainer has her philosophy. A good trainer is going to be flexible in her methods and make the classes fun. Ask people with well-behaved dogs whom they recommend. Perhaps your vet will know someone. Go and observe a class before you sign up and see if it feels like a good fit, then go play!

Important Skills Learned

- One of the most important skills your dog will learn in class is to focus on you—his leader—in a distracting environment.

- When observing a class, ask yourself if both dogs and owners are enjoying themselves. Avoid classes that use choke collars and jerk the dogs around for compliance.

- Punishment should never be a part of any puppy class. Appropriate corrections may be warranted for dogs who have already learned the rules.

Real World Skills

- In class pups start to learn "real world" skills, like ignoring other dogs and tempting items on the ground.

- The dog who must stay still while other dogs are walking by him is called the "honor dog." His job is to stay politely while serv-ing as a distraction for the others.

- In a good class, you can learn from other participants as well as the trainer. Even experienced owners of titled dogs bring beginner dogs to basic classes.

131

"COME"

Puppies naturally come when called; proof your adult dog into an impressive recall

Coming when called is actually two different actions. The dog diverts his attention to you when you call, then he comes to you. The first part—getting his attention—is the most important because that's where the communication often breaks down. Squirrels and interesting smells are just more interesting than you!

Make paying attention to you rewarding. Mealtimes are a good time to do this every day. Wait until he's otherwise engaged, then call him to eat. Make a game out of calling him to you for play, treats, or praise. When you say his name, and he looks at you, immediately praise him for giving you attention. Then encourage him to come to you for extra praise.

Interaction with the Dog

- Crouching down and opening your arms in a welcoming stance while calling encourage a dog to come to you quickly.

- A dog who has never been reprimanded after being called to you might be hesitant. If he understands that coming to you means good things, he'll reliably and willingly obey.

- Training isn't limited to discrete sessions. Day-to-day interaction with your dog determines how attentive and compliant he will be.

Use Your Voice

- Use his name as well as your "come" command and tell him he's a good boy as he runs toward you.

- Sound happy and excited, like this is the best possible thing you two could be doing this very minute.

- Don't do too many repetitions of a recall exercise in a row. It's usually counterproductive to bore a dog. Better to quit all sessions with him wanting more play.

- Extra points go to you for having your dog sit immediately after a recall!

When calling your dog, adopt a welcoming, relaxed stance. If he doesn't come immediately, turn and run away from him; most dogs will follow.

Never call a dog for some unpleasant consequence like reprimanding him or trimming toenails—go get him instead. Avoid repeating "Rover, come, come, Rover, come . . ." until he decides to pay attention because you know what? You're telling him it's OK to blow you off and come when he decides to. Call your dog only when you're certain he will come (or you can haul him to you on a leash) and always praise him when he gets to you. As he progresses, a 20- to 30-foot-long line will be an invaluable tool. Give him the freedom to range to the end of the line on walks and periodically make an enthusiastic game of calling him to you. Use praise, treats, or toys to make coming to you rewarding. Even if you have to tug him to you, praise him all the while. The more often correct behavior is repeated and rewarded, the more it is reinforced.

Use a Partner

- Having a partner restrain your dog for several seconds while you call him builds a little frustration and drive to get to you quickly.

- For a dog who is ho-hum about coming, make sure he sees that you have food or his favorite toy. Have another dog handy whom he loves? Keep that dog with you while you call Rover.

- If he is being restrained while you entice him to come, he will be very eager.

Mix It Up

- Mix it up. Sometimes offer a treat, other times a game as a reward.

- To teach him that coming doesn't always mean the same thing, occasionally wait until he gets to you and stops. Then turn and run away, encouraging him to chase you.

- Games in which your dog chases you are always good. Don't ever play games in which you are chasing him, though. He'll get the idea that sometimes running away from you is desirable.

133

"SIT"

One of the most important basic commands, "sit" teaches your dog self-control

Sitting to eat meals or treats or to have his leash put on teaches your dog both self-control and control of his environment. If he sits, he can make good things happen. Sitting is also an excellent alternate behavior to jumping onto guests or lunging on leash.

Young puppies can learn to sit, and the method for pups is the same. Using a tiny treat or piece of his meal as an appetizer, move it above his head toward his tail while saying "sit." If he backs up or tries jumping, use your hand on his rump to gently sit him. As his butt hits the floor, praise and give him the reward. Do this before feeding every meal, before letting him go through the door, and before giving any

Encouragement

- If you want a perfect straight sit, reward only for correct position and ignore crooked sits.

- To encourage a straight sit, take a step back and encourage your dog into the right position.

- In early stages of training, it's fine to lure him into position with a treat but phase the lure out as soon as he's got the concept.

- Some sighthounds, most notably greyhounds, find sitting uncomfortable. Dogs with arthritis might also find it difficult.

Hand Signals

- Add a hand signal to provide variety and to work at a distance.

- Pair the hand signal with a voice command at first, then phase out the voice. Your dog will soon understand both commands whether given together or separately.

- Hand signals are useful when you can't give a verbal command, such as when talking on the phone or being in a very noisy environment.

- A dog who understands hand signals will transition easily if she loses her hearing with age.

treats. Make it a habit, and it will soon become automatic. Most dogs will learn to sit on command in a day or two.

Next, help him increase self-control by praising him for a few seconds before releasing the treat. Over time increase the sit time up to thirty seconds or so and always have a release word like "OK" or "break" to tell him when he can stop sitting; otherwise you are training him to bounce up again as soon as his rump hits the floor. You are not only training a discrete behavior but also building control.

It appears obvious to us that sitting is a position, but because we almost always teach a dog to sit from a stand, the dog is actually learning specifically to lower his rear. Dogs are very concrete learners. Use a treat initially to lure your dog into a sit, a down, or a stand position, then a hand signal to help him understand "sit" as a position instead of an action.

Straight Sits

- To encourage straight sits, work next to a wall, so that your dog has no choice. This helps build muscle memory.

- Be fair to your dog by slowing down for a few steps before stopping. She needs some signal that you are about to stop, so that she can sit promptly.

- Make it a game by taking a few fast steps, slowing down, and encouraging very fast sits. Get her excited first and praise lavishly for fast sits.

Competition Obedience Sit

- A competition obedience sit is precise and straight, directly in front of the handler or lined up with her left leg next to her. This sit is unnecessary unless you plan on competing. However, it can be a useful exercise.

- This crooked sitting is sometimes called a "puppy sit." It might lose you a few points in competition but otherwise doesn't matter. Most dogs grow out of it.

- Despite what you might hear, this crooked sit doesn't indicate hip dysplasia.

LEASH MANNERS

It's normal for a dog to pull, but it's easy to teach him leash manners

It takes practice and patience to teach leash manners. We are asking our dogs to walk unnaturally slowly at our pace, to ignore tantalizing odors and other dogs, and to curb their enthusiasm when they want to run. Pulling on a leash is perfectly natural, and like people, dogs will resist if pushed or pulled. Often dogs learn to pull because doing so works—we follow them when they do.

The plan of action is two-pronged: (1) Make it unproductive for the dog to pull by stopping and turning each time he pulls and (2) make yourself as interesting as distracting sights and smells. Decide whether you want your dog simply not to pull or to heel with obedience-style precision. For the informal walk, simply not pulling is a realistic goal.

Puppies should be walked on plain collars. Older and more

Basic Commands

- When working with your dog onleash, be sure that he understands the basic commands, first.

- When walking, if you feel the dog tugging on your leash, stop and wait. When the dog stops (either he's gone as far as the leash can go, or he's stopped to see what you're doing), call him back.

- Have him "sit" next to you. Be sure to praise him and reward him with a treat when he does.

Start Out

- Until your dog learns proper leash manners, all walks should be considered to be learning sessions.

- Walk at a quick pace to get the dog to follow you; dogs inherently always want to go fast or get excited, but you must be sure not to let them pull you.

- When you feel the dog tug on the leash, stop. Again, call the dog to "sit" and reward him.

- Soon the dog will pick up on when he is rewarded and when he isn't.

exuberant dogs may benefit from a training collar. Every time the dog puts tension on the leash, stop immediately. The moment the leash slackens, change directions. Be absolutely consistent. You're teaching the dog that pulling will not get him anywhere and that he has to pay attention to you or be abruptly turned around. It may take you thirty minutes to get a block from your house, but that's okay! Vary walking speed and praise him when he is not pulling. It's difficult for a dog to learn this. Start in low-distraction environments and work up to busier environments.

Carry treats and make yourself interesting. Keep his attention by practicing sits at curbs and random, enthusiastic recalls. Walking him before mealtime when he's hungry is a useful strategy. If something utterly distracts your dog, don't get frustrated. Simply walk him away from the distraction and praise him when he finally does pay attention. Be consistent and patient, and he'll get it.

Be Vocal

- When stopping to call your dog, be sure to be clear and have authority in your voice.

- Start each walk with the same command, such as "walk" to establish a routine.

- When providing rewards and treats to your dog, try "good" or "yes."

- Be vocal when changing directions or stopping a pull on the leash. Your dog will soon be familiar with these commands.

Change Directions

- Your dog will need to learn to follow you, not the other way around, so throw in some turns when teaching him to stay onleash.

- Frequent hard stops might frustrate your dog, causing him to act out. Instead, try doing a quick "U turn" turnaround in the opposite direction when a dog starts to pull on the leash.

- The dog will learn that when he pulls, he will only be turned in the opposite direction of his intended destination.

"DOWN"

Teach your dog to lie down and chill out when you need him calm

Having a dog lie down (and then stay) gives him a relaxed way to stay in place during mealtimes or a nonthreatening way to meet kids.

It's easiest to start with the dog sitting down. Although not mandatory, arthritic, older, and fat dogs may find it easier. Wait until your dog is hungry before mealtime. Hold a treat in your hand and slowly lower it to the floor between his feet

while saying "down." He may try to stand up to get the treat, so place your hand on his rump to prevent this. Never try to push him down because he'll automatically resist. You may find it easier to sit on the floor with him. If the dog doesn't lie down quickly, rest your hand on the floor covering the treat and coax him. The instant he is all the way down, give lots of praise, and he gets the treat.

Start in the Sit Position

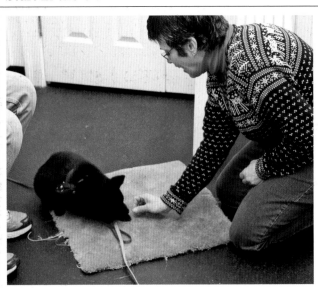

- It's easiest to start with teaching down from a sitting position.

- If his hind end rises as the front lowers, gently hold his rump down and don't give him the treat until he's completely prone.

- If you give him the treat before he's down, you are teaching him that he doesn't need to go all the way.

- Give him several little treats in a row between his feet before telling him "OK" or whatever your release word is.

Use Treats

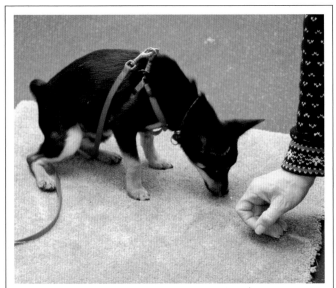

- Luring him down with a treat in front of his nose makes it really easy for him to understand what "down" means.

- To you, it's a position. To your dog, it's an action. Lying from a sit and lying from a stand are two different commands for your

- dog and need to be taught separately.

- Dogs are very concrete thinkers and need to learn how to generalize. After your dog is taught from both positions, he will understand the command either way.

You will spend only a short time luring your dog—as soon as he has the concept, stop luring. Practice down from both a stand and a sit. Get him geeked up for the treat first. "Treat? Are you gonna down for this, gonna down?" Soon he'll start offering the behavior in order to get the reward.

MAKE IT EASY

Being compelled into a down is a submissive position. Some dominant dogs dislike it for this reason, and submissive dogs may feel vulnerable. Make it a game with fast downs and lots of praise interspersed with playing. Let the dog feel that he's accomplished something wonderful by lying down for you.

Moving Down

- Make it even more challenging and fun by teaching a moving down. Start with him walking by your side.

- Slow to a crawl, put your hand in front of his face, and tell him to down while at your side. This will be new because he is probably used to you being in front of him. Big reward!

- With patience, you'll be able to teach him to down fast and stay on command while you keep going without breaking your stride.

Use Hand Signals

- Using a hand signal works well, especially if you're a distance from the dog. Start with just a few feet away and use a well-aimed, thrown treat as a reward.

- Hand signals can come in handy if your dog loses his hearing as he ages, as many dogs do.

- Don't make an older or arthritic dog lie down if he is unwilling. There is never a reason to make a dog do something that hurts him.

139

"STAY"

Another great tool for teaching a dog self-control, "stay" is a useful command

After your dog has mastered sits and downs, the "stay" command can be added to help him increase self-control. It's important to remember to always gave a clear release word for him so he knows when to stop staying and to work up to longer stays around distractions very gradually.

Position your dog, put the palm of your hand in front of his face, and tell him to stay. If he is very bouncy, keep your hand in place, wait a second or two, and tell him "OK!" or "Break!" or any release word you choose—just always use the same word. Make your release word very emphatic. Use lots of praise and treats if you wish. Repeat the exercise until he'll stay in position as you lower your hand. If he moves, simply

Use a Leash

- Start out by using a leash on your dog, so that you can give a gentle tug or restrain him if he decides to wander off.

- Be sure to reward him only after you give the release command. Don't reward him for anticipating you

- and starting to get up before you give permission.

- Use a calm voice and demeanor when teaching stay. Flapping around or sounding excited when you want your dog to be still gives him mixed signals.

Step Away

- After he is steady and can stay reliably for several seconds, start slowly stepping away from or around him.

- Most dogs will start to get up as soon as you take a step. Encourage him to stay in one place and give him lots of praise when he does.

- Work up to being able to walk slowly behind him, to the end of the leash and back, and to moving more quickly around him while he stays.

reposition him and repeat the exercise. Always end on a successful execution of a stay.

As with any training exercise, short sessions are most effective. Using TV commercial breaks is a handy strategy. Slowly work on increasing the time until he can stay in place for thirty seconds. Start adding some movement. Step back and forth, walk slowly around him. Work up to moving all the way across the room.

Add distractions slowly. Toss a toy or a treat. Have someone else run past him. As he gets more solid, proof him by saying words other than your emphatic release word—he should stay until he hears that. Take him outside and practice stays. Put him on leash, go to the park, and practice. A long line will come in very handy to work distance safely. If he seems to be having trouble, he is telling you to slow down and keep the difficulty at a level he can handle for a little longer. Set him up to succeed!

Use Release Words

- Stay is a useful skill for a controlled canine.

- Always use a release word. If you let him get up and wander off without permission, he'll just learn that it's OK to break a stay when he feels like it.

- On longer stays, reinforce the duration by telling him "good stay" and giving him a treat.

- It's more comfortable for him to lie down for longer stays.

Use Hand Signals

- A hand signal is useful for working at a distance or in a noisy environment or if your dog becomes old and deaf.

- Hand signal-trained dogs impress other people with your training prowess!

- Practice short out-of-sight stays with a helper who can correct your dog if he breaks his stay in your absence.

- Use play as well as treats—a thrown ball or a game of tug—as a reward for a successful stay.

"GIVE IT UP"

Your dog should drop whatever is in his mouth, even food, on command

Dogs don't always know what's good for them. A dropped pill bottle or cooked chicken bone can be snatched up in a second, and you want her to drop dangerous items on command. Use a little sneaky bribery and play to teach your dog to give up whatever is in her mouth instantly.

Encourage your dog to take a toy or chewie in her mouth.

Grab one end and hold a fragrant treat in front of her while giving your "drop it" command. The moment she releases the item to take the treat, praise and reward. Enthusiastically return the item, telling her to take it—this way you're teaching her two commands in the same session.

Gradually escalate to more valuable items, like jerky sticks.

Play Tug

- Playing tug is a positive way to teach a dog to release something. Her reward is resumption of play or the occasional treat.

- If your dog understands that it's rewarding to relinquish items when asked, resource guarding will never become an issue.

- Make it a game, but if she doesn't comply, calmly take the item from her mouth and reward her for giving it up.

Reward for Good Behavior

- Stop play before asking her to release something. This gives her a heads-up that you're expecting her to let go.

- Practice dropping a toy onto the floor and making an unpleasant "aack" sound when she tries picking it up.

- Reward her for paying attention and ignoring what you dropped. Using an unpleasant sound is more startling and informative to the dog than saying "no."

- Work up to being able to drop food onto the floor and having her avoid it.

Increase the interval between her release and the reward. Start requiring a sit or down before handing over a treat. If she enjoys tug games or fetch, use the release command during play. Treats are not generally required during play—her reward will be praise and resumption of play with you. Treats should be phased out after she understands the concept. The goal is for her to drop a porterhouse steak on request.

She may decide to turn it into a game by running away instead. Don't play; instead ignore her. Lesson learned? If she runs away with the item, you'll stop playing. If she simply refuses to release the item, place your hand over her muzzle and squeeze until she lets go, then reward.

What is she learning from these exercises? That you control the resources. And that if she doesn't obey, you will either stop being fun or will force her to comply. That interaction with you, on your terms, is rewarding. That is the basis for a deep bond between dog and owner.

Plan B

- If your dog won't release an item, even for an enticing treat, take it away. There's no need to be rough.

- Put your hand over her muzzle and squeeze gently near her back teeth. When she opens her mouth, take the toy and immediately reward or praise her.

- If she growls or guards "her" toy, don't force the issue. Refer to the next chapter on resource guarding and go back to basics with training.

Make It a Game

- If your dog understands that it's rewarding to relinquish items when asked, resource guarding will never become an issue. If she gets away with refusing to give up an item, she learns to disrespect you.

- Make it a game, but if she doesn't comply, calmly take the item from her mouth and reward her for giving it up.

- A dog who growls or threatens is putting both herself and people around her at risk. Find professional help.

JUMPING ONTO PEOPLE
Many dogs are compulsive greeters; teach yours an alternate behavior

Dogs sniff muzzles (and butts) as part of their normal greeting rituals. Puppies and submissive dogs often lick the muzzles of older and more dominant dogs. So when dogs jump up to greet us, they are engaging in very natural, albeit unwanted, greeting behavior. Picking up small dogs in response to jumping encourages more jumping. Giving negative attention by yelling or repeating "down" (which can confuse a dog

taught that "down" is lying down) rarely works. What works is not letting the dog get a reward for the behavior and giving an alternate, acceptable greeting behavior instead.

When she tries jumping, avoid eye contact, cross your arms, remain silent, and quickly turn away. She wants contact and affirmation by jumping, so don't give them to her. Commanding her to get off or pushing her affirms her jumping and is

Do Not Reinforce

- It's important to never reinforce your dog for jumping, and even saying "No jump!" is a form of reinforcement for some dogs. The key is turning away silently and ignoring the dog consistently.

- Don't get mad. Your dog is engaging in very natural behavior.

- If your dog is nipping, mouthing, or displaying any mounting behavior at the same time, it's time to contact a professional. This behavior is crossing the line from over-eager greeting to pushy dominance and is potentially dangerous.

Hold the Paws

- Some dogs are not deterred by being ignored or have gotten away with jumping up for a long time.

- Try holding your dog's paws every time she jumps without speaking or making eye contact. Most dogs dislike this. There is no need to squeeze or pinch her feet.

- Gently drop her after a few seconds and turn away. Praise if she comes back to you and keeps all four feet on the floor.

144

rarely effective. Most importantly, tell everyone she meets to do the same thing or keep her on leash so she simply cannot jump onto strangers and thus reinforce the behavior. Often it is helpful to completely ignore her when you first walk in the door until she has settled down a bit and avoid enthusiastic greetings.

As soon as she has "all four on the floor," praise her calmly. If she jumps up at the praise, turn away again. Start giving her an alternate greeting behavior like sitting and offering a paw. Some dogs like to go fetch a toy when someone walks in the door, others will sit up on their hind legs and look cute. Encourage any natural greeting behavior that doesn't involve jumping up onto people.

Don't allow your dog to jump up onto you or others when they are sitting down either because allowing this gives her a confusing message. The key to curing jumping up is absolute consistency.

Keep Greetings Low-Key

- Keep greetings low-key and always praise for any acceptable actions, like sitting politely or acting neutral.

- Tell children to pretend to be a statue if the dog jumps up. Dogs don't find statues interesting.

- Leash or crate your dog when people visit if the jumping could potentially cause harm or distress.

- Use these techniques with little puppies, too—little puppies learn fast, and it's no fair changing the rules when they get bigger.

Ignore a Hyper Dog

- Some dogs like to greet newcomers with a toy in their mouths. Take advantage of this habit by praising it as long as he's not jumping up.

- Avoid the temptation to respond by immediately playing with him because doing this can condition him to assume that all visitors will start playing with him the minute they walk in the door.

- Having everyone ignore a hyper dog upon walking in the door is a good strategy.

145

LEASH PULLING

Some dogs are "power pullers" and need remedial work on their leash manners

Your dog has been home all day. You come home, feed him, and let him hang around for a while before going for a walk. By this time he is bursting with energy and very eager. Almost every dog pulls on leash, especially high-energy dogs. We walk too slowly. They want to run and explore and sniff. Strolling at your side, at your pace, isn't as much fun. You need to make it fun and realize that it takes two to pull. Remember that every time he achieves forward motion by pulling, he has learned that pulling can work.

Until your dog has learned to walk politely, use a nylon or leather leash instead of a flexi. Training collars and halters are great tools, but teach very sensitive dogs and puppies under

Have Patience

- Leash pulling is one of the most common training hurdles to overcome. The first rule is never to let your dog get anywhere, not a single step, when he pulls.

- This means you might not make it past your block for a while.

- It takes patience, but you have your dog's whole life to teach him.

- Until he learns not to pull, make sure he gets enough exercise by playing fetch or running him in a safe area.

Correcting Leash Pulls

- Making lots of high-speed turns every time he pulls gets his attention. He'll be frustrated in his efforts to charge ahead and will eventually realize it's more rewarding to follow you.

- A training collar or head halter can make a huge difference when used correctly.

- If he pulls or acts aggressive whenever he sees another dog or a person, avoid using a choke or prong collar because doing so will increase his frustration. Head halters work better.

six months old using a regular collar. Jerking on the leash is rarely effective, no matter what collar you are using.

If the basic method involving stopping every time he pulls hasn't worked, go to Phase 2: crazy walking. As you walk, continually change directions. Turn left, right, and do U-turns. Vary your speed. You are not jerking the dog around but rather making him realize that he needs to pay attention to you and to follow in order to keep on walking, so don't tell him you're changing directions, let him figure it out by watching you. Each time he is by your side, praise him like crazy. You may find it easier to practice first in a low-distraction setting like your back yard or an empty parking lot.

Keep the interest up by using treats and toys while walking. Ask him for sits or down at curbs. Encourage him to jump up and off park benches on command. Making walks interactive will keep his attention on you.

Mix It Up

- Mix it up by adding sits, downs, and even hand-shakes for treats. It's all about keeping attention on you.

- Vary your speed if you can. Switch from slow walking to jogging.

- For many dogs, walking with their whole family instead of one person encourages them to stay with their "pack."

- Walking a dog on a long line reduces pulling while getting him used to staying with you on walks.

Use Treats and Toys

- Hold the leash with your dominant hand and use the other for holding toys, giving treats, and touching your dog for attention and praise.

- Keep his interest by asking for other behaviors like sitting at the curb and frequently changing direc-tions. He'll sense frustration, so stay upbeat and don't get mad!

- Getting and holding a dog's attention in a high-stimuli setting like a walk outside are challenging. The more interacting, training, and playing you do, the better his overall attention will be.

BARKING

Some breeds were bred for their vocal skills: How to quiet a barking dog

Understanding why your dog barks excessively is the key to quieting him. We want our dogs to alert us, but we don't want them barking for hours at falling leaves. Boredom and breed tendency, or a combination of the two, are common reasons why dogs bark. Some herding and hunting dogs bark a lot because they were bred to. Bored dogs bark to amuse them-

selves. Hyper dogs start cussing at a squirrel, get wound up, and keep on barking. Nervous or territorial dogs bark to warn away Scary Things.

Don't yell when he's barking; yelling reinforces the excitement level. Allow a few woofs, then calmly say "thank you" and call your dog. Reward and distract him when he comes

Why Dogs Bark

- Dogs commonly bark when they want attention, when they are left behind, or when they spend time alone.

- Puppies are vocal when they are hungry or uncomfortable. They're making noise to get Mama's at-

tention. This is normal. We often continue to reinforce the behavior by responding to it, like letting the dog in or out in response to barking.

- If nobody is present to control barking, a vocal dog can bark all day long.

Territorial Behavior

- Dogs who are triggered by visual stimuli like the sight of people through a window will be quieter if they are not allowed access to the window. Always think of commonsense management solutions!

- Barking at passers-by is usually territorial behavior.

When you're home, call your dog after a couple of woofs and have him do something else, like sit for a treat.

- If he is social, consider taking him outside with a bag of treats to meet people he usually barks at.

to you. Done consistently, doing this can condition him into barking a couple of times, then looking to you for guidance. Make sure he gets sufficient exercise and training or schedule doggie day care periodically—tired dogs don't bark.

If he barks when you're gone, try feeding him his meals in an interactive toy so he has to work for his food. A run or playtime before work will help blow off energy. Excessive barking at visitors is often solved by giving him an alternate behavior, like sitting for a treat, running for a toy, or showing off tricks. If he is being fearful or acting aggressive (these two look simi-lar; if you're unsure, get a professional evaluation), you may have to separate and crate him until he has calmed down.

Barking can often be managed. If a dog barks when left alone outside, bring him in. If he barks at the front window, restrict window access. Antibark collars can be used for some vocal dogs but not for dogs who bark because of separation anxiety or aggression because such a collar can make his behavior worse.

Social Isolation

- Social isolation is a common reason for dogs to bark, especially if they are left alone and bored much of the time.

- Not only is this practice unfair to a dog, but also excess barking bothers neighbors and may be violating local laws.

- Bring the dog inside, train and exercise him, give him interactive toys and chewies daily, teach him tricks, take him hunting—whatever it takes to integrate the dog into your family so he doesn't spend unreasonably long stretches of time alone.

Barking on Command

- Teaching a dog to bark on command can be a handy strategy because then it's easier to tell him to stop. Use a clicker and treats or treats alone to reward only barking on command and silence on command.

- If you have a notoriously vocal breed, you may have to accept some level of barking as part of his personality.

- Dogs who really bark excessively for no apparent reason may need behavioral or veterinary intervention.

149

SEPARATION ANXIETY

Deal with the dog who becomes frantic in your absence through conditioning and management

A common misconception is that dogs who potty in the house or are destructive when alone are "being spiteful." Dogs don't get spiteful. Some dogs get anxious when left alone, and this is called "separation anxiety," and it's not uncommon. A dog may just potty or chew one item—usually her owner's—or she may become terrified and wreak destruction.

Separation anxiety can manifest when there's a change in household schedules or in some dogs from puppyhood. Undersocialized and unconfident dogs are more susceptible.

Chastising her when you find a mess makes things worse because she will associate your homecoming with displeasure and be even more stressed. Crating her will help keep her and

Is This Separation Anxiety?

- Your dog "misbehaves" only when left alone.

- SA could be merely boredom due to lack of exercise and training, so rule this out.

- She potties inside, especially on your bed or in the bedroom.

- She is very distressed when you leave, even during short absences such as when you close the bathroom door and leave her out.

- She howls and barks when you leave and gets overexcited when you return.

- She does any of the above and is untrained and seems generally anxious or fearful.

Preventing Anxiety

- Crating or confining a dog with some great toys and chewies may help her feel less anxious.

- Dogs are natural pack animals. Being left alone means potential starvation and fear of being vulnerable to larger predators.

- Owners often unwittingly contribute by being lax in training and allowing a dog to follow them everywhere. Doing this creates underconfidence. Well-trained dogs used to occasional absences deal better with stress.

your belongings safe but won't cure anxiety, and some dogs get so distraught they'll hurt themselves trying to escape.

Depending on the severity, curing SA may take a multi-pronged approach. Keep all arrivals and departures low-key. It's OK to completely ignore your dog for a while when you come home. Don't get angry and don't coddle her for being anxious. Have a word you use every time you walk out of the door, even to take out the trash, so she starts associating that with your coming back eventually. Give her a hard rubber toy filled with food or frozen yogurt when you leave the house.

Practice short absences and work on the stay command. Get her confident in your return, even from another room. Increase general training and consider classes because trained dogs are more confident and in control. Make sure she gets plenty of exercise and play.

It may not hurt also to talk to your vet about anti-anxiety medication to calm her. Used short term and in conjunction with behavior modification, this medication can be very effective.

Anxiety Medications

- Talk to your vet about anxiety medications. For more severe cases, meds can really help.

- Medication alone is never enough. You must also make behavioral changes.

- There are herbal remedies that may help but could be worth a try. If your dog is on any other meds, make sure it's OK to give both simultaneously.

- Be careful about using herbal essential oils, especially on toy dogs. Check first with your vet because some can be toxic.

Ground Rules

- Train, don't coddle, your dog. Anxious dogs are comforted by clear rules and fair training, not by being spoiled.

- Make sure she gets daily exercise.

- Get her used to a crate, x-pen, or baby gate.

- Practice short absences.

- Keep coming and going low key.

- When you leave, give her a long-lasting chew.

- Ignore her on your return until she calms down.

- Never get angry with her. She is frightened, not spiteful.

RESOURCE GUARDING

Guarding food, toys, and people is a potentially serious problem to be addressed immediately

We all protect what is valuable to us, and dogs are no different. Guarding items from other dogs in the house is natural and can be managed, but a dog who gets growly over food or other resources is assuming entirely too much power in the household. The key is to request obedience for every treat or praise and do a little training every day and not to give her petting and attention for simply looking cute.

Control all resources from day one so she doesn't see you as competition but as a "benevolent dictator" who hands out good things like food and play as long as the rules are followed. Avoid free feeding. Instead, call your dog to you and request a sit before feeding. Don't allow anyone, particularly

Guarding Property

- As benevolent dictator, you provide good things for your dog, including food.

- Apart from simple exercises to add food or treats to her bowl, don't pester her while she is eating. You could make her feel that her food is always threatened, which will make her feel justified in guarding it.

- It's OK for dogs to protect their food from other dogs. If this is an issue in a multiple-dog household, crate or separate the dogs during mealtime.

Make Dogs Work for Food

- Request that your dog "work" for all food and treats. She must understand that you provide everything good in her life as long as she behaves nicely.

- Teach her to take treats nicely. Close your hand around the treat and let her have it only if she's not being grabby. Use tiny little crumb-sized treats so she doesn't get too eager.

- Practice "take it nice" after meals, when she is already full.

152

children, to pester her during mealtimes. Instead, walk up to her while she is eating, drop a hot dog piece or treat into her food, and walk away again. If she growls, feed her all meals by hand while demanding a sit or down for a week and try again.

Chewies, particularly high-value ones like rawhides, can trigger snotty behavior. Don't avoid the problem by simply not giving these items because that solves nothing, and you still have a disrespectful dog who will take advantage when she can. Start with a lower-value toy. Wait until she is playing with it and approach her with a better toy or treat. Tell her to drop it, and when she does, she gets a treat and praise; give the toy back. Work on the "give it up" exercises every day.

If your dog is threatening, and you fear she may bite you, get professional help. These situations might be manageable with some help.

Trade with Dogs

- The point of trading with a dog is to let her know that she doesn't have to guard items from you and that your proximity often means a reward for her.

- She should willingly trade, especially if she gets a good treat for letting you take something away and then gets it back.

- If she growls or shows teeth, you need to re-evaluate your day-to-day interactions.

Use Treats and Games

- Some dogs guard furniture (or laps!). First, don't allow her up without permission. Use bubble wrap or plastic carpet protectors to deter her.

- Make a game out of getting up and off furniture. Use a leash at first if you have to. Have a command like "hup!" for getting on and "off!" for getting down. Use treats to reward jumping off only.

- Don't attempt to drag or force a threatening dog from her place. This could get you bitten.

AGGRESSION

Dogs express several drives through aggressive behavior, and it should not be taken lightly

Aggression takes many forms. A dog may be aggressive to other dogs or other animals but trustworthy with people. Some tend to be dog-aggressive, and many terriers and hounds have a strong prey drive to chase and kill smaller animals. Animal-aggressive dogs don't have to be friends with animals they meet but can be taught to control themselves.

Frustration and overeagerness on leash often look like belligerence but really aren't, and jerking or yelling is futile. Group classes led by an experienced trainer will teach a dog self-control.

Fear-aggressive dogs cringe and may bite when they feel threatened. Dominant-aggressive dogs are pushy and often

Types of Aggression

- Fear/defensive: The dog is taking a pro-active stance, warning away anything that scares him.

- Territorial: This is a natural guarding instinct exhibited to varying degrees from merely barking to attacking.

- Dominance: This is shown by a dog who perceives himself as ranking higher than many people and other dogs.

- Interdog: Some dogs are aggressive toward other dogs, particularly those of the same sex.

- Prey/predatory: Many dogs have a strong hunting instinct to chase and kill small animals, including smaller pets.

Modifying Aggression

- Most types of aggression can be avoided, modified, or managed. The size and breed are irrelevant—any dog can bite.

- The fear-aggressive dog is the least predictable. What we perceive as harmless she may well perceive as threatening.

- A dominant dog who threatens his owners in any way is not properly trained and does not respect them.

- Dominant, aggressively territorial and fearful dogs are potentially dangerous and need intervention with a knowledgeable trainer.

show warning signs. Overly "protective" dogs who resource guard and growl at family members give a clear signal that they don't respect their humans. All types benefit from consistent training and having to comply with a command before eating, getting a treat, or being petted. They're not allowed onto furniture and don't get carried around or cuddled. Coupled with ongoing obedience training, this practice teaches a dog to be confident in her place in the family.

The root of most aggressive behavior is genetic and may be modified for the better or worse through training. Dogs who are unsocialized, untrained, or chained up can become aggressive. Dogs who are untrained and spoiled, even doted on, often become aggressive, too. This condition is common with small, pampered dogs. Dogs love those whom they respect and those who give them guidance. This is why basic training and socialization are so important. Aggression in dogs may be managed, but it shouldn't be ignored.

Aggressive behavior toward humans needs professional intervention. Ask your vet or local training facility for a recommendation to a behaviorist or knowledgeable trainer.

Avoid Fight or Flight Situations

- Don't put an aggressive dog into a "fight or flight" situation. If yours is comfortable with other dogs at 30 feet away but not at 10 feet, maintain distance while you work on keeping her attention on you.

- Interdog aggression and predatory behavior do not mean there is anything wrong with your dog. They are natural behavior. These can often be moderated and managed but rarely eliminated.

- Aggression toward animals and aggression toward people are two separate dynamics.

Dealing with Aggression

- Get a consultation with a good trainer or behaviorist.

- Clearly understand whether the aggression needs to be modified through training or must be managed for life.

- Training consists of setting and enforcing very clear rules.

- Don't correct aggression with punishment. Doing this usually makes matters worse.

- Management depends on the aggression type. It could mean not letting your dog around any small animals, providing secure containment, or even muzzling the dog in public.

- The safety of others should be your primary concern.

EXERCISE REQUIREMENTS

If your dog has her exercise needs fulfilled, other behavior problems may disappear

There's an easy cure for many behavioral problems: exercise. Dogs are pack animals like wolves who spend much of their time interacting and hunting. They have been bred for centuries to herd, hunt, and guard. Modern dogs don't work much and adapt to spending most of their time inside or in small yards, often alone. This is fine, but owners need to in-

vest a little time exercising Fido for both weight and behavioral management.

Active breeds like Labradors, goldens, collies, and many terriers are better behaved and easier trained when they get plenty of exercise, especially in their first few years of life. Activity level is not determined by size, although it's easier to

Dogs Need Plenty of Exercise

- Exuberant retrievers are easy to wear out with a tennis racquet or tennis-ball thrower.

- Few dogs get much exercise by merely being outside by themselves, even in a large yard. They benefit from aerobic and muscle-building activity.

- Friendly dogs benefit from having another dog to play with sometimes. Try play dates and day care.

- Small dogs are easy to exercise indoors. Unlike bigger dogs, they can run full speed inside.

Use a Treadmill

- Dogs can learn to use a treadmill, either one designed for dogs or one that people use.

- Start very slowly when introducing a dog to a treadmill. You might need to get on with him and use lots of treats or even start

by feeding him there when it's turned off.

- Keep treadmill sessions short and don't let your dog run himself into exhaustion.

- This can "take the edge off" before practicing leash manners on a walk.

exercise a little dog inside. Jack Russell terriers are small but have extremely high exercise requirements, whereas great Danes are laidback enough to be content with minimal daily exercise.

Exuberant dogs left to their own devices may bark, dig, be destructive, or develop anxiety or even aggressive behaviors. Exercising doesn't have to be a time-consuming chore. Play fetch in the back yard or even in the house. Put a backpack on the dog and take a short, brisk walk. Train him to run with a bicycle or roller skates. Teach the dog tricks and do some obedience play-training. Arrange play dates with friends' dogs or look into doggie day care. Sign up for classes in obedience or dog sports. Take your dog to a beach or a river. Find a pet sitter or neighbor to take your dog for walks when you're at work. Look for interactive, problem-solving dog toys. Dogs can learn to run on a treadmill. Start a fitness walking routine for yourself and bring the dog along. Remember the saying: If you're overweight, your dog isn't getting enough exercise!

Controlled Jumping

- Controlled jumping is a fun game for dogs but don't let them overdo it and avoid repeated jumping with a growing pup.

- Keeping jumps at elbow height or lower is generally safe.

- Toss toys and treats over for him to get.

- If he's unwilling to jump, start by having him jump over something flat on the ground or setting up a very low jump in a hallway so he has no choice.

Mental Exercise Is Important

- Although physical exercise is important, mental exercise can wear a dog out as well.

- Hide treats and let your dog find them. Put a treat under little cups and see how quickly she finds the right cup.

- Use games like this to reinforce basic commands like "come," "sit," and "stay."

- Play hide and seek, get a book on clicker training (see the resources chapter), teach tricks, and work on quick obedience exercises.

EXERCISE

WALKS
Walking with a dog is one reason why many people get a dog to begin with

Dogs' wild cousins, like wolves, travel 10 or more miles per day hunting. Chances are your dog doesn't need to walk farther than across the kitchen floor for her dinner, but roaming is an instinctual desire in dogs. Walks help satisfy that desire. Being walked regularly gets your dog used to other dogs, people, sights, and smells. It keeps her muscles and heart strong and calms her down. And, of course, the human on the other end of the leash benefits, too.

A dog who is already good at walking on leash can be walked on a retractable leash, but such a lease doesn't offer enough control and tension to teach a dog. Until she has learned, a 20-foot cotton leash is great for providing a bit

Country Walks

- Every dog loves a country walk, but be aware of wildlife dangers. Dogs can get bitten by snakes and ticks or take off after deer or get stung by insects.

- Carry a basic first aid kit on hikes and keep your dog under control.

- Make sure she is wearing ID, especially when hiking in unfamiliar terrain where she could get lost.

- See Chapter 8 for more on doggie backpacks. Using one can maximize the effectiveness of a walk.

Long Leashes

- Dogs tend to pull less on a longer leash because they have more room to walk at a natural speed.

- For trained dogs, a flexible leash gives them room to walk at their own pace and stop and sniff and is less likely to be tangled.

- Be careful not to let your dog run or swim while dragging a leash. There are too many things, including her legs, it can get caught on.

more freedom in rural settings, and a 6-foot leash is perfect for city walks.

It's worth it to stick with obedience classes and leash training; otherwise you end up with a dog who rarely gets to leave her property. There is a plethora of collars and halters to make walking easier until she knows the rules. Putting a backpack onto an exuberant dog gives her a job and an enhanced workout. Load the pack with water and collapsible drinking bowls and take a hike. Find other dog owners and make it a group exercise.

Overweight or out-of-condition dogs won't be able to do extended day hikes right away—you'll need to work up to it. Dogs are much less heat tolerant than humans, especially if they have short snouts or heavy fur. When your dog is getting tired or overheated she'll slow down and pant excessively. And although larger, furry dogs love snowy weather, smaller, lighter-coated dogs can get quite chilled, so watch for shivering and limit exposure in extreme cold.

Walks in a Group

- Walking in a group is fun, and dogs walking with other people and dogs tend to walk better on leash because they feel like part of a pack.

- Ask friends and neighbors if they'll start a walking program with you and your dog.

- When dogs are introduced during a walk, they're much more relaxed. Don't let them spend a lot of time getting introduced—just start walking.

Hikes

- If you hike alone in back-country, always make sure you let someone know where you will be headed.

- Carry a fully charged cell phone and take common-sense precautions for the weather and terrain.

- Obey leash laws. Dogs can disturb other hikers and wildlife when off leash, and most parks that allow dogs have leash laws.

- Always carry a poop bag, whether hiking in the wilderness or strolling in your local park.

BIKING

Bicycling with your dog is an effective and healthy way to wear her out

Biking with a dog is an efficient way to wear her out fast and give her the flat-out running she needs. Most dogs are quickly trained to run safely next to a bicycle. There are several bike attachments on the market that require virtually no training, and even large, rambunctious dogs are held safely next to the bike. Mountain bike enthusiasts often ride with high-endurance dogs, but a more sedentary dog relishes the change of pace, too.

Dogs should be biked only on trails or in quiet suburban areas, not in traffic. Let your dog set the pace and have her run on grass or dirt as much as possible because extended running on hard surfaces can crack paw pads. Exuberant dogs

Bike Attachments

- It's possible to bike while holding your dog's leash, but this is an accident waiting to happen.

- Bike attachments are fairly inexpensive and, despite their lightweight look, are designed to keep the largest dog under control without pulling you off the bicycle.

- Biking allows a larger dog to trot at her natural gait instead of adjusting to a slower human pace.

Other Bike Attachments

- Some models attach to the rear axle, some to the frame, and some to the seat post.

- Look for a bike attachment that allows your dog to run right beside you instead of slightly behind.

- Most are designed to keep the leash well away from moving parts while giving the dog just enough reach to run next to the bicycle.

- Most dogs are so intent and satisfied with running that they don't want to stop and sniff or chase anything.

may want to race at full speed until they're exhausted. Slow her down if you think she's overdoing it and carry water if you'll be going more than a few miles, especially on warmer days. Avoid biking with a dog until she is about one year old because that pavement pounding can be damaging to young joints.

Follow packaging instructions if you get an attachment. Most attachments can be put to use right away. Teaching a dog to run on leash next to a bike does require a dog with basic leash manners, and it's not a bad idea to use a training collar and halter at first. Start with walking your dog alongside the bicycle and don't let her cross in front of the wheel. Some dogs will have to be trained not to nip or "herd" the bicycle wheels at first, and some might be nervous about the whole experience. Start slowly in a safe area. If you have good balance, ride one-handed while holding the leash in the other for better control.

Be Mindful of Your Dog

- Avoid busy roads or those with higher speed limits.

- Whereas a cyclist may be visible, drivers are less likely to notice a dog alongside. Having your dog wear a brightly colored vest makes him instantly visible.

- Although a short bike ride is almost effortless for the rider, an accompanying dog is working hard. A few blocks might be a good distance to start out with, depending on your dog's age and condition.

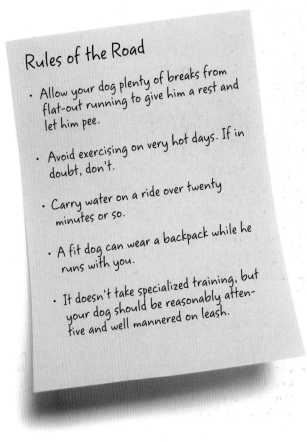

Rules of the Road

- Allow your dog plenty of breaks from flat-out running to give him a rest and let him pee.

- Avoid exercising on very hot days. If in doubt, don't.

- Carry water on a ride over twenty minutes or so.

- A fit dog can wear a backpack while he runs with you.

- It doesn't take specialized training, but your dog should be reasonably attentive and well mannered on leash.

TRICKS

Tricks can be silly or useful, but your dog will amaze you with her abilities

It might seem silly to teach a dog to shake hands or roll over—after all, that's not real work. But your dog doesn't know that. Teaching tricks, along with providing obedience training, helps her learn to learn.

The easiest tricks are whatever your dog does naturally. Smaller dogs often find it easy to sit up on their haunches or stand on their hind legs, whereas larger dogs may need a hand. Offer your big dog both hands and encourage her to jump with her paws in your hands—call it "dancing." Almost any dog will shake hands. Put your dog in a sit and ask her to shake while nudging the back of her front leg until her paw is up. Praise or treat and repeat. Most dogs are either right-

Costumes

- Don't forget proper costumes for maximum impact, especially for parties and special events.

- Make sure any costume doesn't impede your dog's movement and bear in mind that some can get in the way of pottying!

- Most dogs adjust fine to wearing ridiculous clothing, especially if they are already used to wearing coats or backpacks. If yours seems distressed by the idea, perhaps stick with a simple bandanna or understated string of pearls.

Fun Tricks

- Waving hello and bye-bye is a perennial favorite. Start with a simple paw shake and gradually ask your dog to raise the paw higher. With rewards, he'll start doing this on command without your offering your hand.

- Approach trick training with a fun attitude and never use corrections. This is not crucial training, although it can help with overall skills. It's just for entertainment and amusement.

- Some movements and positions are uncomfortable for arthritic dogs.

or left- "handed," or you'll find she'll have a preference. After she's got it, work on right and left, paw and other paw, wave bye-bye, or high five.

Make tricks cute by having creative commands. Teach "roll over" while your dog is lying down by luring her with a treat into being belly up, then give big praise. You can call it "bang," "belly rubs," or "would you rather be dead than [use your imagination!]?" If she barks, put an arithmetic cue to it. Tell people your dog can do calculus by figuring out the square root of 1, or if she lets out a volley of barks, come up with a question with "really a lot" as the answer. Lure your dog into a spin with a treat, then reverse the direction and call it "nips."

Impressive tricks, like having your dog fetch a drink from the fridge are just simple tricks strung together. If your dog does easy tricks, she can do the really cool ones.

Tricks on Command

- Is this cocker spaniel counting on command or about to roll over and play dead?

- The beauty of trick training is that by being creative with commands, you can turn almost anything into a trick.

- Choose behaviors that she does willingly, like rolling over, barking, or retrieving, and put creative commands to them.

- If your dog is having a hard time understanding a particular command, don't force the issue. Just find something that's easier for her to do.

Natural Ability Tricks

- Use your dog's natural abilities to teach suitable tricks.

- Standing up, and even walking on their hind legs, comes easily for many smaller dogs. This is not something that most large dogs can do.

- Use treats as a lure at first to get her into position, then phase them out until you're rewarding only intermittently. Beware: A trained dog will start offering her repertoire of behaviors in order to get a treat out of you!

STRUCTURED PLAY

Training doesn't have to be boring; turn it into structured play time

Incorporate play into regular obedience training for a more willing worker who is attentive to you. Using play in training strengthens the bond between you and your dog and is a nice alternative to dry commands or frequent use of treats. Play training encourages interaction with you and increases his enthusiasm for training. Dogs have an innate play drive, and if your dog likes to play fetch, play with squeaky toys, or play tug, playing is a really useful tool in your training toolbox.

Use a special, favorite toy for training only. As with any type of training, keep sessions short and high energy and quit while the dog is still eager for more. Always remember that you control the toy, so if he plays keep away or runs with it, get it back and end the session and avoid setting him up so he can get control.

Tug Toys

- Using a tug toy you can teach "take it" and "give it up." The tug can be used as a lure to shape behavior and as a reward for a job well done. Use a simple piece of knotted rope to increase drive and focus.

- Although many dogs play-growl fiercely while tugging, a dog who growls or refuses to give it up is resource guarding.

- Control the game by initiating and ending it.

Toys as Rewards

- Children should never play tug or chase with a dog because doing so can set up a dominance or prey mind-set.

- For enthusiastic tuggers, stop, relax, and say "out" in a growly voice. Most dogs will let go, especially if they sometimes get the toy back as a reward.

- Use a toy instead of a treat as a reward for holding a sit or down stay. For toy-oriented dogs, doing this can be just as rewarding as food rewards.

Despite what you might have read, tug is an excellent way to teach several commands. Use a fast game of tug as a reward for sit, down, or come. Teach him to take something on command by saying "take it" and offering it to him. Work on "give it up" by encouraging him to tug. Then stop tugging, be still, and give the command in a low, growly voice. If this doesn't work, pry his jaws away from it and praise him the moment the toy is free. His reward? He gets the toy right back.

Leashwork is learned more readily if it's interactive. Vary your walking speed. Use treats intermittently and bring a favorite toy along. Put treats inside an empty pop bottle for a little variety. Instead of doing training sessions standing up, try doing them while sitting or lying on the floor and see how your dog does. Mix it up and make it fun.

Your Dog, a Willing Worker

- The most important benefit of using play in training is turning your dog into a willing worker who is attentive and joyfully looks to you for direction.

- Just because you're playing doesn't mean she isn't learning! Toys and play build drive and focus.

- Alternate letting your dog run off leash with having short leash sessions, giving lots of treats, praise, and play while she is on leash. This gives her the idea that being leashed doesn't mean being bored.

Distraction Proofing Toys

- Use toys for distraction-proofing stays. If your dog can hold a stay command while a toy is thrown in front of her, you're doing very well.

- Increase the distraction level slowly. Start with rolling a ball and slowly work up to throwing it or using an enticing squeaky toy.

- If she realizes that she gets rewarded for controlling herself, she'll comply—but set her up to succeed by taking things slowly.

EXERCISE

DOG SPORTS

Whether you take classes just for fun or compete, use your dog's natural abilities

You don't have to be athletic, and your dog doesn't need to be impeccably trained to get involved with dog sports, and mixed-breed dogs can train and even compete in most venues. Dog sports are becoming increasingly egalitarian and popular, and training facilities and organizations offer an ever-increasing list of activities.

Some competitive sports are breed (or group) specific. Lure coursing lets sighthounds chase a mechanical lure at high speed over fields. Earthdog lets small terriers negotiate tunnels after quarry. Field, hunting, and herding trials are usually open only to herding and hunting breeds. Whether your dog is purebred or mixed breed, finding a way to let him use his

Freestyle

- Agility, obedience, and canine freestyle take a lot of training, with dog and handler working closely as a team. It is a true working partnership.

- Depending on your dog and your training, you could be ready for competition in six months.

- The primary goal of most sports should first and foremost be to have fun with your dog.

- Earning placement ribbons and titles can be addicting and not as hard as you may think.

Natural Instinct Sports

- Some sports, like earthdog, weight pulling, and lure coursing, require little or no training, relying primarily on the dog's natural instincts.

- Some competitions are breed specific. Earthdog is an AKC sport, and only terriers are eligible. Lure coursing is open to sighthounds through several organizations, although some clubs will let nonsighthounds practice for fun.

- Several organizations sponsor most sports, and mixed-breed dogs are often eligible for competition.

natural potential is an outlet for his energy and a great way to broaden your social horizons, too.

Many dog sports are open to any suitable breed. Dogs of any size who like to throw their weight around can pull carts and sleds and compete in weight pulling. Flyball, Frisbee, and agility are great fun for high-energy dogs. Water-loving canines can train and compete in dock diving, in which dogs race off the end of a dock after a thrown toy and compete for jump length. Canine freestyle pairs dog and owner in musical dance routines. Tracking puts a dog's nose to the ground, using his formidable scenting abilities for fun, competition, or search and rescue. Macho dogs can be trained in schutzhund or other protection sports.

Call training facilities or go online to find activities. Training can be done just for fun or for competition. Junior handling and 4-H allow children to get involved with hands-on training and healthy competition. Visit any dog sport event, and you'll see schlumpy middle-aged people with bad knees alongside kids and retirees having fun with their dogs.

Sports That Need Little Training

- Sports that require some, but not extensive, training are tracking, Frisbee, dock diving, and hunting or field trials.

- You will get the most out of an activity that lets your dog use his natural instincts. Most terriers will be lousy herding dogs, and a nonswimming dog wouldn't enjoy water retrieving.

- If you get involved with a sport, consider joining a club. You will help with sponsored trials, make new friends, and often get reduced entry fees to club events.

Sports That Need Practice

- Most training facilities hold obedience, rally, and agility classes.

- Use the Internet to find opportunities to practice. Look up local or state organizations to locate classes for less-known activities like canine freestyle and earthdog.

- If you'd like to compete, find classes taught by someone who is active in the sport.

- Don't be intimidated! Most participants, even at high-level competition, are just regular folks enjoying a hobby.

NUTRITION 101

Is your dog a carnivore or an omnivore? Take a trip through a dog's digestive system

Domestic dogs are carnivores with a long history as scavengers, and they have adapted well to an omnivorous diet in most parts of the world. Had dogs had very specific dietary needs, it probably would have been impractical to domesticate them. They are opportunistic eaters and have evolved for thousands of years eating human leftovers.

Dogs' primary ancestor is the wolf, and their basic digestive anatomy is essentially unchanged. They have carnivorous teeth, designed for tearing and crushing food instead of chewing it. Their saliva contains no digestive enzymes but lubricates food so it can be gulped. Their jaws cannot move side to side for chewing; rather they can rip large chunks of

KNACK DOG CARE AND TRAINING

Dog Teeth

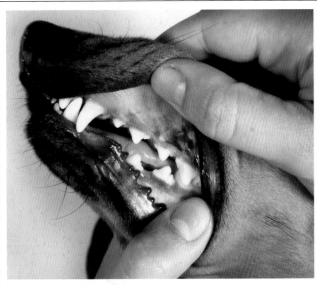

- Dogs' teeth are designed for killing prey, tearing meat, and pulverizing bones.

- Dogs don't naturally chew food carefully because they don't have flat-surfaced chewing molars like omnivores and herbivores do.

- The standard for a correct bite in most breeds is a "scissors bite" in which the incisors slightly overlap each other. This bite allows for efficient use and less wear as the dog ages. Some breeds, like bulldogs, have been bred for an undershot jaw.

Dog Diets

- A good diet provides a healthy coat, few gastrointestinal issues, and one or two bowel movements a day.

- There is no one perfect diet for all dogs. Their needs change with age, pregnancy, whelping, and sometimes breed type.

- If you got your pup from a quality breeder, she will give you feeding guidelines.

- Unlike cats, who are carnivores and need meat proteins to survive, dogs are more easily fed a vegetarian diet, although few veterinary nutritionists recommend doing this.

food and swallow them whole. Although dogs' eating styles can differ, it is completely normal for most dogs to "inhale" their meals. This is probably because as hunters they've adapted to gorging on large amounts of food, never knowing when they'll bring down the next meal.

Their stomachs are highly acidic. Like most carnivores, they can digest bones, fats, and quite disgusting things, usually with few ill effects. Dogs are very efficient at throwing up, as most dog owners know, and can quickly regurgitate unsuitable meals. Digestion time varies a great deal depending on the individual dog and the type of food. It can be anywhere from eight to forty hours, with large dogs tending to digest food more slowly.

Dogs need proteins, minerals, amino acids, and fats to survive. They have no dietary need for carbohydrates or fiber, although they can utilize and digest them. The fact that millions of dogs eat kibble and that most live quite healthy, long lives on kibble is proof of that, although they thrive on other diets as well. With a varied diet, dogs have very sturdy and adaptable digestive systems.

Dog Digestive Systems

- No matter what size the dog, the digestive systems are anatomically identical.

- Puppies and adult dogs utilize some nutrients differently. Adult dogs can excrete excess calcium or tolerate inadequate calcium in the diet for a while. Growing pups need more calcium, and incorrect amounts can lead to serious bone and joint abnormalities.

- Puppies, especially large breeds, should be encouraged to grow slow and lean. Often they benefit from lower protein levels in the diet while growing.

The Digestive System

- When food is swallowed, it passes down the esophagus into the stomach.

- Food is churned and dissolved into a soupy mess called "chyme." Fats, carbohydrates, and proteins are broken down as the chyme moves through the small intestine.

- Most of the nutrients are absorbed through the walls in the small intestine.

- What is left passes into the large intestine, where water is absorbed, and the resulting feces is eliminated.

COMMERCIAL DIETS
The array of products is dizzying, but following some basic rules simplifies feeding choices

For thousands of years most dogs have eaten whatever people didn't want, like table scraps, leftovers from butchering, and cooked grains. The first commercial dog food was made in the 1860s in America, and it has led to the pellets most people now recognize as kibble. Rising concerns about additives to pet food, along with the resurgence in popularity of home-cooked and raw diets since the 1980s, have led to a wide array of commercial foods.

There are hundreds of kibble choices. Generally speaking, the cheaper brands don't provide an optimum daily diet and can result in dull coat, doggie odor, and poor overall condition. Naturally preserved kibbles, using more meat and whole

Finding the Right Food

- Although the cheapest kibble is never a wise choice, the most expensive kibble also may not be the best choice for your dog.

- Some manufacturers charge a premium for dry foods that have "everything and the kitchen sink" in them. Organic cranberries may indeed be good for dogs, but the small amounts processed into kibble may not be useful.

- Some of the best have a short, simple list of ingredients, using whole meat and grains.

Meat

- Better pet stores carry whole-meat canned food in varieties like rabbit, duck, and venison.

- The apparent meat chunks in cheaper canned foods are probably not meat but rather grain gluten processed to look like meat.

- Dog food is also available in rolls, like large salamis.

- Although some foods may seem expensive, it can take several times the amount of low-quality food to provide adequate nutrition compared with high-quality, denser food.

grains instead of meat and grain by-products, are a better choice. Low-quality kibble may be a false economy because more must be fed to provide enough nutrition. Pay attention to labels and don't automatically reach for the expensive "natural" and "holistic" food. These are just marketing terms and have no legal definition.

Moist and canned food can be an excellent addition to the diet. Again, the choices range from poor-quality, chemically laden, semimoist foods to good-quality, meaty canned food. Canned foods are not a great choice for the bulk of the diet because they provide zero dental benefits, but they're great for variety.

There are now grain-free kibbles and kibbles containing freeze-dried meats and vegetables. Some kibbles are formulated to have raw or cooked meats added to them for added nutritional punch. Some foods have extra supplements and nutraceuticals for everything from brain development to joint health (but do your research—many don't contain a useful dose). Go to good pet stores for most of these foods because they won't be on the supermarket shelves.

Read the Ingredients

INGREDIENTS:
Beef, Beef Meal, Cracked Pearled Barley, Brown Rice, Millet, Rice Br (preserved with mixed tocopherols), Ocean Fish Meal, Tomato Pom Natural Flavor, Salmon Oil (source of DHA), Choline Chloride, Taurine Root, Parsley Flakes, Pumpkin Meal, Almond Oil (preserved with mixe Sesame Oil (preserved with mixed tocopherols), Yucca Schidigera E Blueberries, Cranberries, Carrots, Broccoli, Vitamin E Supplement, Iro chelated source of iron), Zinc Proteinate (a chelated source of zinc), Copp chelated source of copper), Ferrous Sulfate, Zinc Sulfate, Copper Sul Iodide, Thiamine Mononitrate, Manganese Proteinate (a chelated source Manganous Oxide, Ascorbic Acid, Vitamin A Supplement, Biotin, Calciu Manganese Sulfate, Sodium Selenite, Pyridoxine Hydrochloride (vitam B12 Supplement, Riboflavin, Vitamin D Supplement, Folic Acid.

GUARANTEED ANALYSIS:
Crude Protein .... 22.00% ....
Crude Fat .... 12.00% ....
Crude Fiber .... 4.00% ....
Moisture .... 10.00% ....
DHA (Docosohexaenoic Acid)........... 0.05% .....*.......
*Not recognized as an essential nutrient by the AAFCO Dog Food N

CALORIE CONTENT (calculated):
Calories (ME) .... 387 kcal/cup..............

- Look for animal protein to be listed more than once in the top five ingredients. Meats should be identified by type (chicken, beef, lamb) instead of as "animal digest" or "meat meal."

- Whole grains (millet, rice, oats) are better than grain by-products (gluten, brewers' rice).

- Avoid foods with added colorants.

- A good barometer of how your dog does on a kibble brand is his stool. It should be firm, small, and fairly low odor.

Canned Foods versus Dry Foods

Liver, Chicken & Rice Formula Mixer
Formule foie, poulet & riz pour chien
For Adult Dogs
Chicken Liver, Chicken, Veggies, Flaxseed & Canola Oil
Simmered in Broth
NET WT 13 OZ/POIDS 369g

- Use the same ingredients quality criteria for canned food as for dry.

- Read the label carefully. Some canned formulas are not meant to be fed as a complete diet but rather are meant to be added occasionally to the regular diet.

- Feed new foods in small amounts at first, although dogs used to variety usually take new foods in stride.

- A dog who eats some moist food daily will require less water than a dog who eats an all-dry diet.

171

RAW FEEDING

This food is becoming increasingly popular and is not as hard as you think

Raw feeding is also referred to as "BARF" (biologically appropriate raw food). The premise is that because dogs evolved from wolves and still have the same digestive anatomy, the ideal canine diet is one of raw meat, bones and organs, and no grains. Proponents claim their dogs have improved health, healthier teeth, and lower incidence of chronic health problems from allergies to cancer. Detractors say that the potential problems caused by eating whole bones and raw meat are not worth the risk and that the diet is a fad. Although some vets actually promote the diet (and two have written books about it), many are skeptical.

Because feeding whole elk and snowshoe rabbits isn't prac-

Switching Diets

- Any changes made to the dog's diet should be gradual to avoid stomach upset and diarrhea.

- Chicken is easy. Buy a whole chicken and whack it into meal-sized parts. To start out with, peel off the skin and fat where possible.

- Hand this meat to your dog. Most take to it immediately.

- Feeding outside or on a towel will ease your fear of bacteria.

- Strict hygiene should be observed when handling and feeding raw meat.

Meat

- Meats have different nutrient profiles, so feeding a variety, both red and white, over time is important.

- There is no need to have every meal "complete and balanced." Balance is achieved in the overall diet instead of in every meal.

- Butchers can order inexpensive meats for you. Hunters, grocery sales, and wholesale buying clubs allow for cheap or free food.

- Strict attention should be paid to balancing the diet, especially calcium needs.

tical for most people, the diet usually consists of a variety of cuts of meat meant to roughly approximate a "prey model" diet consisting of 10–15 percent bones and 5–10 percent organ meats, with the balance being muscle meat. Many people add pulverized vegetables in small amounts. Like vegetables, supplements are considered optional, just as they are with a kibble diet. An adult dog eats roughly 2 percent of his ideal weight in raw food per day, depending on metabolism and activity level. Buying meat from butchers and grocery stores is generally the most economical way to feed.

Commercial pet food companies and local purveyors have also stepped into the market, offering ground raw diets that eliminate the possibility of injury from eating whole bones. Raw mixes are now in many pet stores along with freeze-dried and minimally processed canned foods.

There are several books and thousands of websites about raw diets. Avoid relying on a single source for information and research the topic very well before diving in. Those who feed raw claim it takes little time and effort after you get into a routine.

Raw Bones

- Chewing meaty bones satisfies a primal need in addition to keeping teeth and gums healthy.

- Just as with any diet, dogs of all sizes—even toy breeds—can eat raw.

- Dogs may do just fine on a raw diet, but they should be closely monitored for problems with undigested bones or pathogenic bacteria found in raw meat.

- Feeding ground bones is an option for the nervous, and home grinders are relatively inexpensive.

Provide a Balanced Meal

- A variety of meat, bones, and organs provides many of the protein, minerals, amino acids, and fats a dog needs.

- Commercial raw dog food companies offer products from the mundane to the exotic. You can buy optional bison, goat, rabbit, and emu for the discriminating dog along with chicken, beef, pork, and other basic meats.

- Many commercial raw dog food companies sell preground raw, complete food.

COOKING FOR DOGS
Meals can be done simply ahead of time with some basic recipes

Home cooking is another option, with zero risk of complications from feeding whole bones and raw meats. Proponents make claims similar to those of people who feed raw—improved overall condition, fewer chronic ailments, and greater vigor. Additionally, special diets can be formulated for various illnesses. The arguments against home-cooked dog diets include the cost and time involved and the dif-

ficulty in finding reliable, properly formulated recipes.

Although recipes for cooked diets vary, most authors recommend roughly equal parts cooked whole grains, cooked vegetables, and cooked meat and organs. Because cooked bones are unsafe for dogs, a calcium supplement is essential. Other ingredients like fruit in small amounts, cottage cheese, eggs, and canned fish may be added. Most cooked diet re-

Custom Diets

- Most ingredients except for some supplements can be bought inexpensively at the grocery store.

- Just as with raw or commercial dog food, a variety of proteins is important.

- Some veterinary nutritionists can help dog own-

ers put together cooked custom diets for dogs with chronic conditions like food allergies, cancer, or diabetes.

- If you have freezer space, take advantage of meat sales and stock up.

Calcium

- No canine diet is complete without calcium. Add 1,000 milligrams of calcium powder to each pound of food.

- A pressure cooker offers a good way to add calcium in the form of whole bones, cooked until completely soft.

- Never give cooked bones in any other form to your dog. They are not properly digested and can cause impaction or perforation.

- Other supplements can be added, but many experts claim they're not necessary as long as the diet contains a healthy variety.

gimes include supplements to supply amino acids and oils.

It is more time consuming, but those who cook for their dogs make up large batches and freeze them for later use, so feeding can be done quite efficiently. Buying in bulk and having enough freezer space make it more affordable. Again, research this diet thoroughly first and make sure the recipes you use are from current, reputable sources. There are several books on the market that have withstood the test of time, and, of course, the Internet is a great resource.

ZOOM

A safe way to feed cooked bones to dogs is to make dog stew using a pressure cooker until the bones are very soft. Many of the recipes that call for cooking and then deboning meat can be pressure cooked instead. Chicken bones become soft after two or three hours of cooking.

Diet Staples

- Other staples may include eggs, cottage cheese, and canned fish. The bones in canned fish are pressure cooked and perfectly safe.

- Animal protein should make up a minimum of one-third (more is fine) of the diet.

- Some cooked leftovers can be added to the meal.

- Until relatively recently in history, dogs had evolved and been quite healthy eating cooked or raw diets and table scraps instead of dried pellets.

Cooking and Storage

- Cook the ingredients in the largest pot you have. Up to a month's worth of food for a small dog can be prepared in an hour or two.

- Use plastic zip-tie freezer bags or containers to store food, one to four meals at a time. It will be fine in the freezer for at least two days.

- Don't worry if food gets freezer burned. It doesn't affect the nutritional value.

175

DOGGIE DINNERS

BLENDING DIETS
No rule says a dog must eat the same thing for every meal

Contrary to advice you may hear, it is perfectly fine to give your dog "people food" sometimes. No organism on Earth was naturally meant to eat nothing but pellets. Dogs have naturally sturdy digestive systems, made sensitive by the common practice of feeding one brand of dry food for life.

Many people add fresh foods to their dog's dry food or combine raw or cooked meats with kibble, and, in fact, sev-

eral dry foods on the market are meant to have meat or eggs added. Allergies and food intolerances are becoming more common, and some experts think that challenging the system by feeding a varied diet helps. Animal protein like yogurt, meats, fish, and eggs can be added to dry food in small amounts. Many don't think twice about large amounts of dog treats upsetting the "balance" in dog food, and adding a

Blending Commercial with Homemade

- Some commercial foods are formulated to have fresh, raw or canned meats mixed in for extra nutrition, palatability, and variety.

- Most commercial gravies available for adding to dry food have little nutritional benefit. Adding a little

cooked meat, egg, or cottage cheese is better.

- If your dog won't eat her kibble unless something is added, she may truly dislike it. Experiment with different flavors or brands.

Rotating Food

- Rotating several varieties allows your dog a wider choice of proteins, which can reduce the chance of allergies and intolerance.

- To rotate types (even different brands), feed one for a month or two and then switch to another.

- Avoid routinely mixing brands. It is better to rotate two to four types, feeding one at a time.

- Adding vegetables like beans can add flavor without calories.

little fresh food certainly won't.

There are, of course, potentially harmful foods for dogs. Grapes and raisins, cooked bones, large amounts of cooked fat, chocolate, caffeine, and some products containing natural sweeteners are just some. Some people worry that feeding a dog "people food" leads to begging, but begging is a behavioral issue. Feed your dog in her bowl, never from the table, and she won't beg. When you give her something new, feed a very small amount until you're sure she can handle it without diarrhea. Dogs who grow up eating a healthy variety can handle just about anything edible, though, and through most of their history with humankind, dogs have shared our food.

Diet Insurance

- Some people feel more comfortable feeding kibble along with a raw or cooked diet as "insurance."

- Although it is generally all right to feed both together, and many people do, some dogs can have digestive upsets if fed meat and bones along with kibble.

- Alternating meals makes it easier. It's fine for a dog to have her kibble for breakfast and a raw or cooked meal in the evening.

Mixing

- Canned foods are another way to add protein variety. They can be fed alone or added to dry food.

- Dry food is considered better for keeping teeth clean because of abrasive action.

- Canned food generally has fewer calories than dry dog food in a volume-to-volume ratio, so you can add it for taste and to help your dog feel full while trying to cut weight.

- Canned food is more expensive than dry, but it has fewer preservatives.

177

TREATS & PEOPLE FOOD
Choose healthful and nutritious treats by thinking outside the box

Unless you are using them for training, treats are optional. The massive treat industry doesn't want you to think so, of course! But with widespread obesity in dogs, showing your love with food may well be killing to be kind. However, most of us like to spoil our dogs a little bit, and there is nothing wrong with that. Just don't overdo it: Make sure your dog works for her treats, and choose healthful ones.

Walk down the treat aisle, and you will notice a trend: The main ingredient advertised in most treats is meat. Read the ingredients, and although there are some excellent treats, there are many with a long, incomprehensible ingredients list of chemical additives, high fat and little nutritional value, and even less actual meat. Now figure out the price per pound of some of these, which can exceed the price of a

Cooked Meats

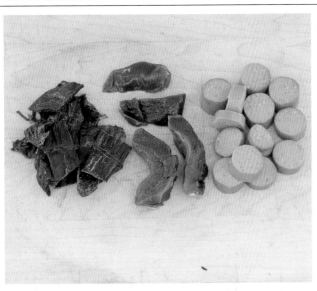

- Hot dogs, jerky, and other cooked meats are a healthful and often inexpensive choice and can be kept in the fridge or freezer.

- Treats ought to be nutritious, low-calorie, or both. Treats that add nothing to your dog's health but load her up with preservatives and low-quality ingredients are a waste of money.

- If you give a lot of treats to your dog, reduce her regular food a little to compensate.

Fruits and Vegetables

- Many vegetables and fruits (except grapes and raisins, which can be toxic) make good low-calorie treats.

- Try chopping fruits and vegetables and keeping them in the fridge for crunchy frozen treats.

- Unsalted popcorn, oat cereal, ice cubes with swirls of peanut butter, yogurt, or other tiny pieces of food mixed in (use your imagination), unsalted almonds, and pieces of low-fat cheese all make excellent low-fat snacks.

prime porterhouse steak. Just as with food, read ingredients with a critical eye and remember that your dog doesn't care about color, shape, or price.

If you want something meaty, tasty, and somewhat nutritious, low-fat hot dogs are an excellent price, and you're paying mostly for human-grade meat instead of mystery ingredients. Cut the hot dogs into small pieces, nuke in the microwave until crispy, and keep them in the fridge. Beef jerky sold for people is fine for dogs. Some dogs go crazy for carrot pieces, string cheese, or raw sweet potato slices. Try unsalted popcorn, unsweetened oat cereal, and unsalted almonds (almonds are good for dogs, but some other nuts, like macadamias, may be toxic).

There are plenty of books and websites with ideas for making some more complex treats, like liver-banana brownies or mackerel and peanut butter cookies. And with homemade treats, at least you know how to pronounce the ingredients!

New Dog Treat Recipes

- Cooking snacks for your dog can be a great way to use up brown bananas and lunch meat that has lost its luster.

- If your dog is used to a varied diet, just wing it. Make an omelet using whatever crazy (and nutritious) items you can find or add meat or canned fish.

- There are countless books and Web sites with recipes and ideas for dog treats. Check the resources chapter for some.

What Not to Feed Fido

- Grapes and raisins

- Onions

- Macadamia nuts

- Uncooked dough

- Chocolate

- Caffeine

- Alcohol

- Anything containing the sugar substitute xylitol

- Very spicy, salty, or sugary foods (a little here and there is OK)

179

NAILS

Trimmed nails look great; let your dog walk comfortably and save your floors, too

Unless your dog gets a lot of exercise on hard surfaces, the nails need attention. Too-long nails make walking uncomfortable and can deform the dog's feet if left unattended for a long time. It's not that difficult to convince dogs that getting their nails trimmed is no big deal. Many dogs dislike having their feet handled, but nail clipping doesn't hurt one bit.

When your dog is calm or sleepy, handle his feet. Reward him for being calm. You can use treats. Don't stop if he fusses or wiggles—that lets him know that fussing and wiggling work. No part of the nail should be touching the ground as the dog walks. If you hear toenails clicking on hard floors, it's time. There are three tools for trimming nails. The guillotine clip-

Cutting Nails

- This too-long nail will be easy to cut because it's light colored, and the quick is visible.

- On dark-colored nails, you can both see and feel where the extra nail meets the nail bed from underneath. The excess nail will feel flatter and be concave, curving beyond the nail bed.

- The quick stays well receded if the nails are trimmed regularly. When nails are allowed to grow really long, the quick grows long, too.

Using a Vet

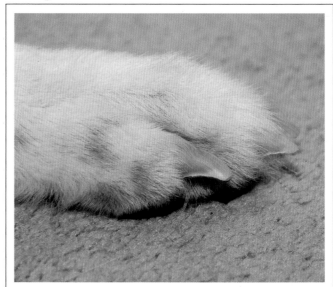

- Just like a good pair of shoes, nicely trimmed nails indicate good grooming!

- Some dogs put up an incredible fuss despite an owner's best efforts, and they simply won't let you do nails.

- At this point, there is no shame in having your vet or groomer take over. These professionals are used to this, and some dogs can be absolute drama queens about their nails for reasons we will never understand.

pers are the easiest to use. For large dogs with thick toenails, scissors-type clippers do a better job. Grinder tools take a little more time, but there is less risk of hitting the sensitive quick.

Choose a time when your dog is calm, even napping. It's easier to get a better cutting angle when he is lying down and best to cut the nails from underneath, so you can see the quick. Dogs with white toenails are simpler because the pink quick is visible. Viewed from underneath, it's easier to see the overhanging claw on a black nail and make small nips.

When a small gray area shows in the center of the nail, you're approaching the quick. Although cutting too far hurts and produces a lot of blood, the bleeding will stop in about five minutes and even quicker with styptic powder. Resist the temptation to make a big show of pity for your dog. It's kinder to tell him he's brave, clean up quickly, and continue.

Where to Cut

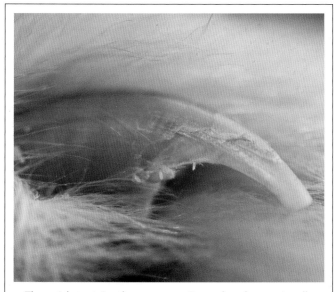

- The quick contains the blood supply and bony base of the nail, and it's fairly easy to see on light nails. Cut as close to the quick as you can.

- Cut at an angle, so the trimmed nail is roughly parallel to the floor.

- Some dogs have naturally high-knuckled toes, and the trimmed nail will jut forward well above the ground. Other dogs have flatter feet, and the nails don't have to be very long at all before they start touching.

What to Use

- Scissors-type clippers can be used on most dogs but are ideal for big dog nails. As long as they're sharp and properly aligned, these clippers will cut cleanly without mashing the end.

- Both guillotine and scissor-type clippers are available with guides to help prevent

getting the quick, although they're not fail-safe.

- A battery-operated grinder takes a little more time but does a professional job with less risk of hitting the quick.

EARS

Keeping ears clean and dry is easy and will prevent infections

No animal in the wild has floppy, furry ears. This trait in dogs has been selectively bred for centuries and requires maintenance. Fur on the inner ear traps dirt and moisture, and floppy ears don't let air circulate, allowing bacterial buildup. Ear infections are painful and can lead to complications, including deafness. Routine ear care can prevent infections.

Trimming hair from the underside of the ear, particularly around the ear canal, improves air flow. If your dog gets groomed regularly, make sure your groomer does this or use small, sharp clippers to do it yourself. Check ears about once a week. A small amount of brown wax or dirt in the outer ear is normal and can be cleaned off with cotton or gauze.

The Dog's Ear

• The ear flap is also called the pinna, and it covers the opening of the ear canal.

• Dogs have a narrow ear canal, which bends at a 90-degree angle. This is where dirt and debris often get caught.

• The ear canal is separated from the middle ear by a thin membrane, which can be easily ruptured by using a swab to clean the ear.

• The inner ear is where nerves connect to the brain, controlling balance and allowing the dog to hear.

Cleaning the Ears

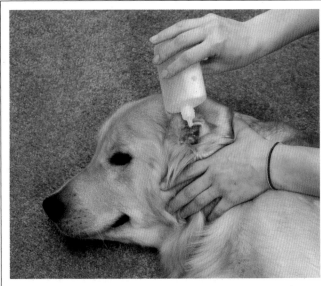

• Drop in ear cleaner by pulling the ear gently up and out. This might be easier with your dog lying down and relaxed.

• Don't poke her or squirt anything down her ear because doing this hurts and can even rupture her eardrum.

• Be ready to massage the base of her ear before she gets a chance to shake her head.

• Use only white vinegar, not apple cider vinegar, or a vet-approved ear cleaner as an ear douche.

Douche your dog's ears every few weeks with a veterinary ear wash or a mixture of 50/50 tepid water and white vinegar. It's best to do this outside because she'll shake her head, and gunk will go flying everywhere. Using a cup or turkey baster, hold back the ear flap, and gently pour a generous amount down the canal.

Massage the base of the ear until you hear a squishy sound, then let her shake. It is fine to use gauze wrapped around your finger to clean the visible parts of the outer ear, but never poke anything down the ear canal— dogs' ears are designed differently from ours, and it's easy to cause damage.

Chronic ear infections can indicate food or environmental allergies, especially if the dog is generally "itchy." Your vet should be the first stop when you suspect allergies. If the inside of her ears are reddened, if she scratches her ears a lot or shakes her head, or if there's any strong odor or discharge, she needs a vet visit.

Using a Vet

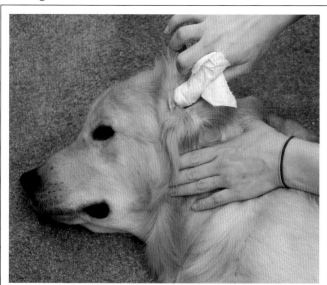

- It's normal to see a little black or brown discharge in the folds of the outer ear.

- Clean it with a moistened cotton ball or gauze wrapped around your finger. Most dogs enjoy this.

- If your dog is pulling away or unwilling to let you handle her ears, have your vet take a look down there.

- Grass seeds and other foreign objects can get worked down into the ear canal, especially with floppy-eared dogs.

Ear Problems

- Long-haired, floppy-eared dogs often have the fur on the underside shaved to increase air flow.

- A lot of fur around the base and underside of the ear also traps dirt, moisture, and foreign objects, which can work down into the canal.

- Chronic ear infections in dogs are not only extremely painful but also can cause scarring and deafness if untreated.

- Anytime you suspect an ear problem, have your dog checked by your vet.

TEETH

What you can do at home to keep your dog's teeth and gums healthy

"Doggie breath" is not normal. A majority of adult dogs have poor dental health, and bad breath is a primary symptom, indicating gum disease and bad teeth. Bacteria from inflamed gums and infected teeth infiltrate the blood stream, weakening organs and compromising overall vigor. Often the dog adjusts to having a sore mouth, so you may not notice anything but bad breath. The good news is that it's easy to prevent and not difficult to treat.

Brushing teeth daily, or at least several times a week, prevents plaque buildup. Using toothbrushes for dogs with doggie toothpaste do a fine job, as does wrapping a piece of gauze around your finger and rubbing the teeth down.

Dental chews and bones will help a great deal. Some people swear by raw turnips or crunchy vegetables—

Regular Brushing

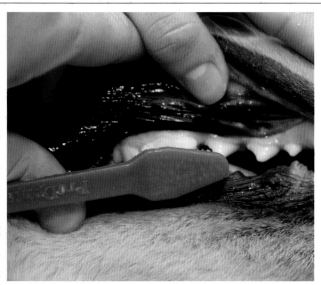

- Regular brushing with a doggie toothbrush or gauze will keep tartar from turning into hard plaque.

- Pet stores carry doggie toothpaste, as do many vets. Look for one with enzymatic additives to help dissolve the tartar.

- Concentrate on the outside of her teeth because that is where tartar is more likely to build up.

- Just like people, some dogs are more prone to plaque buildup and dental problems than others.

Large Dogs versus Small Dogs

- Large dogs tend to have healthier dentition than smaller dogs, although a few larger breeds, like greyhounds, are notorious for dental problems.

- A healthy dog's gums are pink, without any swelling or reddening along the gum line.

- Teeth should be white. If you notice discoloration on one side and not the other, this could indicate chewing on one side because of a cracked tooth.

- Slight yellowing is tartar and can be removed by brushing and feeding dental chews and soft bones.

try them if your dog will chew them. If you have a breed prone to dental problems, like greyhounds or many toy dogs, talk to your vet about enzymatic rawhide chews or spray to control bacteria and plaque. Food matters. Higher-quality dry dog food is precisely formulated to shatter as the dog eats and to provide abrasion to help "scrub" teeth.

However, most dogs don't chew much, so the benefits are minimal. Cheaper kibbles are no better than crackers at keeping teeth clean and smush between the teeth to fer-

ment after eating. Brushing after meals will help, as will giving your dog something to chew for dessert. Advocates feel that raw or home-cooked diet may be better, but definite proof is lacking and remember there is a danger of larger bones cracking teeth.

Have the vet cast an expert eye on your dog's teeth when you take her in for checkups. Few dogs can go their whole lives without needing a dental cleaning; most need a professional scaling almost annually as they get older.

Dental Problems

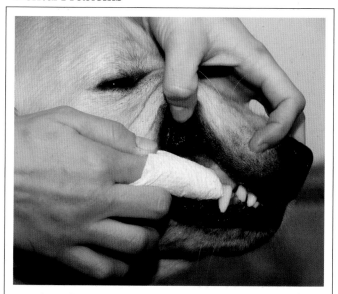

- Without dental care, most dogs will have dental disease by middle age. This is an undertreated problem for dogs. It leads to many illnesses and compromises the immune system.

- If your dog's breath smells horrible or his teeth have any brown discoloration, he needs veterinary attention.

- Like many animals, dogs often don't show pain. This is especially true when the pain comes on gradually, like with slowly worsening teeth.

- Drooling and dropping food are signs of mouth pain.

Maintain Dental Health

- Talk to your vet about products to help maintain dental health. Chews and mouthwashes containing antimicrobials may help reduce inflammation.

- Large, hard "butcher" bones sold for dogs are often too hard and can crack teeth if the dog is an aggressive chewer. Look for natural chews like bully sticks or tendons or nylon bones.

- Some nylon bones are flavored, and you can flavor your own by soaking them overnight in meat broth to get your dog's interest.

BRUSHING

This is a good way to bond with your dog and keep her coat tangle free

Brushing your dog eliminates tangles and keeps her coat shiny. It removes dead hair—the more you brush out, the less in your house and on your clothes. Most dogs love it, and it's a good way to bond. Many dogs have double coats with a dense, insulating undercoat. Short-haired, double-coated dogs like German shepherds are generally worse culprits than long-haired dogs, and some very sleek dogs like Dalmatians and Jack Russell terriers will leave white hairs everywhere. Long-coated dogs don't tend to shed as much.

Dogs shed a little year around, with a big spring "blowout" as the winter coat loosens and another shedding in fall as the winter coat comes in. Dry indoor heat in win-

Spring and Autumn Coats

- During the spring and autumn, a double-coated dog will "blow coat" by shedding the old winter coat. Dogs with heavy coats, like huskies and chows, can lose an astonishing amount of dead fur.

- For chow and Pomeranian-type coats, you may have to first brush in sections against the direction of the coat growth, pulling as much fur as possible. Finish by brushing in the direction of growth.

- Consider a professional grooming session during shedding season.

Tangles and Mats

- Areas where tangles form quickly on long-haired dogs are along the backs of the legs, under the ears, and the tail.

- Mats can be removed with a mat rake, which gently separates and pulls out the wad of dead fur. Severe mats might have to be clipped off; be careful with scissors, as it's easy to cut the skin—if left, they pull on the skin.

- A few minutes of daily brushing prevent tangles and mats as well as keeping oils distributed through the coat to keep it shiny.

ter can make the coat look patchy and dull, and brushing stimulates skin oils and lubricates the fur. Stress from illness, pregnancy, or anxiety can make a dog shed temporarily. Long-coated dogs should be brushed several times a week to prevent mats; short-coated dogs less often as needed. Use an undercoat rake or mat comb for the tangles in long fur along with a firm slicker brush to pull out dead undercoat. Dematting sprays loosen matted fur for easier removal. A soft-bristle or slicker brush can be used on very short-haired dogs. Shedding blades work very well for heavier short coats,

like those of German shepherds and Labradors. Be gentle, especially in sensitive areas around the inner thighs.

When you brush your dog, pay attention to her overall condition. Feel for skin lumps. Check her ears, teeth, eyes, and paws. Assess her weight, which can be hard to monitor in long-haired dogs. Even if you also take her to the groomer, ongoing maintenance keeps down dog hair volume as well as making the groomer's job easier.

Therapeutic Grooming

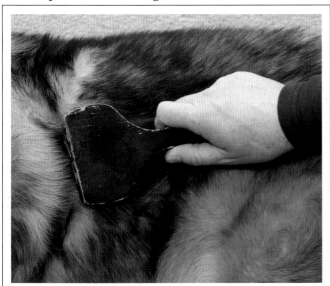

- For long-haired dogs, you'll need a rake or comb to remove tangles and a slicker-type brush to pull out loose undercoat.

- Most dogs enjoy being groomed and find it very relaxing.

- While your dog is relaxed and enjoying a grooming session, check her ears and do nails at the same time.

Double Coats

- Most dogs have a double coat—that is, a softer undercoat, which will shed in spring and autumn, and a coarser, glossy top coat.

- Some long-haired dogs, like poodles and Maltese terriers, have no undercoat. Although they shed less, they still need regular grooming to prevent tangles.

- Dobermans, among some other smooth-coated breeds, also have a single coat and shed minimally. Brushing them doesn't take long but keeps the fur gleaming.

CLIPPING

Home clipping and trimming are not that difficult with the right tools

The worst that will happen while you're learning to clip your dog is a bad haircut, and it will grow out within a month. Scissor-cutting is a bit more of an art. Unless you're very proficient and have the right scissors, you can end up with a chopped look. Scissors are best used just for trimming ear and face hair in a well-behaved dog. Electric clippers are more goofproof for doing a full body cut and are safer for wiggly dogs.

Your fluffy dog won't be cooler in summer with shorter fur; in fact, long fur helps regulate her temperature. Never closely shave a dog because dogs can sunburn and get skin cancer when the sensitive body skin is exposed. Look online or in breed books to get an idea of different looks for your breed.

Clipping

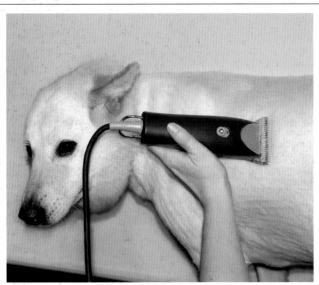

- This dog isn't thrilled about being clipped, but she is stoically accepting it. Give her a treat and tons of praise when you're done.

- Clipping can be done in short sessions to give your dog a break and let her know she's doing great.

- Most electric clipper kits come with a full set of instructions for basic clips and have all the blades you need for different parts of the dog.

What to Use

- Use grooming scissors instead of regular scissors. They are very sharp and have blunted ends to prevent accidentally jabbing the dog.

- Thinning shears, with their fine cutting teeth, are used after doing the heavy-duty clipping. Use them to blend the fur after clipping or scissoring to avoid a choppy look.

- Decent scissors are not cheap, but there is no need to spend a fortune for home-grooming use. Look for good midrange scissors.

A standard puppy clip leaves the fur a similar length over the whole body and is the simplest to maintain. A show clip is what you'll see in the show ring and isn't necessary for a pet.

Most electric clippers come with instructions, and you can buy kits containing the different blades needed for basic clips. The blades will be numbered. The higher the number, the shorter the blade will cut, but brands differ in their numbering system, so refer to the owner's manual to choose the right blades. Typically you will use a longer-cutting blade for the body and shorter ones for the feet, face, and sanitary areas. Guide combs attached to the blade will help give a uniform cut.

Your dog should be clean, dry, and brushed out before you start. Always clip in the direction of the fur growth, using long, even strokes. The blade will get hot, so use cooling lubricant while you work. Start with the longer blades until you get a feel for the best look.

What to Use, Continued

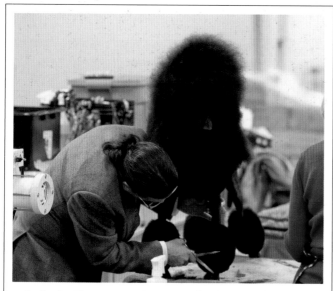

- Professionals use grooming tables, which keep their canine clients at a convenient height.

- If you don't invest in a grooming table, put a non-skid mat on a regular table or counter to protect the table and prevent your dog from slipping.

- Taking your dog for a good walk before her beauty session will use up excess energy and make her easier to work with. Make sure she doesn't need to go potty before you start working with her.

Types of Clips

- Unless you are showing your dog, there's no need for elaborate show clips, although you can certainly experiment with different looks.

- A basic "puppy clip" leaves the fur on the body short and longer but neatly trimmed on the head and tail.

- Look online for instructions or find a book on clipping your particular breed. There are many subtleties and styles, depending on breed, coat type, and even head shape.

BATHING

Dogs don't need many baths, so make the ones they get really count

Dogs shouldn't be bathed more than once a month because bathing can strip the skin and coat of natural oils. Some dogs can go months between bathing, and short-haired dogs can be rubbed down with a damp towel. Bathing during shedding season will loosen a lot of dead fur. If yours has a strong doggie odor or oily-feeling fur, a vet check is a good idea to rule out skin problems.

Use dog shampoo and avoid ones that are highly scented or contain pesticides. There is a wide array of shampoos for every task from enhancing coat colors to soothing itchy skin, but generally speaking, the milder, the better. It's fine to use conditioner, but some leave a tacky residue on the fur that will attract dirt, and conditioning really isn't necessary.

Small dogs can be bathed in the kitchen sink, especially

Bathing

- Put down a rubber bath mat for tub bathing. Dogs are not naturally sure-footed, and the combination of wet dog and soap suds is a recipe for a sliding dog and potential injury.

- Use tepid water and, unless your dog really enjoys play-

ing with water, avoid spraying him in the face or ears. Use a washcloth instead.

- Water-loving dogs can be bathed outside in warm weather, using a bucket of sudsy water, a sponge, and a garden hose.

Use Shampoo

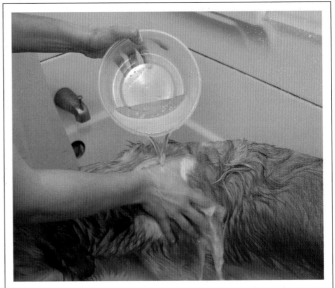

- A squirt bottle filled with diluted shampoo helps distribute it over his body.

- Make sure fluffy dogs are completely wetted down before shampooing, so that the shampoo gets to the skin.

- Use a sponge—a car wash sponge works for large dogs—to work up lather.

- Rinse thoroughly because unrinsed shampoo can be irritating. Pay attention to his "underarms" and belly.

handy if you have a faucet sprayer. Larger dogs can be bathed in the bathtub, and buying a spray attachment will make rinsing much easier. Use a drain screen to catch dog hair. Water-loving dogs who enjoy playing with the water hose can be bathed outside in warm weather using the hose and a bucket of warm, shampooey water.

Wet him down thoroughly and lather him up. It's easier to dilute the shampoo first so you don't get big blobs in one spot, which are harder to rinse out. Do his head last because he'll instinctively shake off when he gets water in his ears.

You can put a cotton ball at the ear opening if he has droopy, furry ears. Rinse completely and towel dry or use a hair dryer at low setting, being careful not to get too close to his skin.

Drying Him Off

- Your dog will shake. Draping an oversized towel over him as he exits the tub or sink will contain most of the water.

- It's a guarantee that if you let a wet dog outside, he'll immediately roll on the ground.

- Underlying skin, ear, or dental disease can cause the return of body odor shortly after a bath. Have it checked out.

- Some hound breeds have naturally oily skin and a stronger doggie odor.

Types of Doggie Shampoos

- Medicated, herbal, or essential oil shampoos can help with conditions from bacterial skin infections to itchy skin from summer allergies.

- Color-enhancing shampoos are formulated for just about any coat color.

- Flea and tick shampoos are not as effective as prescription "spot" treatments and may be quite harsh.

- Soothing shampoos for dogs with a tendency to sensitive skin and runny eyes are especially suitable for puppies.

- Conditioning shampoos can make brushing out a long-haired breed easier.

191

NEWBORN TO WEANED

Puppies develop and even learn at an incredible rate from birth to weaning

Like most carnivores, puppies are born very vulnerable—blind, deaf, and unable to regulate their own body temperature. They cannot urinate or defecate without stimulation from the dam cleaning them. However, they have a keen sense of smell and taste. Between ten and twelve days, their ears and eyes open. They grow rapidly, usually doubling their weight in the first week. Puppies respond immediately to touch from birth and, because they need warmth, will sleep in a pile with their littermates.

At about three weeks old, they can start digesting soft food and are completely weaned by six weeks. This used to be the age when puppies were commonly sold or given away.

Brand New Puppies

- Like most higher-order mammals, puppies are completely dependent on their dam at birth and for several weeks thereafter.

- Although they respond to touch and temperature, newborns show no recognition of littermates or strange objects placed in the whelping area.

- Their ears and eyes are closed at birth. They do have a sense of smell, but there is dissent about how keen their sense of smell is at first.

- They don't begin to wag their tails until the third week. Breeds who are docked have the tails removed at two or three days old.

Two- to Four-Weeks-Old

- From two to four weeks, they are gradually gaining other senses, and their puppy teeth start to emerge. They become more vocal and start to walk and play.

- They start investigating their environments using all their senses and begin toddling around at about three weeks.

- At three weeks, if a potty area is set aside for the puppies, they can begin to understand the early stages of housebreaking by pottying away from the feeding and sleeping area.

Later research indicates that puppies left with the dam and littermates until at least eight weeks are better socialized and healthier and have learned to interact properly with other dogs by learning manners from their siblings. In some states it is illegal to sell puppies younger than eight weeks old.

Puppies learn from their environment from birth. Handling and even talking to very young puppies have a beneficial effect on their adult temperament. Puppies who are isolated from birth to weaning tend to be less resilient, shier, and more prone to behavior problems. The U.S. military developed the "Super Puppy" program, which exposes very young puppies to mild stressors, like being briefly held upside-down, placed onto a chilled towel for five seconds daily, and tickled between the toes. It's been found that challenging a puppy's system early promotes increased neurological development, resulting in more emotionally and physically resilient adults.

Because early handling matters, puppies raised in cages and sold in pet stores are often not as sturdy as their more carefully bred peers. Although basic temperament and health are partly genetic, they are also strongly influenced by environmental factors.

Five- to Six-Weeks-Old

- By five weeks, eyesight is developed. They are recognizing people and learning social structure by playing and interacting with their littermates, dam, and human caretakers.

- It is not uncommon for little puppies of either sex to hump other puppies or inanimate objects. It is not sexual but rather a phase. They are experimenting with ways to interact with their environment. Redirect them if they do it to a person.

- Puppies are weaned by six weeks old.

Early Socialization

- From three to six weeks of age, toddler puppies learn a lot from both littermates and dam. They practice body posturing, biting, and being bitten and start establishing social rank.

- When the puppies are about five weeks old, the dam will begin disciplining them. This is how they learn to respect seniority.

- Without these early experiences, a puppy misses critical development and may have lifelong problems interacting with other dogs.

- Puppies who are never given consequences for biting too hard at this age often lack "bite inhibition" and can be very mouthy as adults.

TAKE-HOME AGE

At eight weeks puppies are still growing babies with critical social and environmental needs

An eight-week-old puppy is a little learning sponge. Between two and five months he will learn very rapidly. How he interacts with people is determined at this age, which is why continuing socialization is so important. Keeping his vulnerability in mind until he has received all his puppy shots (usually by sixteen weeks old), give him positive exposure to as many types of people possible to ensure a confident adult. Expose him to different sounds, sights, smells, and walking surfaces. Start teaching him right away: He can learn basic commands at eight weeks.

Some puppies potty train quickly; others, like many toy dogs, take longer. A very rough rule of thumb is that the

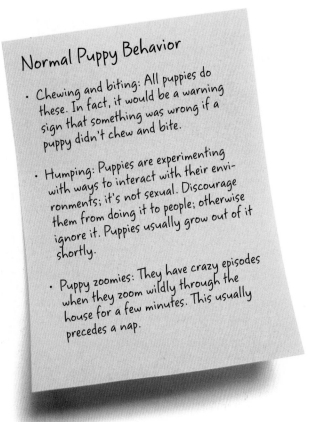

Normal Puppy Behavior

- Chewing and biting: All puppies do these. In fact, it would be a warning sign that something was wrong if a puppy didn't chew and bite.

- Humping: Puppies are experimenting with ways to interact with their environments; it's not sexual. Discourage them from doing it to people; otherwise ignore it. Puppies usually grow out of it shortly.

- Puppy zoomies: They have crazy episodes when they zoom wildly through the house for a few minutes. This usually precedes a nap.

Puppy Kindergarten Classes

- Puppy kindergarten classes get a pup off on the right paw. Between three and four months, a pup may start testing his pack position, and dominant puppies in particular need a lot of structure.

- Submissive or nervous puppies also benefit from struc- ture and rules. Knowing the rules and achieving praise and a sense of accomplishment for following them breed confidence.

- This is an excellent time to reinforce self-control through training.

puppy's age in months is equal to the number of hours he can hold it, so a three-month-old puppy can hold it about three hours. He will sleep hard and play hard at this age and has a short attention span. Teething lasts from about four to eight months of age, and during this time he really needs to chew and can be destructive unless monitored and given appropriate chewies.

Some puppies experience a fear period between eight and twelve weeks, when they may startle quickly and be nervous about new experiences. It is critical that you don't coddle or reassure a fearful puppy because doing this reinforces the fear and can set a pup up for a lifetime of being scared of new things. Assuming he's nervous about something innocuous like a tricycle or new person, encourage him to be brave. Touch and talk to the scary object. Be cheerful. Use treats and praise for any show of confidence and don't acknowledge fear.

When he is three months old, take him to puppy kindergarten classes to learn proper play with other dogs and continue learning manners.

Teething

- During teething, you may see your puppy's ears go crooked —one up and one down or sitting sideways across his head. This is completely normal, as is bad breath during teething.

- Some puppies go through "ugly" stages. Rear legs get longer than front legs, ears get disproportionately large, and coat looks scraggly. Don't worry: All his parts will eventually catch up to each other!

- A knowledgeable breeder can tell puppy buyers what to expect because some lines mature differently from others.

Punishments

- Never punish a puppy; just redirect him. It is not fair to punish when he doesn't yet know the rules.

- Pushy pups can have temper tantrums and even growl at you. This is normal in high-drive puppies and welcome by many working dog owners. Be very clear and firm with rules and don't punish them for being bratty.

- Socializing with people doesn't mean he has to enthusiastically love everyone he meets. He just needs to be calm and confident.

195

ADOLESCENCE

The terrible teens affect a puppy, too—he looks like an adult, but he's still developing

The larger the breed, the slower it tends to develop both physically and mentally. A little dog can be "all grown up" by a year old, but a large dog can take over three years to mature. The period between four to eighteen months can be trying, more so if a good foundation with manners and socialization has not been laid early. Puppies acquired at this age are certainly trainable but might need more work if they've not received good early training.

Your dog may question your authority and forget what he has been taught, like coming when called. This is normal and requires you simply to take a few steps back in training and go back to basics. Intact males will have very high testoster-

Sexual Maturity in a Female Puppy

- The first estrus, or heat, can come as early as five months old.

- Heat lasts approximately three weeks. Be vigilant because no pup should have a litter on her first heat.

- She may become "bitchy" or more affectionate, go off her food, and forget early training. Be patient with her.

- The first physical signs will be swelling of her vulva and increased urination.

- She will probably spot blood. Get some protective bloomers from the pet store.

Pediatric Speutering

- Large-breed puppies can grow in alarming spurts, sometimes gaining several pounds seemingly overnight.

- Food requirements will keep changing. Monitor his condition, letting him get neither too plump nor too skinny.

- Puppies go through lanky stages, and it's fine to see some ribs, but hip bones shouldn't be prominent.

- Puppies can be "fixed" as young as eight weeks old. There are both risks and benefits to pediatric speutering. Research the issue and talk to your vet.

one levels during adolescence and may start challenging other males as they approach sexual maturity.

Spayed and neutered dogs may also challenge others, and not all intact dogs will do so—neutering will not guarantee a nonreactive dog, although it usually helps. This is an excellent time to take him to obedience classes to help him learn dog manners.

Keep him well occupied with outlets for chewing until he's done teething. Continue making sure he has lots of positive interactions with the outside world so he remains confident.

Mental Maturity

- Mental maturity usually comes after physical maturity, meaning a large dog may still have some puppy traits at two or even three years old.

- Your teenage dog may periodically try testing you by disobeying or ignoring you. Taking a few steps back in basic training and reminding him of his manners are the best strategy.

- Teenagers have abundant energy and really benefit from both physical and mental exercise to channel energy and calm them down.

Have daily play and training sessions.

Most dogs are sexually mature by a year old. A female will usually come into heat between five and ten months old and should never be allowed to breed this young, so you need to be very vigilant to keep her safe. Males are capable of breeding at six months old. Owning intact dogs of either sex requires responsible stewardship to prevent unplanned litters. If you never plan to breed, talk to a vet about the best age to sterilize your dog.

Sexual Maturity in a Male Puppy

- His testicles should descend between two and six months. If they're undescended at six months, talk to your vet because this condition can lead to serious complications.

- He is capable of siring a litter at six months.

- Testosterone will make him lift his leg, possibly be challenging with other males, and be very responsive to bitches in heat.

- With the exception of junior handling, conformation show dogs must remain intact.

- Intact dogs of both sexes need responsible management to avoid unintended litters.

197

MATURITY

Now your labor really bears fruit: A calm, sensible adult dog

It can seem like adolescence lasts forever. Then the final brain shipment arrives, and you realize that your dog is finally a sensible, well-behaved adult. This doesn't mean that he doesn't still have needs, but he won't be as much work.

Older dogs can learn tricks, so don't stop teaching him new things. If he is an energetic, intelligent dog he can still develop behavior issues if not mentally and physically exercised. Keep him fit with regular walks and playtimes. Consider participating in dog sports, taking ongoing training classes, or volunteering your gentle, well-mannered canine as a therapy dog. Teach him tricks to amuse him and impress your friends.

As he matures, his territorial instincts may develop if so predisposed. Making sure your dog is confident and friendly with visitors won't affect his ability as a protector. A confident

Routine Care

- Daily or weekly: Groom him regularly and keep his teeth clean.

- Every one to three months: Heartworm preventative is usually given monthly. Flea and tick meds, depending on the product, can be effective for up to three months.

- Annually: Get a routine wellness check, including a heartworm blood test if you live in an at-risk area.

- Every one to three years: Vaccinate responsibly and follow your state law when it comes to rabies vaccines.

Provide Different Environments

- Make sure your dog gets out in different environments at least once a week.

- On cool days, take your dog along in the car while you run an errand.

- Positive exposure to people of different ages, races, and abilities helps your dog remain confident and gives him better judgment as a watchdog or guard dog.

- A dog who is relegated to the house and yard is more likely to become nervous about new people and situations and potentially aggressive.

dog has better judgment, and an isolated dog tends to be fearful or potentially dangerous. A dog who growls or barks at friendly visitors is not being protective but rather aggressive, and professional help should be sought.

Occasional doggie playdates or day care will keep his dog manners honed. Dog parks may be almost a necessity for big-city dwellers, but exercise diligence. They are controversial for a reason, and although you may be able to control your own dog, you cannot control others' dogs, and dogs in packs can behave differently than they do at home.

Vaccinate responsibly, groom regularly, and use a vet-approved preventative for parasites and heartworms when indicated. Develop a good working relationship with a veterinarian you trust. Feed the best diet you can and keep your dog lean—overweight dogs are prone to many increased health risks and have a shorter lifespan and an overall reduced quality of life. Sterilized dogs may need slightly less food to maintain a healthy weight.

Keep a Dog Healthy

- One of the most important and easiest things you can do to keep an adult dog healthy is to keep her fit and trim without extra weight.

- It's easy to pay less attention to an adult, well-behaved dog. Keep her involved in family activities and keep her mind and body exercised.

- As a general rule, smaller dogs mature faster and have longer lifespans. The larger the dog, the slower he matures and the shorter his average lifespan.

Learning Is for Life

- Learning doesn't stop with adolescence. Even the best-behaved dog needs refreshers on obedience.

- Obedience classes can be repeated. Most dogs enjoy classes and enjoy learning. It's usually cheap entertainment as well as useful for both dog and owner!

- Teach tricks. It's surprisingly easy to teach simple tricks, especially if you capitalize on behaviors your dog does naturally, like fetching, rolling over, or even barking.

SENIOR DOG
These dogs need special attention now that they've lived long enough to deserve it

Very large dogs may be considered senior as young as five years old, whereas small dogs may not reach that status until about ten. Determining senior status in a dog depends very much on the individual, and the best way to determine if your dog is "senior" is by physical indications.

Early signs of aging include a general slowing down in energy and increased napping. She may start lagging on walks that never tired her before. She will move a little more stiffly. Some dogs' muzzles start turning gray early, others not until they're quite old. She may gain weight and will need smaller meals. Her eyes might start taking on a slightly hazy cast due to hardening of the lens. You may find fatty lumps under her

Signs of Aging

- Signs that your dog is aging appear so gradually that they can be easy to miss. The first thing you might notice is more time spent napping.

- A willing companion on 5-mile hikes might start slowing at the 3-mile mark now. Don't force her to overexercise but rather adjust to her pace.

- Age-related changes might be inevitable but treatable. Talk to your vet about ways to keep your senior dog comfortable.

Keep Your Dog Limber

- Easy daily exercise helps keep muscles toned, which in turn can compensate for arthritic joints.

- Swimming and even walking in water are great. Regular short walks, especially on softer surfaces like grass, will help, too.

- Keep playing with her. Many older dogs retain a willingness to play, whether it's leisurely games of fetch in the back yard or tug-of-war in the living room.

- Do something every day with your old dog to keep her limber.

skin or warts and skin tags around her face.

Any unusual changes need to be discussed with your vet. It is a good idea to have a full health screening, including diagnostic bloodwork, on any dog moving from middle to senior years. Most vets recommend an annual screening for senior dogs to check teeth, eyes, and organ function.

If she eats dry dog food, a high-protein, low-phosphorus, easily digestible food will promote good health and prevent constipation. Make sure she stays lean. Older dogs still need exercise, even if their tolerance is lower. Swimming is an excellent, low-impact way to keep her mobile. Supplements for joint health are a good idea because arthritis is very common, especially in dogs who have led active lives. Make sure she has a warm, soft bed because senior dogs don't regulate their body temperature well.

Hearing, eyesight, and sense of smell often become compromised as dogs age. Cognitive dysfunction, or "doggie Alzheimer's," is not uncommon, and effective medications are available.

Comfort Your Older Dog

- Older dogs need a soft surface to sleep on. There are many dog beds on the market for elderly, arthritic dogs.

- Putting rubber-backed throw rugs on slick flooring will help keep her foot-sure.

- If she's been used to training or dog sports, continue to have short, fun sessions with her as tolerated.

- Stay alert to signs of failing hearing and eyesight, which can be subtle at first. Dogs adjust very well, but she may need some help from you.

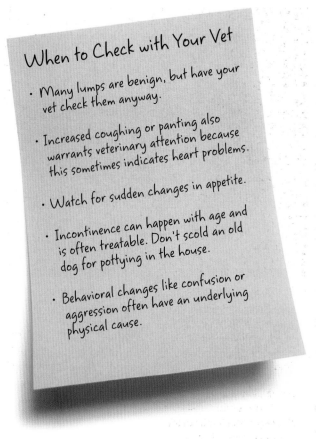

When to Check with Your Vet

- Many lumps are benign, but have your vet check them anyway.

- Increased coughing or panting also warrants veterinary attention because this sometimes indicates heart problems.

- Watch for sudden changes in appetite.

- Incontinence can happen with age and is often treatable. Don't scold an old dog for pottying in the house.

- Behavioral changes like confusion or aggression often have an underlying physical cause.

SAYING GOODBYE
One of the hardest decisions you will ever make is also one of the most important

To own dogs is to accept the hard fact that they live much shorter lives than we do. No matter what the circumstances, making the decision of when to let go and euthanize is a wrenching one. Death is a more loaded concept for us than it is for a dog, and it's important to honestly ask yourself if you are delaying the inevitable for your own benefit or your

dog's. People may say you'll "know when it's time," but this is not always the case. Dogs are naturally stoic animals and may eat, drink, and respond normally despite being in terrible discomfort. We may hope that she'll quietly pass in her sleep, thus sparing us having to make the decision, but that, too, is often not the case.

Physical Signs of Aging

- Very old dogs lose muscle tone, start accumulating fat deposits around the neck, and joints may become misshapen from arthritis.

- Graying of the muzzle and face is determined by genetics, just as with people. Some dogs start going gray early, others not until their very senior years.

- Some dogs can reach a great old age without too much discomfort or loss of vital functions.

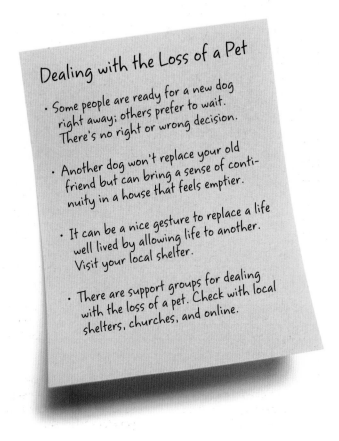

Dealing with the Loss of a Pet

- Some people are ready for a new dog right away; others prefer to wait. There's no right or wrong decision.

- Another dog won't replace your old friend but can bring a sense of continuity in a house that feels emptier.

- It can be a nice gesture to replace a life well lived by allowing life to another. Visit your local shelter.

- There are support groups for dealing with the loss of a pet. Check with local shelters, churches, and online.

If your dog has a terminal illness, talk to your vet about options. Know that there is no shame in making a decision based on funds—end-of-life care and intervention can be prohibitively expensive and may not increase quality of life for the dog.

Assessing whether a dog's enjoyment in life is outweighed by pain is difficult because he cannot tell us. If you've run out of options to control pain, if he is no longer eating, drinking, or pottying without help, if she appears afraid or confused, or if she can't stand or walk by herself, she is suffering, and it's probably kindest to let her go.

Many vets will make a house call to euthanize a pet, and this might be the least-stressful option for everyone. You may want to have friends or family around, or you may want to be alone. You may not want to be there for the death at all. There is no right or wrong way if you are acting in your dog's best interest.

Remembering a Pet

- If the dog has had a show or sporting career, have a quilt made from the win ribbons.

- A photo album or framed photo of your dog honors her memory, as does an online journal.

- An urn, a stepping-stone, or even jewelry made from her ashes can be a comforting memento.

- Be honest with children about the death of a pet appropriate to their ages and your family beliefs.

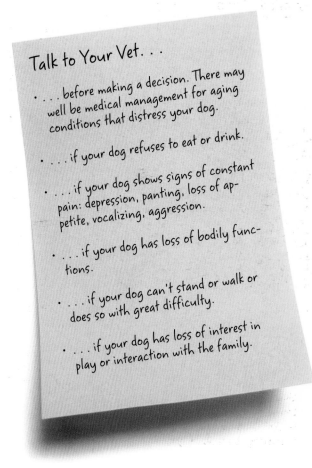

Talk to Your Vet. . .

- . . . before making a decision. There may well be medical management for aging conditions that distress your dog.

- . . . if your dog refuses to eat or drink.

- . . . if your dog shows signs of constant pain: depression, panting, loss of appetite, vocalizing, aggression.

- . . . if your dog has loss of bodily functions.

- . . . if your dog can't stand or walk or does so with great difficulty.

- . . . if your dog has loss of interest in play or interaction with the family.

FIND A GOOD VET

All vets are not created equal, so find one who will give excellent care for life

The single best way to find a good vet is by asking for recommendations from dog-savvy people. Breeders, dog trainers, groomers, and experienced dog enthusiasts usually set high standards for a vet, and you should, too. Don't choose a vet just because she's close to your house or has a large Yellow Pages ad.

It's fine to interview a vet and ask about pricing policies, the types of vaccination, parasite protocols he recommends, and whether he's experienced with your breed and dog behavior in general. Visit the office, with your dog if possible, and get a feel for the staff members and the amenities. Although it's not their job to be chatty, a relaxed, competent atmosphere

Establish a Relationship with Your Vet

- An advantage to establishing a relationship with a single vet is having all your veterinary records in one place and having a vet and staff familiar with you and your dog.

- A good vet takes the time to answer questions and

keeps current on veterinary research.

- Some problems can be stubborn to treat or require a specialist. Don't hesitate to ask for a referral if a health problem isn't getting resolved.

Vets and Insurance

- Veterinary care can be expensive, especially if you need to be referred to a specialist. Consider veterinary insurance. There are many available plans, so research and compare carefully.

- Your vet can probably give you good feedback on in-

surance companies that her office has dealt with.

- There is nothing wrong with price shopping if you get a high estimate for a procedure. Vet charges can vary widely. Better to do that than forego a necessary procedure for lack of funds.

indicates a relaxed, competent visit for your dog. You want a vet who will take the time to answer questions and explain procedures to you and who is willing to refer to any specialist if something is outside her area of expertise. The office and exam rooms should be clean and well organized and the caging area odor free, with comfortable housing for recuperating pets.

Be a good client to get the best service. Keep appointments and have a well-behaved, friendly dog or give fair warning to the vet and her staff if your dog gets stressed and may bite. Have a list of questions ready when you bring your dog in so you don't pester the staff later with phone calls. Bring your dog in for scheduled checkups and be diligent in general care and grooming so you're not bringing the dog in for preventable problems. If your dog is getting supplements or vitamins, let the vet know, especially if she is prescribing medication.

Know where the nearest emergency vet clinic is if your regular vet doesn't offer twenty-four-hour care.

A Well-Ordered Vet's Office

- A clean, well-ordered office and kennel area are important.

- If your dog stays overnight after surgery, ask if the vet has staff available overnight, if someone visits after hours to check on the animals, or if they are unattended outside of business hours. Somebody should at least check kenneled animals on nights and weekends.

- You may not get the time you need if the vet's office is always very busy.

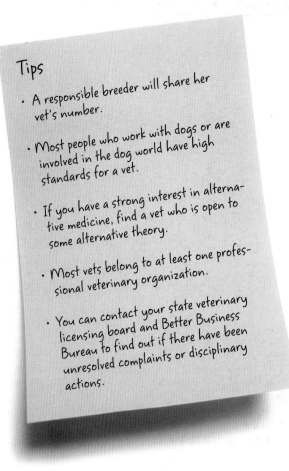

Tips

- A responsible breeder will share her vet's number.

- Most people who work with dogs or are involved in the dog world have high standards for a vet.

- If you have a strong interest in alternative medicine, find a vet who is open to some alternative theory.

- Most vets belong to at least one professional veterinary organization.

- You can contact your state veterinary licensing board and Better Business Bureau to find out if there have been unresolved complaints or disciplinary actions.

PARASITE CONTROL

Controlling fleas and other pesky bugs is not as difficult as you might think

Where you live largely determines which parasite regimen you use. Indoor dogs in colder climates may never need flea treatment, whereas dogs in warm, dry areas may need it year around. Outdoorsy dogs need to be checked for ticks frequently. Heartworms transmitted by mosquitoes are common in warm climates and easily prevented. Puppies almost always need to be treated for internal parasites and worms, although adult dogs don't often get them.

The best flea and tick control is available from your vet. The "spot" treatments are put onto the skin between the shoulder blades and disperse through the epidermis, never entering the bloodstream. There are several types, effective from one

Parasite Medications

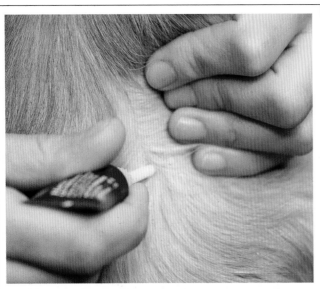

- The safest and most effective parasite meds are available through your veterinarian.

- If cost is an issue, they may also be purchased online. Remember to factor in shipping costs and buy only through a reputable

company with a long track record.

- Dogs with extremely heavy coats might need to have a small area of fur shaved off to get the med right to the skin.

Ticks

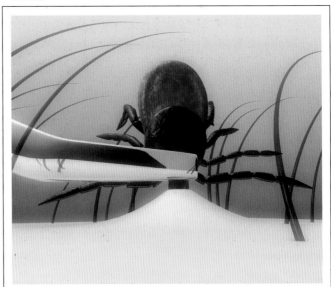

- Most spot treatments also repel ticks. Ticks carry Rocky Mountain spotted fever, ehrlichia, and Lyme disease.

- Because they can be very small and almost impossible to find on long-haired dogs, the only sure way to control them is with meds.

- Removing them with tweezers is the only safe method. If the head is embedded in the skin and won't come out, that's OK. Watch the spot to make sure a small abscess doesn't form; but usually the head falls off.

to three months. Flea collars, shampoos, and store-bought spot treatments are not as effective, and some contain harmful pesticides. Although some people swear by garlic or vitamin B supplements to deter fleas, research indicates otherwise, and regular doses of garlic may be harmful to dogs.

A dog gets heartworms in the blood when bitten by an infected mosquito. The immature worms migrate to the heart, where they slowly grow and breed. A dog can have no symptoms for years as the worms develop, but over time the worms gradually damage the heart and can kill him. The most common preventative is a monthly chewable pill, which works by killing any microfilaria present but does not work on adult worms. Prevention is simple and low risk, whereas treatment is very expensive and hard on the dog. Annual testing is recommended because no treatment is 100 percent effective.

Most puppies have worms and are routinely wormed at least twice. Untreated worms can cause diarrhea, dehydration, and even death to some puppies. Healthy adult dogs are usually resistant to most intestinal parasites, but most monthly heartworm pills also kill intestinal worms.

Fleas

- If your dog starts scratching, consider the possibility of fleas. Fleas can live through cold winters inside, and some dogs are very allergic.

- You may not see fleas, but little specks of "dirt" in your dog's coat may be flea feces. Treat all animals in your house at the same time—if there is one flea, there could be hundreds.

- Consider treating your house if fleas are an ongoing problem.

Heartworm Disease

- Check with your vet for prevalence. Heartworm medication protocols vary by region.

- Annual blood testing is inexpensive and highly recommended, even if your dog has taken the pills.

- A single undetected episode of diarrhea, vomiting, or some other malabsorption can leave your dog unprotected.

- Signs of heartworm disease include lethargy and exercise intolerance, coughing, panting, weight loss, and poor coat.

- There are several types of preventative. Collies and collie mixes may experience side effects on ivermectin and should be given an alternative.

VACCINATIONS

Protocols have changed. What does your dog need and what does more harm than good?

For decades conscientious dog owners took their dogs to the vet for annual booster vaccinations. Vaccine companies told vets that all vaccinations had to be given annually, and vets complied. Research—some by pharmaceutical companies themselves—indicates that most vaccinations are good for many years, just like childhood vaccines for people. Not only

are annual boosters unnecessary, but also they are a suspected causal factor in several conditions, from cancer to allergies, although the extent is unknown. In 2003 the American Animal Hospital Association stated that "revaccination every three years or more is considered protective," and several international veterinary organizations are in agreement. No vet

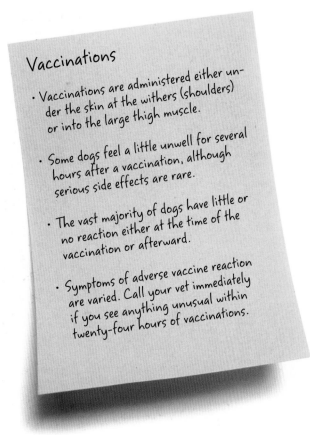

Vaccinations

- Vaccinations are administered either under the skin at the withers (shoulders) or into the large thigh muscle.

- Some dogs feel a little unwell for several hours after a vaccination, although serious side effects are rare.

- The vast majority of dogs have little or no reaction either at the time of the vaccination or afterward.

- Symptoms of adverse vaccine reaction are varied. Call your vet immediately if you see anything unusual within twenty-four hours of vaccinations.

Keep Records

- Keep a copy of all vaccinations handy. If you need to take your dog to an emergency clinic, if there's a bite incident, and if boarding, training, or grooming, you will need a copy.

- If you travel with dogs or attend shows and working

events, keep a copy in your vehicle or traveling gear.

- Results of blood titers (showing the levels of immunity in the dog's system) should also be kept handy, especially if you have no vaccination records.

school in North America recommends annual boosters, yet many vets still do them.

Experts agree that all puppies need a series of core vaccines: parvovirus, distemper, adenovirus-2, and rabies. Depending on geographical risk assessment, some vets may want to give several others, but giardia, coronavirus, Lyme, and adenovirus-1 are generally not recommended. Being revaccinated for core vaccines every three years is good for adult dogs, although some owners prefer to forgo adult vaccinations in lieu of blood titers to check for immunity. Rabies vaccinations are required by law in most areas and are important for every dog.

Be cautious if you research online because there is a lot of misinformation on vaccines. Although some dogs do indeed suffer severe vaccine reactions, and some breeds are more susceptible, the vast majority do not, and overall vaccines have prevented countless deaths. What is known is that annual boosters are unnecessary; what is not known is what harm overvaccinating does. It's best to get information from veterinary school websites and organizations, and if you have questions, bring them up with your vet. The correct vaccinations depend on your dog's breed, lifestyle, health, and age.

Rabies

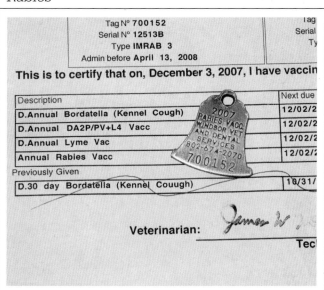

- Rabies in domestic dogs has been all but eradicated in the United States because of legally mandated, widespread rabies vaccine use. Other countries, like the United Kingdom, are virtually rabies free for all species.

- North American urban wildlife, like skunks and bats, can carry rabies. Don't assume that living in a city protects your dog.

- Not only will the vaccination protect your dog, but also, should your dog ever bite someone, you could face legal complications if he's unvaccinated.

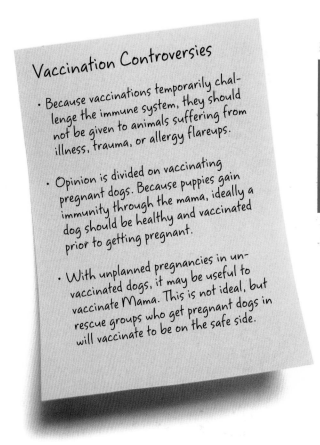

Vaccination Controversies

- Because vaccinations temporarily challenge the immune system, they should not be given to animals suffering from illness, trauma, or allergy flareups.

- Opinion is divided on vaccinating pregnant dogs. Because puppies gain immunity through the mama, ideally a dog should be healthy and vaccinated prior to getting pregnant.

- With unplanned pregnancies in unvaccinated dogs, it may be useful to vaccinate Mama. This is not ideal, but rescue groups who get pregnant dogs in will vaccinate to be on the safe side.

MEDICAL EMERGENCIES

Know when it's OK to wait until morning and when you need to act immediately

No book can tell you when a situation is a veterinary emergency. Some things are obvious. If your dog has been hit by a car, has been bitten by a snake, is wounded and bleeding badly, is convulsing, if you've just watched him drink antifreeze or eat rat poison, get him to the vet immediately. A dog in shock may be panting, shivering, and have cold feet and pale gums and needs veterinary attention right away.

Vomiting and diarrhea happen, and sometimes they are no big deal. Repeated vomiting or diarrhea that doesn't improve within twenty-four hours warrants a vet visit and the sooner, the better if your dog is refusing food and water and seems lethargic. If possible, bring a stool sample with you.

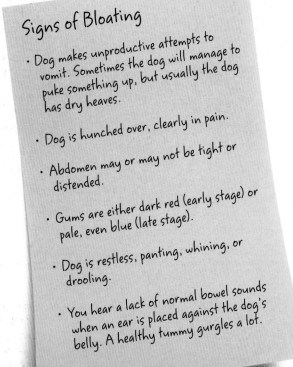

Signs of Bloating

- Dog makes unproductive attempts to vomit. Sometimes the dog will manage to puke something up, but usually the dog has dry heaves.

- Dog is hunched over, clearly in pain.

- Abdomen may or may not be tight or distended.

- Gums are either dark red (early stage) or pale, even blue (late stage).

- Dog is restless, panting, whining, or drooling.

- You hear a lack of normal bowel sounds when an ear is placed against the dog's belly. A healthy tummy gurgles a lot.

Emergency Room Trips

- Dogs frequently end up in emergency rooms because they've swallowed something inappropriate, leading to poisoning, obstruction, internal injuries, or choking.

- If your dog is choking, try removing a foreign object only if you can actually see it. Never attempt to feel for and remove something.

- A Heimlich maneuver can be done much like it is for people. Steady the dog, make a fist, and make sharp thrusts upward on the belly below the ribcage.

Any deep-chested dog is prone to bloat, or torsion of the stomach. The signs include unproductive attempts to vomit, extreme discomfort, pacing, drooling, and sometimes a tight or distended abdomen. This is a dire emergency, and your dog can die very quickly. Go immediately to the closest vet, preferably calling ahead to say that you are bringing in a possibly bloating dog.

A dog who is having difficulty breathing and is drooling heavily needs immediate attention. This condition could be anything from aspiration pneumonia to poisoning. Other signs of poisoning are having dilated or constricted pupils, staggering or acting "drunk," showing extreme lethargy, or suffering agitation and convulsions. Never induce vomiting because some poisons cause even more harm coming up.

Fights with other dogs or with cats may result in puncture wounds almost impossible to see. After an altercation, watch your dog very carefully and feel every part of him for signs of swelling. Cat bites in particular can get badly infected. If you think he may have been bitten, contact your vet because a prophylactic antibiotic prescription may be indicated.

Poison

- Antifreeze tastes good to dogs and is commonly ingested. It can be fatal. If you suspect your dog has ingested antifreeze or any other possible poison, contact a vet immediately.

- Eating rat and mouse poison, or even eating an animal that has been poisoned, can also kill your dog.

- Never induce vomiting unless you're assured that the substance won't cause even more harm coming back up. Caustic or sharp objects may need to be neutralized or removed by a vet.

Signs of Emergencies

- Extreme lethargy, sudden aggression, or any unfamiliar and sudden behavior could have a physical cause.

- Very dark or very pale gums indicate shock. A distressed dog will often pant, drool, vocalize, try to hide, or be unwilling to walk or move normally.

- Generally, if you're unsure whether you have an emergency, get to a vet instead of second guessing. It truly is better to be safe than sorry.

FIRST AID KIT
Every dog owner should keep one in the house

Use a plastic container for your dog's first aid kit and write the emergency vet's phone number in Magic Marker on the lid. Keep a copy of your dog's vet records in the kit and let anyone watching your dog know where it is.

For wound care, keep gauze bandaging, sterile pads, disinfectant, and antibiotic ointment. Sanitary napkins are good for wounds that are bleeding profusely. A soft muzzle can come in handy because even the sweetest dog may bite when in pain or shock.

Several "people" medications are safe for dogs, but it's wise to check with your vet for dosing, especially if your dog is on a prescription. Antihistamines can be used for allergy symptoms and can be megadosed for dogs who have a life-threatening reaction to an insect sting. Stomach-settling liq-

Maintain Your First Aid Kit

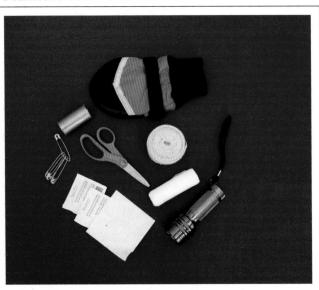

- Many of the items needed will do double duty for human use.

- Every few months, check the expiration dates on everything in the first aid kit and replace whatever is out of date.

- Ask your vet for suggestions for supplies particular to your dog and her breed, age, or condition.

- Some people keep a spare credit card in their first aid kit for veterinary emergencies.

What to Store in Your Kit

- Your medicine cabinet can contain supplies that your dog and your family can share.

- Although regular bandaging equipment is fine, buy a roll of vet wrap to keep on hand. It adheres without sticking tightly to fur.

- Check with a vet about any "people" medications you give your dog, especially if your dog is already on meds.

- This tip applies to herbal remedies and supplements, too. Some can interact with either prescription or over-the-counter medications.

uids containing bismuth can be used for diarrhea, nausea, and motion sickness. Electrolyte fluid is useful for rehydrating dogs with diarrhea. Aspirin can be used for mild pain control. It should be given with food, and enteric-coated aspirin shouldn't be used because a dog's digestive system can't dissolve the coating. Ibuprofen can be toxic to dogs; only aspirin is safe. Most eye ointments are fine for dogs, although they should not be used if there's a foreign body in the eye.

An ear syringe works for administering liquid medications. Small, sharp scissors or clippers can be used for trimming fur from around wounds; keep tweezers for removing splinters from paws and faces. A rectal thermometer will help assess your dog's condition if you are trying to decide whether to take him to the vet. His temperature should be between 100 and 102.5 degrees Fahrenheit.

Where to Keep your Kit

- Keep your first aid kit in a safe, easily accessible place out of reach from dogs or children.

- Write the phone numbers of your own vet, the nearest twenty-four-hour clinic, and the poison control center in indelible marker on the lid. In a real emergency you can waste precious moments looking up phone numbers.

- If you need to take your dog in for treatment, let the vet know what you have done for her and what medications you've administered.

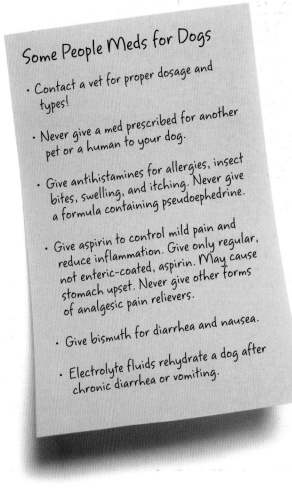

Some People Meds for Dogs

- Contact a vet for proper dosage and types!

- Never give a med prescribed for another pet or a human to your dog.

- Give antihistamines for allergies, insect bites, swelling, and itching. Never give a formula containing pseudoephedrine.

- Give aspirin to control mild pain and reduce inflammation. Give only regular, not enteric-coated, aspirin. May cause stomach upset. Never give other forms of analgesic pain relievers.

- Give bismuth for diarrhea and nausea.

- Electrolyte fluids rehydrate a dog after chronic diarrhea or vomiting.

213

PREVENTATIVE MAINTENANCE
Routine care, a good diet, and supplements keep your dog healthy

Preventative maintenance saves you money in lower vet bills and helps your dog live a longer, happier life. A proper vaccination schedule lowers the risk of communicable disease. Controlling how much your dog eats not only saves on food costs but also drastically lowers the risk of conditions linked to obesity, like diabetes and joint problems. Taking care of ears, nails, teeth, and coat prevents a host of complications.

A fit, well-exercised dog enjoys the same benefits that fit humans do—longer life, increased strength and endurance, and better emotional health. Feed the best food you can. If your dog is healthy with a shiny coat, her diet is working. Train your dog because trained dogs are a pleasure to live with and care for.

If you have a purebred dog, be aware of congenital health

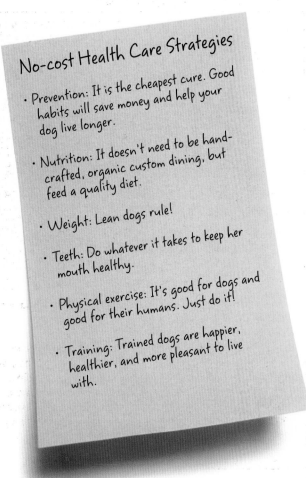

No-cost Health Care Strategies

- Prevention: It is the cheapest cure. Good habits will save money and help your dog live longer.

- Nutrition: It doesn't need to be hand-crafted, organic custom dining, but feed a quality diet.

- Weight: Lean dogs rule!

- Teeth: Do whatever it takes to keep her mouth healthy.

- Physical exercise: It's good for dogs and good for their humans. Just do it!

- Training: Trained dogs are happier, healthier, and more pleasant to live with.

Prevent Arthritis and Joint Pain

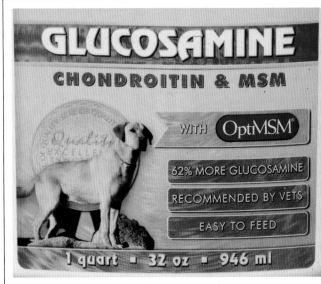

- Arthritis and joint pain are almost inevitable as dogs age. Research supplements and talk to your vet. There are so many pain-control choices now.

- Many supplements formulated for people, like fish oil or glucosamine, are fine for dogs.

- Over half of the nation's pet canines are overweight. They have more health problems, are in more arthritic pain, and live shorter lives. Is this what you want for your dog?

problems she may be prone to and do what you can to prevent them. Mixed-breed dogs are not free from inherited conditions, either, so consider the breed mix. Research spaying and neutering because there are both risks and benefits to the procedures. If you elect to keep your dog intact, be responsible and don't allow unplanned breeding.

Supplements are often touted as miracle workers, but avoid the temptation to go overboard and look to research instead of marketing hype. Some supplements, such as omega-3 fat-ty acids in fish oil, probiotics, and joint support supplements, are probably nothing but beneficial. Others, like multivitamin supplements containing calcium, can seriously unbalance a commercial diet, which is especially risky for puppies.

Complementary therapies, like homeopathy or acupuncture, can be a valuable part of your dog's health maintenance, especially when used in conjunction with modern medicine. Some vets are open to different approaches, and if you have chosen your vet well you can talk about this with her.

Skin and Coat Maintenance

- Routine grooming, whether you do it yourself or hire a groomer, not only makes your dog look great but also maintains a healthy skin and coat.

- While grooming, be aware of any lumps or changes in your dog's body.

- Regular brushing keeps skin oils distributed through long fur, keeping it glossy and healthy.

- Grooming is a nice way to bond with your dog. This long-haired Chihuahua is relaxed and enjoying the session.

Maintain Good Dental Hygiene

- Apart from keeping your dog fit and lean, maintaining good dental hygiene is one of the more important things you can do for her overall health.

- This border collie is getting physical and mental satisfaction from chewing a bone while keeping her teeth clean.

- Some very hard butcher bones, like soup bones, can crack a dog's teeth. Take fresh bones away before they become dried out and give softer chewies to aggressive chewers.

ALLERGIES
How to deal with the allergy-prone dog

Dogs can be allergic to inhalants, foods, and fleas. The primary symptom of any canine allergy is itchy skin, sometimes with a visible rash. Food and inhalant allergies can also cause chronically itchy and infected ears. Flea bites cause an allergic dog to itch intensely and chew himself raw, usually around the hindquarters. Allergies can be frustrating to pinpoint, and there is no real cure. However, most allergies can be man-

aged with a range of approaches.

Inhalant pollen allergies are often seasonal, but if the dog is also allergic to house dust, he will have year-around symptoms. He may scratch and chew his body and feet and rub his face on the ground. Secondary to allergies are bacterial skin and ear infections. Make sure your vet does a culture on irritated skin so the proper medication can be prescribed. A

Inhalant Allergies

- Inhalant allergies are more common than food allergies, and both types can manifest in itching or skin problems, including reddened, itchy feet.

- Treatment is two pronged: Identify and manage the allergen, and relieve the miserable dog's symptoms.

- Some breeds, like bulldogs and bully breeds, retrievers, poodles, and some terriers, are more prone to allergies.

- A genetic predisposition for allergies is often passed on to puppies. Dogs with allergies should not be bred.

Allergic Responses

- Watery, red eyes and frequent ear or bladder infections are often indicators of underlying allergies.

- Allergic dogs can be susceptible to infections and illness because irritated and damaged skin has less protection from bacteria.

- You may never know precisely what the allergens are, but talk to your vet about managing symptoms.

- Too-frequent vaccinations can exacerbate allergy symptoms by triggering an immune response. Minimize vaccinations and consider titers instead.

dermatologist can isolate the allergens and mix a custom "cocktail" injection to lessen symptoms, although this can be expensive. Ask your vet about antihistamine dosages for your dog. Also consider supplementing with fish oil, a natural anti-inflammatory. Some medicated or oatmeal shampoos can help itchy skin. An air purifier in the house can help as well.

Food allergies are usually in response to a meat or grain protein and sometimes to additives. Food allergies are less common than inhalant allergies and are not the same as intolerance, which tends to manifest in vomiting or diarrhea.

Food allergies present very much like inhalant allergies. They are diagnosed by strict elimination diets, so the offending proteins can be removed from the diet.

Flea allergies are the easiest to prevent. Use prescription flea preventative regularly and keep your home flea free. Steroids can be prescribed for the short term in severe cases, but long-term use can suppress the immune system and result in serious unwanted side effects.

Prevent Infections

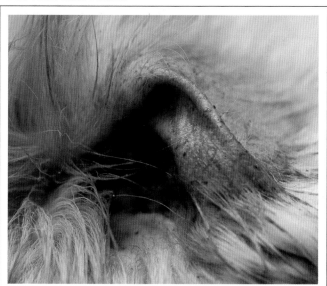

- Regular ear cleaning to keep yeasty buildup in the ear canal can prevent infections.

- Although cranberries or cranberry extract capsules don't cure bladder infections, they can prevent such infections from occurring in the first place.

- Good diet, medicated shampoo, and fish oil capsules can all help soothe itchy skin.

- Wash your dog's bedding every week, keep the home vacuumed, and use non-toxic, natural cleaners.

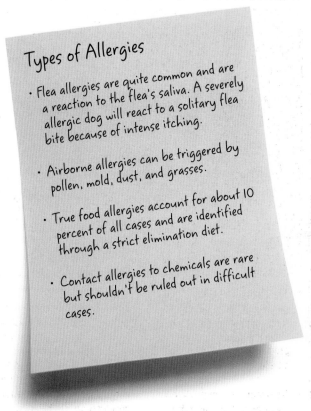

Types of Allergies

- Flea allergies are quite common and are a reaction to the flea's saliva. A severely allergic dog will react to a solitary flea bite because of intense itching.

- Airborne allergies can be triggered by pollen, mold, dust, and grasses.

- True food allergies account for about 10 percent of all cases and are identified through a strict elimination diet.

- Contact allergies to chemicals are rare but shouldn't be ruled out in difficult cases.

SKIN PROBLEMS

The skin is the largest organ, and health problems often manifest in skin and coat

Skin problems are common, and there are so many causes besides allergies that only a vet can diagnose them. Some skin conditions are linked to a malfunctioning thyroid, Cushings syndrome, or autoimmune disease; others are hereditary. With any stubborn skin problem, you can ask for a referral to a dermatologist for a second opinion because problems can be complicated to diagnose and treat.

Bacterial and fungal skin infections often are found in allergic dogs and can be stubborn, requiring long courses of medications. It is important that the vet does a skin scraping and culture so that the correct medications can be prescribed. Some infections can be resistant to common antibi-

KNACK DOG CARE AND TRAINING

Skin Problems

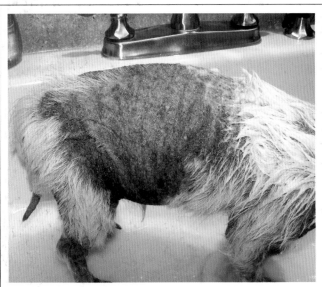

- Although many skin problems are fairly easy to diagnose, some can baffle even experienced vets.

- A plethora of conditions can manifest as itchy, discolored, reddened, or irritated skin.

- If your vet can't find a remedy in a few tries, get a referral to a dermatologist.

- It could be cheaper and bring faster relief to your dog than unsuccessfully trying to treat a stubborn case.

Fungal Skin Problems

- Some fungal skin problems can be transmitted to other animals or people. Ringworm is a classic example.

- Fungal skin problems can present as crusty, red bumps but can also appear as red swollen skin or black or thickened, discolored skin. It can be similar in appearance

- to bacterial skin infections or mange, and a strong odor is associated with it.

- The only way to diagnose many skin problems is with a skin culture and biopsy.

- Be careful handling your dog and wash your hands afterward.

otics. The ringworm fungus is contagious to humans. Other fungus, like yeast, usually infects damaged skin and is not as contagious. A dog who gets persistent skin infections may benefit from a change in diet, particularly to a meat-based or home-cooked diet or premium, grain-free commercial food. Coat supplements containing fish oil can also help, as will regular bathing with antifungal shampoo.

Several types of mites can be passed on to humans. Itching, patchy hair loss, and flaky skin can indicate mites. Some, like sarcoptic mites, are difficult to diagnose because they live burrowed deep in the hair follicle. They cause intense itching and can be misdiagnosed as allergic dermatitis.

Hot spots start as small skin irritations (like flea bites) that become open sores when the dog continuously licks them. They are treated by trimming surrounding fur and applying a drying agent and relieving the itching/licking cycle. Chronic hot spots can advance to acral lick granulomas, which are caused by incessant licking of one spot on the feet or legs. In either case exercise or distraction to redirect the dog's attention from the sore will help.

Bacterial Infections

Serious Disorders and Illnesses

- Several types of mange, caused by microscopic mites in and on the skin, cause intense itching.

- Some skin problems are symptoms of serious disorders and illness, including glandular and hormonal diseases and cancer.

- Your vet may suggest a steroid injection to give your dog relief. Steroids may have side effects, but sometimes they are the only way to make your poor dog more comfortable.

- Steroids can break the biting and scratching cycle, which can make the problem worse.

- For stubborn bacterial infections, a long-term course of antibiotics may be the only way to get them under control.

- It is common for dogs to improve while on medication, then have symptoms return as soon as the meds are stopped. In that case, look for underlying causes like allergies, glandular, or hormonal conditions.

- Talk to your vet about giving antihistamines to your dog to provide temporary relief from miserable itching. These usually work best for inhaled allergies, not for food allergies or infections.

DENTAL HEALTH

Poor dental health can lead to serious health problems, especially in older dogs

It is estimated that millions of dogs die earlier than necessary due to neglected teeth. If soft tartar is not removed regularly, it turns into hard, bacteria-laden calculus. The bacteria and calculus cause chronic gum inflammation, leading to infection, abscessed teeth, and mouth pain. They lodge in the liver, kidneys, and heart, where they accumulate, forming growths and damaging the organs. A dog's immune system is put under constant stress fighting the bacterial overload, and the dog is more susceptible to any illness.

The good news: Removing all the calculus is a fairly simple procedure. The dog is sedated, and calculus is scraped and ground off, and the teeth are polished. The vet will be able to

Teething

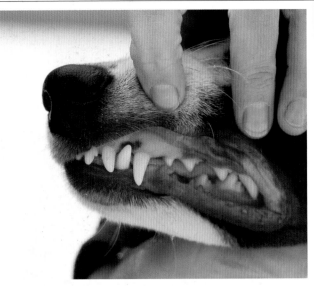

- Periodically check a puppy's mouth during teething. If a baby tooth is not dislodged when the adult tooth comes in, call your vet.

- Small dogs are most prone to retaining baby teeth and poor dentition in general.

- Puppies are born toothless. Twenty-eight puppy teeth are formed by birth and will cut through the gums by about five weeks of age.

- Adult dogs have forty-two teeth: twenty in the upper jaw and twenty-two in the lower.

Dental Exams

- Healthy teeth are white, with smooth, pink gums.

- If your dog is ever scheduled for surgery, ask your vet if she needs a dental check-up and cleaning at the same time.

- Many conditions, like loose or cracked teeth, are not al-

ways easy to see. With your dog sedated, the vet can do a thorough exam.

- Having a dental exam and cleaning at the same time as another procedure can save you considerable money.

carefully inspect the teeth for cracks and exposed roots and can extract teeth that are beyond repair. (Dogs can chew and eat quite well with missing teeth.) The dog may be put on a course of antibiotics following a cleaning to counteract the bacteria released during the procedure.

Bad breath is the first sign of dental disease, and if you can see brown deposits on the teeth, that is the cause. Infected gums will be reddened or puffy along the gum line. A dog will indicate a painful mouth by drooling, refusing to eat, or eating slowly. If teeth look worse on one side of the mouth, this indicates he's chewing only on the other side because it hurts.

Some dogs can reach their middle years with great teeth; others will have calculus very early in life. Small dogs have a predisposition to dental disease. It's best to be proactive and maintain dental health to avoid more serious problems.

Cracked or Loose Teeth

- Teeth that are infected, extremely loose, or broken to expose the sensitive pulp should probably be removed.

- A dog can eat surprisingly well, even with many missing teeth. Most can manage dry food without a problem because their teeth are not used much for chewing food in the first place.

- Make sure you get at least a few days of pain medication after dental surgery or tooth removal and stock up on soft foods for the healing process.

Dental Health Risks

- Teeth can be saved by treating gingivitis before the teeth become infected or loose.

- Regular veterinary cleaning is not expensive. Dental surgery can be quite costly.

- A dog with periodontal disease and an infected mouth is in constant pain.

- The heart, kidneys, liver, and other organs are weakened by having to fight off a steady flood of bacteria.

- Dental disease is linked with shorter lifespans and increased chance of chronic ailments.

JOINT PROBLEMS
You can help your dog stay strong and flexible

Joint pain is indicated by stiffness, lameness, or an abnormal gait. Hip and elbow dysplasia usually present in younger dogs while their bones are still growing. Rear lameness or "bunny hopping" can indicate hip dysplasia, diagnosed by manipulation and X-rays. Front lameness can be elbow dysplasia, which is a little more complex and tricky to diagnose. Keep a young limping dog confined and calm. Ligaments,

muscles, and tendons can be pulled or torn during exercise. Often rest and anti-inflammatory medication heal the injury. If the lameness persists for more than a few days, get a veterinary opinion. If surgery is suggested, always get a second opinion from an orthopedist.

Mild dysplasia may not require surgery. Keeping a dog very lean is critically important for any joint problems. Exercise as

Bones in a Dog

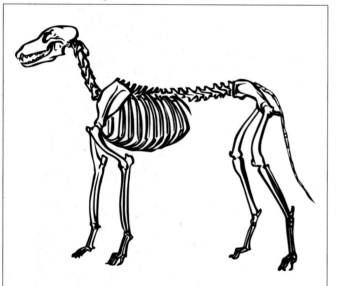

- Dogs have about 320 bones —humans have about 206. The number of bones depends on whether the dog has a tail and how long it is and whether the dog has dewclaws.

- A growing pup reaches his full height before his body fills out.

- The larger the dog, the slower he grows. Although exercise is important, avoid overexercising and encouraging jumping until the pup has done growing so as not to stress or damage growing bones.

Elbow and Hip Dysplasia

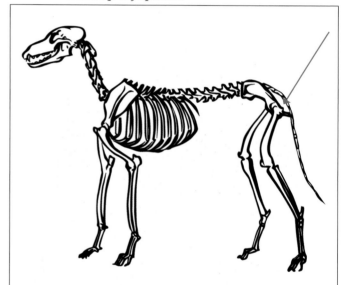

- Elbow and hip dysplasia is unfortunately common, particularly in larger dogs. Both mixed breeds and purebreds alike can be affected.

- Males and females are equally affected by hip dysplasia, but more males have dysplastic elbows.

- Stiffness, hopping, and abnormal gait should be checked. Dysplasia is usually first noticed in growing pups under one year old.

- Orthopedist will have the most up-to-date information on new medications and procedures; canine orthopedics is a fast-growing field.

tolerated, especially swimming, builds muscle that protects and compensates for weak joints. Supplements and nutraceuticals like glucosamine/chrondritin, MSM, and fish oil may be very helpful in lubricating joints and reducing inflammation. Some studies have shown that sterilization while bones are still growing, particularly in males, may increase the risk of joint injury and abnormality by reducing the testosterone that develops bone density. Dysplasia is often hereditary, so choosing puppies from tested parents is important.

Luxating patellas, or slipping knee joints, are painful and can affect any dog, although toy breeds are more susceptible. If the condition is mild, it can be managed, but severe cases can be fixed surgically.

Arthritis is common in older dogs and can affect the spine or any joint. As with dysplasia, there is plenty you can do to ease pain. Acupuncture and chiropractic care can bring great relief, and many pain-control medications can be used in conjunction with supplements. Be sure your dog has a soft, warm place to sleep.

Joint Supplements

- An overwhelming number of joint nutraceuticals are available, and many can help. Buy from trusted sources and be skeptical of "miracle cure" formulas.

- Most joint-support supplements sold for humans contain the same active ingredients and work just fine for dogs.

- Liquid formulas are easier to give because they can be drizzled over food.

- Unless they are time-release capsules, pills can also be dissolved in water or ground up and mixed with food.

Alternative Joint Support

- Some veterinarians are certified acupuncturists. Acupuncture can be very helpful for arthritis.

- Physical therapy, including exercises and underwater treadmill sessions, is often recommended for surgery recovery and arthritis.

- Chiropractic care and massage therapy can help. Look for therapists who have trained specifically on animals.

- Most herbal, holistic, and nutraceutical supplements are safe, but effectiveness and quality vary. These remedies should be treated with the same respect as regular medications.

OBESITY
Help your dog maintain a healthy weight for a long, healthy life

Overweight dogs are so common that many people now think a fit dog looks underweight. Pudgy dogs have become the norm, which is unfortunate because excess weight significantly affects health, longevity, and enjoyment in life. An overweight dog will have a heavy fat layer over the ribs. Regardless of body type, you should be able to feel every single rib quite easily. The dog should have a trim waist and

tummy. Hip bones and spine should not be prominent, but you should be able to feel them. Some dog fanciers bemoan the acceptance of hefty dogs like Labradors and rottweilers in the show ring and make a distinction between "working" and "show" condition. Our pet dogs should be in "working" condition, lean and fit.

Some dogs can seemingly gain weight just by looking at

A Fit Dog: Ribs

- You should be able to either see or feel all ribs.

- Despite popular opinion, slightly visible ribs do not mean a dog is underweight.

- People with fit, athletic dogs complain that other people often remark that their dogs are too thin.

Many people have become so accustomed to seeing pudgy dogs that they consider this condition normal.

- A dog's ribs should feel like the skin covering the back of a person's hand: easily felt, with a layer of skin covering them.

A Fit Dog: Waist

- A fit dog has a defined waist when seen both from the top and side.

- Feel a long-haired dog. You should be able to detect a well-defined waist, no matter what the breed.

- For most breeds, if you can grab a handful of fat at the

side of the waist, the dog is overweight.

- Breeds like the stocky English bulldog or wrinkly shar-pei do have naturally looser skin, and ribs may not be as easy to detect.

food; others burn through calories. Feeding suggestions for commercial dog foods are simply rough guides. Although some dogs self-regulate and can be free fed, most don't, so it's best to have measured feeding.

Weight-control dry food works for some dogs if fed as directed. However, it is not designed for long-term use because it's high in fiber and carbohydrates and lower in fat and protein. A better option to take off moderate amounts of weight is to simply feed a little less of your dog's regular quality diet. There really isn't a need to let him fill up on low-nutrition bulk, but adding canned green beans and a little canned pumpkin to his reduced meals is a healthy option. Curtail treats or use low-fat ones like fat-free popcorn or carrot or string cheese pieces.

Don't forget exercise. As little as fifteen extra minutes a day will help. Expect weight loss to be slow because dogs don't naturally drop weight quickly.

Other Diseases

- The great Dane and Chinese crested, with their short coats (or no coat at all!), are easier to monitor than fluffy dogs because you can more easily see their condition.

- Although breed types can be either naturally slim or bulky, there shouldn't be rolls of fat on any part of the body.

- Diabetes is on the rise in dogs because of the obesity epidemic. Diabetes is associated with chronic pancreatitis, which is also becoming more common.

Diet Control

- Cook and add any of the following to a reduced portion of his regular food: green beans, pumpkin, any squash, white rice, or sweet potatoes. Mix a little canned fish if he won't eat the food otherwise.

- Cutting too much fat for too long not only leads to poor skin and coat but also can lead to poor overall health. Dogs need fat in their diets.

- Increase exercise. Even a little bit every day will help.

GASTROINTESTINAL ISSUES
How to deal with vomiting and diarrhea

Vomiting and diarrhea seem to be popular canine pastimes, usually on carpeting. An isolated bout of either is nothing to worry about if all else is normal, but it could indicate a more serious problem if frequent. Extreme listlessness, abnormal pain, or weakness is a medical emergency. Any diarrhea or vomiting that lasts more than twenty-four hours needs veterinary attention.

Some vomiting is caused by irritation of the stomach. Some dogs vomit small amounts of yellowish fluid at night. This is probably bile irritating an empty stomach, and if the dog is otherwise healthy, a solution is a later dinner or bedtime snack. Other dogs vomit when they are stressed or have eaten too fast. Try behavioral management and techniques like putting a very large rock into the food bowl to slow eat-

Cleaning Up Messes

- Messes happen. Have pet stain and odor remover on hand so you have it if you need it.

- In a pinch, a mix of water and vinegar makes a good odor remover. Making a paste of baking soda and water and using it to blot up the remaining mess usually works for stains.

- Dogs often eat grass just because they like the taste or texture, but sometimes they eat it deliberately prior to throwing up.

Soothing an Upset Stomach

- For a dog who has a mildly upset tummy not warranting veterinary attention, feed small meals of boiled white rice and cooked lean meat.

- If the upset isn't resolved in twenty-four hours or is a frequent occurrence, collect a fresh stool sample and your dog, and go to the vet. Your vet can check for parasites and abnormal bacteria.

- Intestinal parasites are a common cause of diarrhea and sometimes vomiting. There are many types of parasites, some too small to see.

ing. Vomiting can also be a symptom of cancers, pancreatitis, parasites, and inflammatory bowel disease (IBD). Have your dog vet checked and ask about home solutions like a diet change, digestive enzymes, probiotics, or over-the-counter medications.

Most diarrhea is caused by irritation of the intestines. There are too many causes to list here, but isolated incidences are usually caused by eating something unsuitable. Diarrhea may be caused by parasites or a viral or bacterial infection. Chronic diarrhea can indicate colitis, IBD, or pancreatitis. Al-ways take a stool sample to the vet to help with the diagno-sis. Ask her about remedies like a temporary diet of cooked rice and meat, spoonfuls of pumpkin added to meals, probi-otics, and herbs like slippery elm.

Chronic diarrhea, and to a lesser extent vomiting, can be dan-gerously dehydrating to young puppies and toy dogs. If skin pinched between the shoulder blades doesn't spring back immediately, the dog is dehydrated. You can offer ice cubes or replacement electrolyte solutions, but get to a vet as soon as possible; this degree of dehydration is life-threatening.

Soothing the Digestive System

- A spoonful of plain canned pumpkin (a teaspoon for a small dog, a heaping tablespoon for a large dog) added to the food can help with diarrhea by absorb-ing excess water from the colon.

- Digestive enzymes may be helpful for dogs who frequently have gastroin-testinal problems, espe-cially vomiting. They can't hurt and will help food get digested in the stomach.

- Probiotics help repopulate the intestine with beneficial bacteria. Again, they cannot hurt and may help, espe-cially with diarrhea.

Diarrhea

- Watery or bloody diarrhea, especially in conjunction with lethargy and un-willingness to eat or drink, is a medical emergency, especially in puppies and toy dogs.

- Mucus in the stool occasionally is nothing to worry about and usually in-dicates a mild, temporary inflammation. Frequent mucus warrants a vet visit, along with your bagged stool sample.

- A black tarry stool could be from eat-ing too much liver or, more seriously, bleeding into the intestines.

- Being a dog owner means sometimes monitoring poop!

MORE ABOUT DOGS

The world of dogs is vast and diverse. The following list of resources will provide you with a good start for finding further information.

Adopting
Adopt a Pet
www.adoptapet.com

The Humane Society
www.hsus.org/pets

Pet Finder
www.petfinder.com

The Senior Dog Project
www.srdogs.com

World Animal Net
www.worldanimal.net

Breed Organizations
American Kennel Club
www.akc.org

The Kennel Club
www.thekennelclub.org.uk

United Kennel Club
www.ukcdogs.com

The World Canine Organization
www.fci.be/home.asp?lang=en

Disabled Dog Resources
D2Care
d2care.org

Deaf Dog Education Action Fund
www.deafdogs.org

Pets with Disabilities
www.petswithdisabilities.org

Mixed-breed Organizations
American Mixed Breed Obedience Registration
www.ambor.us

Crossbreed & Mongrel Club
www.crossbreed-and-mongrel-club.org.uk

Mixed Breed Dog Clubs of America
www.mbdca.org

Puppies

Books

Dunbar, Ian, *Before and After Getting Your Puppy: The Positive Approach to Raising a Happy, Healthy, and Well-behaved Dog*, New World Library, 2004

Kern, Nancy, *The Whole Dog Journal Handbook of Dog and Puppy Care and Training*, The Lyons Press, 2007

Monks of New Skete, *The Art of Raising a Puppy*, Little, Brown and Company, 1991

Web sites

Breeding Better Dogs
www.breedingbetterdogs.com

Theory and Breeds

Books

Budiansky, Stephen, *The Truth about Dogs*, Viking Penguin, 2000

Coppinger, Raymond, and Lorna Coppinger, *Dogs: A Startling New Understanding of Canine Origin, Behavior and Evolution*, Scribner, 2001

Coren, Stanley, *Why We Love the Dogs We Do*, Simon & Schuster, 1998

Web sites

Dog Breed Info Center
www.dogbreedinfo.com

Just Dog Breeds
www.justdogbreeds.com

GEAR

Check out these Web sites for some unique gear for your pup.

Bedding and Housing Gear

Jeffer's
www.jefferspet.com

La Petite Maison
www.lapetitemaison.com

MidWest Homes for Pets
www.midwesthomes4pets.com

Collars and Leashes

Annie's Sweatshop
www.anniessweatshop.com

Thayer & Ridge
www.thayerandridge.com

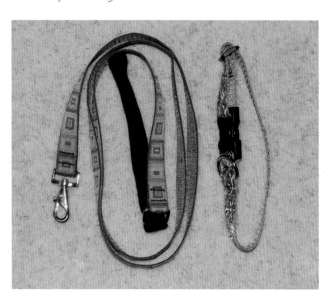

Eco-friendly Gear

A Natural Home
www.anaturalhome.com

Belladog
www.belladog.com

Branch
www.branchhome.com

Earth Dog
www.earthdog.com

Earth Doggy
www.earthdoggy.com

EcoAnimal
www.ecoanimal.com

Great Green Pet
www.greatgreenpet.com

Green Dog Pet Supply
www.greendogpetsupply.com

Natural Pet Market
www.naturalpetmarket.com

Planet Dog
www.planetdog.com

General

Dogstuff
www.safe-servers.co.uk/~dogstuff/acatalog

8 in 1
www.eightinonepet.com

Jeffer's
www.jefferspet.com

Palmetto Pet Gear
www.palmettopet.com

Robbins Pet Care
www.robbinspetcare.com

Grooming
Only Natural Pet Store
www.onlynaturalpet.com

SitStay
www.sitstay.com

Toys
Branch
www.branchhome.com

Earth Dog
www.earthdog.com

Simply Fido
www.simplyfido.com

West Paw Design
www.westpawdesign.com

Training
Invisible Fence
www.invisiblefence.com

Leerburg's Video & Kennel
www.leerburg.com

Petsafe Instant Fence
www.petsafe.net

Travel Gear
High Country Plastics
www.highcountryplastics.com

Orvis
www.orvis.com

Pup Life
www.puplife.com

SPORTS, BEHAVIOR, & TRAINING

Behavior and Training Organizations

Books

Aloff, Brenda, *Canine Body Language: A Photographic Guide Interpreting the Native Language of the Domestic Dog*, Dogwise Publishing, 2005

Ammen, Amy, and Kitty Foth-Regner, *Hip Ideas for Hyper Dogs,* Howell Book House, 2007

Donaldson, Jean, *The Culture Clash,* James & Kenneth Publishers, 1996

Millan, Cesar, *Cesar's Way: The Natural, Everyday Guide to Understanding and Correcting Common Dog Problems,* Three Rivers Press, 2007

Miller, Pat, *The Power of Positive Dog Training,* Howell Book House, 2008

Monks of New Skete, *Divine Canine: The Monks' Way to a Happy, Obedient Dog,* Hyperion, 2007

Rugaas, Turid, *On Talking Terms with Dogs: Calming Signals*, Dogwise Publishing, 2005

Web sites
Association of Pet Dog Trainers
www.apdt.com

Clicker Training Lessons
www.clickerlessons.com

K9 Deb
www.k9deb.com

National Association of Dog Obedience Instructors
www.nadoi.org

Dog Sports and Shows

American Kennel Club
www.akc.org/events/index.cfm?nav_area=events

Dog Play
www.dogplay.com

The Kennel Club
www.thekennelclub.org.uk/activities

United Kennel Club
www.ukcdogs.com/WebSite.nsf/WebPages/
DogWhatKindsOfShows

Working Dog Web
www.workingdogweb.com

Therapy Dog Organizations

Assistance Dogs International
www.assistancedogsinternational.org

Caring Canines
www.caringcanines.org

Delta Society
www.deltasociety.org
(425) 679-5500

Land of Pure Gold Foundation
www.landofpuregold.com

Therapy Dogs International
www.tdi-dog.org
(973) 252-9800

NUTRITION & HEALTH

Dog Food Analysis
www.dogfoodanalysis.com

The Dog Food Project
www.dogfoodproject.com

Westie Rescue Houston
www.westierescuehouston.com

General Information

Books

Billinghurst, Ian, *The BARF Diet*, SOS Printing, 2001

Dye, Dan, *Three Dog Bakery Cookbook*, Andrews McMeel
  Publishing, 1998

Pitcairn, Richard, *Dr. Pitcairn's New Complete Guide to Natural
  Health for Dogs and Cats*, Rodale Books, 2005

MacDonald, Carina, *Raw Dog Food: Make It Easy for You and
  Your Dog*, Dogwise, 2003

Web sites

Dog Feeding Information
http://dogaware.com/dogfeeding

DEVELOPMENT & GROOMING

Books

Bonham, Margaret, *Dog Grooming for Dummies*, For Dummies, 2006

Eldredge, Debra, *Dog Owner's Home Veterinary Handbook*, Howell Book House, 2007

Fennell, Jan, *The Seven Ages of Man's Best Friend*, Collins Living, 2007

Goldstein, Martin, *The Nature of Animal Healing*, Ballantine Books, 2000

Web sites

Altvetmed.com
www.altvetmed.com

American Veterinary Medical Association
www.avma.org

DoLittler
www.dolittler.com

The Pet Center
www.thepetcenter.com

Whole Dog Journal
www.whole-dog-journal.com

World Veterinary Association
www.worldvet.org

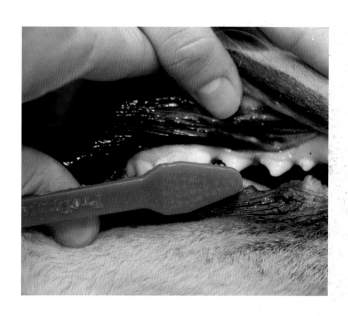

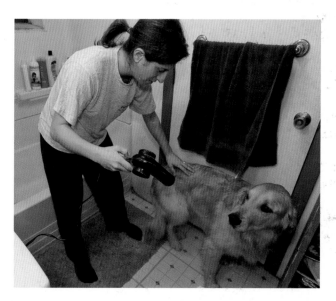

GLOSSARY

Agility: Dog sport in which handler and dog navigate an obstacle course, being judged on technique and speed.

American Kennel Club: An American purebred dog registry that promotes and sanctions dog shows, sporting, and working events.

Assistance dog: This is an umbrella term, like *service dog*, referring to dogs trained to work with disabled people.

BARF: Acronym for *bones and raw food* or *biologically appropriate raw food*. A term coined by Australian veterinarian Dr. Ian Billinghurst to describe a raw meat- and bones-based diet for dogs.

Bitch: The technical name for an adult female dog.

Canadian Kennel Club: The Canadian purebred dog registry, promoting and sanctioning dog shows, sporting, and working events.

Clicker, clicker training: A clicker is a small handheld device that makes a distinctive "click" sound as a marker when a dog has performed the correct action. Clicking is paired with a treat reward to reinforce behaviors.

Conformation, dog show: Purebred dogs who are competing in the show ring for the distinction of which conforms most closely to the ideal breed standard.

Dam: The mother of a litter of puppies.

Deep chested: This term describes the depth of the dog's chest. A deep chest usually extends to or below the elbows. Examples would be Dobermans, dachshunds, and Irish wolf-

hounds. The depth of the chest has nothing to do with the width, and many deep chested dogs are rather narrow across the front.

Designer dog: A dog bred by breeding two dogs of different breeds (or breed mixes) for sale as a pet rather than for any working purpose.

Dewclaws: Extra toelike digits on the inside of a dog's ankles above the foot. A pup may be born with or without them, and they are sometimes removed from very young puppies. Some breeds, like briards, are born with double dewclaws.

Dock diving: A relatively new sport in which dogs run and leap from the end of a dock into deep water after a thrown toy, competing for distance.

Double coat: Most dogs have a double coat. A softer, denser undercoat insulates the dog, and the coarser top coat provides some water resistance. All double-coated dogs shed to some degree.

Drive: A drive is a dog's urge to fulfill a working or instinctual need, such as herding, chasing, or defending territory. In very general terms, a high-drive dog is less suitable for an average family pet because of high exercise and training needs. Lower-drive dogs are more laidback and often easier to live with.

Dysplasia: Malformation of either the hip or elbow joints. Can be asymptomatic to crippling.

Earthdog: A terrier sport in which the dogs are dispatched down a narrow humanmade hole to find a caged animal, usually a rat. The rat is unharmed.

Freestyle, canine freestyle: A sport in which the dog and handler perform a dance routine to music. It often includes

some very complex moves and elements of formal obedience training, like precise heeling.

Handler: Any person who is training or showing a dog. A handler can be a paid professional at a dog show or the owner training or showing her dog.

Kennel Club: Usually referred to as "the Kennel Club," it is the United Kingdom purebred dog registry that promotes and sanctions dog shows, sporting, and working events.

Kibble: A food product for dogs, made by combining grains, meat products, and other ingredients and cooking them into dry pellets.

Lure coursing: A sport, primarily for sighthounds, that allows them to chase a lure via mechanized trolleys over a large field.

Neutering: This is technically the correct term for sterilizing a dog of either sex, although it is usually used to refer to male dogs. The testicles are removed, reducing testosterone production and making the dog unable to breed.

Obedience trial: A sanctioned event in which dogs compete for points toward obedience titles or championships.

Pack: The family, human or canine, that the dog lives with. Three or more dogs are a canine pack and may exhibit different behaviors as a group than singly.

Pedigree: The dog's family tree. Every dog has a pedigree. In purebred, registered dogs it is recorded with the registry.

Positive reinforcement: Any training technique that involves rewarding a dog for correct behavior with praise, treats, or play.

Puppy mill: There is no legal definition of the term. Usually considered to be a high-volume dog-breeding operation for profit. The dogs' value lies only in their worth as breeding stock.

Purebred: Any dog with parents and ancestors of a single recognized breed, registered or not.

Registry, registered dogs: Any dog or litter that is registered with an outside organization. The importance of the registration papers depends entirely on the validity of the registering body.

Schutzhund: A dog sport originating in Germany for working and police dogs. It gives equal importance to obedience, tracking, and protection.

Sighthounds: Dogs in the hound group who hunt primarily by sight, like greyhounds and whippets.

Single coat: Dogs like poodles, greyhounds, and some terriers have a single coat, with no undercoat. They tend to shed minimally.

Sire: The father of a litter of puppies.

Spaying: The medical procedure in which the ovaries and uterus are removed from a female dog, reducing estrogen and progesterone, eliminating heat cycles, and making her sterile. Sometimes only the uterus is removed, but complete removal of all reproductive organs is the most common procedure.

Speutered: A portmanteau word combining the words *spaying* and *neutering* to apply to dogs of either sex.

Therapy dog: A therapy dog provides comfort to others, usually in assisted living homes, hospitals, and schools.

Undercoat: The thick, dense insulating coat that many dogs have, covered by the top coat.

United Kennel Club: An American registry for both purebred and mixed-breed dogs. Although it sanctions and holds dog shows, its emphasis is on working and sporting events.

Weight pulling: A sport in which harnessed dogs compete to pull the most weight on a wagon or sled.

Whelping: Giving birth to puppies.

Withers: The top of the dog's shoulders. Height of a dog is measured from the withers to the ground.

X-pen: A portable mesh pen for containing dogs.

PHOTO CREDITS

INDEX